8633764

B/LER

-0 AUG 1978

KELLY, L.
6.50

LERMONTOV

HERTFORDSHIRE LIBRARY SERVICE

This book is due for return on or before the date shown. You may extend its loan by bringing the book to the library or, once only, by post or telephone, quoting the date of return the letter and number on the date card, if applicable, and the information at the top of this label.

RENEWAL   **The loan of books ~~is~~ and cannot be extended.**

INFORM-

Please renew/return this item by the last date shown.

So that your telephone call is charged at local rate, please call the numbers as set out below:

From Area codes 01923 or 0208:	From the rest of Herts:
Renewals: 01923 471373	01438 737373
Enquiries: 01923 471333	01438 737333
Minicom: 01923 471599	01438 737599

L32b

7112

27 JUN 2002

18 JUL 2002

−6 AUG 2002

27 AUG 2002

17 SEP 2002

−8 OCT 2002

29 APR 2005

L33

D1345882

Lermontov
Tragedy in the Caucasus

LAURENCE KELLY

Lermontov

Tragedy in the Caucasus

Constable London

First published in Great Britain 1977
by Constable and Company Ltd
10 Orange Street London WC2H 7EG
Copyright © 1977 by Laurence Kelly

ISBN 0 09 461710 4

Set in Monotype Fournier 12pt
Printed in Great Britain by The Anchor Press Ltd
and bound by Wm Brendon & Son Ltd
both of Tiptree, Essex

HERTFORDSHIRE
LIBRARY SERVICE

B/LER

8633764

JAN 1978

To Linda

Contents

Illustrations

The most detailed Catalogue of Lermontov's own paintings and drawings is by N. Pakhomov, *The Artistic Heritage of Lermontov*, published in 1948 by the Academy of Sciences, Moscow, and wherever possible references have been given to his work. The most comprehensive illustrated book about him and his period is by E. A. Kovalevskaya and V. A. Manuilov, *M. Yu Lermontov in Portraits, illustrations and documents*, Leningrad 1959. Reproductions of pictures at present in State Museum collections in the USSR are by Courtesy of Novosti Press Agency.

M. Yu. Lermontov, as Cornet, Life Guards Hussar Regiment. By Kirill Gorbunov, oil, 1883. (*Institute of Russian Literature, Pushkin House Leningrad.*) *Frontispiece*

M. Yu. Lermontov, as Lieutenant, Tenginsky Infantry Regiment. By K. Gorbunov, 1841. Lithograph by F. I. Jordan from original watercolour. Institute of Russian Literature, Leningrad. *Frontispiece*

Between pages 32 and 33

Portrait of Varvara A. Lopukhina, 1814–1851, as a Spanish nun. Aquarelle 1835 by Lermontov. Formerly in collection of Countess Beroldingen.

Elisaveta Alekseyvna Arseniyeva (born Stolypina), 1773–1845, oil painting by artist unknown. Lermontov's maternal grandmother (*State Literary Museum, Moscow.*)

Nicholas I, Tsar of all the Russias, 1796–1855. Watercolour by Samsonov. (*State Literary Museum, Moscow.*)

Count Aleksandr Christoforovich Benckendorff, 1783–1844. Chief of the Gendarmes, General Adjutant. Oil, in possession of Countess Benckendorff and Mrs Humphrey Brooke, London.

Grand Duke Mikhail Pavlovitch, 1798–1848, Colonel of the Life Guards Hussar Regiment. Print from painting by T. Cherikov, in Author's collection.

Varvara Alexandrovna Lopukhina by Lermontov, c 1835. Aquarelle. (*Institute of Russian Literature, Leningrad.*)

Self-portrait in uniform of Nijegorodtsy Dragoon Regiment. Painted by Lermontov in 1837 as a gift for Varvara Lopukhina – Bakhmetieva in 1838. (*State Literary Museum, Moscow.*)

Pyatigorsk, 1834. View of Nikolayevsky, Aleksandrovsky and Yermolov Baths. Lithograph from the drawing of I. Bernadazzi. (*Institute of Russian Literature, Leningrad.*)

View of Pyatigorsk and Mount Elborus. Oil, by Lermontov, 1837. (*State Literary Museum, Moscow.*)

The headquarters of the Nijegorodtsy Dragoon Regiment near Kara-Agatch, Kakhetia, ?1840. Oil by Prince G. G. Gagarin. (*State Russian Museum, Leningrad.*)

Between pages 96 and 97

Highlander armed with rifle. Sketch by Lermontov, ?1835–6.

Daghestan Highlander wearing helmet. Sketch by Lermontov, ?1835–6.

Circassians and Cossacks fighting. Sepia sketch by Lermontov, 1835–6. (*Album, State Public Library, Leningrad.*)

The Daryál Gorge and Tamara's Castle. Pencil sketch by Lermontov, 1837. (*Institute of Russian Literature, Leningrad.*)

Two Russians firing at a Highlander. Drawing of Lermontov's, copied by Prince G. G. Gagarin. (*State Russian Museum, Leningrad.*)

Illustration for A. Bestujev Marlinsky's '*Ammalat-Bek*' by Lermontov: '*Ammalat-Bek kills Colonel Verkhovsky.*' (*Institute of Russian Literature, Leningrad.*)

View of Tiflis. Oil by Lermontov, 1937. (*State Literary Museum Moscow.*)

Maidan Square and Bazaar in Tiflis, by Prince G. G. Gagarin and Baron E. Von Stackelberg, published in *Le Caucase Pittoresque*, Paris 1847.

Garden near Tiflis, girls dancing in the 'Lesghinka', by Prince G. G. Gagarin. Published in (*Le Caucase Pittoresque*) Paris 1847.

Resting Room at the Baths of Shemakha, by Prince G. G. Gagarin.

'*Djigitovka*' or Tournament. Oil, by Prince G. G. Gagarin. (*State Russian Museum, Leningrad.*)

Feast at Mtskheta, Georgia, by Prince G. G. Gagarin and Baron E. Von Stackelberg. (Published in *Le Caucase Pittoresque*, Paris 1847.)

Between pages 160 and 161

The village of Sioni near Kobi and Mount Kazbek, Caucasus. Sketch by Lermontov, 1837. (*Institute of Russian Literature, Leningrad.*)

'Souvenir of the Caucasus'. Oil, by Lermontov, 1838. (*Institute of Russian Literature, Leningrad.*)

Taman. Pencil drawing by Lermontov, 1837. The hut and rowing boat feature in the chapter, 'Taman', in *A hero of our Time*. (*Institute of Russian Literature, Leningrad.*)

Caucasian view with buffaloes and mounted Circassians. Oil, by Lermontov, 1838. (*State Literary Museum, Moscow.*)

'*Bataille de Valerik, 11 Juillet, 1840*'. '*Dessin de Lermontoff, aquarelle par moi pendant une convalescence à Kisslovodsk.*' '*Lermontov delineavit, Gagarin pinxit.*' (*State Russian Museum, Leningrad.*)

'At the Valerik, 12 July, 1840: The burial of the dead', Lermontov and Gagarin. Aquarelle (*State Public Library, Leningrad.*)

Major N. Martynov (Lermontov's opponent), 1843, by Thomas Wright, 1792–1849. Watercolour. (*State Russian Museum, Leningrad.*)

Prince A. I. Vasiltchikov, by Prince G. G. Gagarin. Attributed by Dora M. Nigdal. (*State Russian Museum, Leningrad.*)

M. Yu. Lermontov in army forage cap, by Baron D. P. Pahlen, pencil drawing. Campaign of July, 1840. (*Institute of Russian Literature, Leningrad.*)

M. Yu. Lermontov on his deathbed in Pyatigorsk, July, 1841. Sketch by P. K. Shvede, 1806–1871, later coloured. (*Institute of Russian Literature, Leningrad.*)

Acknowledgements

At different times over the last five years, I have received en-
couragement or help from the following, to whom I wish to
record my gratitude: The late W. E. D. Allen, Monsieur Boris des
Aubrys, Professor Abayev, Mr David Barrett, Oxford, Mrs
Humphrey Brooke, Hon. Adrian Berry, Mr William Carey,
Mr J. Dobbs, Princess Djordjadse, Mr Arthur Edmondson,
Mr Denys Edwardes, Mr Michael Evans, Professor Donald
Fanger, Professor John Fennell, Professor John Freeborn,
Madame Giraud, Mr Mark Hamilton, Mr Max Hayward, Mrs
Ellen de Katt, Mr Michael Katz, Madame N. Lermontova,
Mr David MacDonald, Mrs Anne Mytton, H.E. Monsieur Jean
Laloy, Ministère des Affaires Etrangères, Paris, Professor Lam-
pert, Keele University, Stafford. Mr John Morgan, Foreign
Office, Mr William Marsden, Mr Andrew Mylett, Mr Neil
Malcolm, Mr & Mrs Paul O'Bow-Hove, Mrs Helen Michailoff,
Professor Arnold McMillan, Monsieur Nicholas Rayevsky, Mr
John Roberts, Mr John Simmons, Mr P. Selegey, Mr Harry
Willetts, Mr Igor Vinogradov, Mr Alexander Zghenti.

During a visit to Moscow and Leningrad in January 1977, to
obtain the illustrations for the book, I received much encourage-
ment and practical help from the Directors of the State Literary
Museum in Moscow, of the Literary Museum at Pushkin House
in Leningrad, from the Curators of the Drawing, Watercolour
and Oil Painting departments at the State Russian Museum in
Leningrad, and from the experts in the Institute of Russian
Literature in Leningrad; and I should like to express my gratitude
to them, as also to the appropriate officials in the Ministry of
Culture and the Soviet Academy of Sciences who made these visits
possible.
I must especially thank Prince George Vasiltchikov of Geneva

and London for his generosity in allowing me to print, for the first time, extracts from Prince Boris Vasiltchikov's unpublished Memoirs relating to Lermontov's last duel and minutes on this earth; and Professor V. Manuilov for his kindness in giving me a number of valuable books from his own library in Leningrad; my mother for her patience in reading earlier drafts of the book; Mrs Shila Ladak for her good temper and patience in typing and retyping those selfsame drafts; Philip Longworth, without whose suggestions there would have been probably no drafts at all; Valerie Pakenham for proof-reading, and my wife Linda.

Permission has been received, and is acknowledged, from the following publishers, to reproduce quotations and extracts as follows: Associated Book Publishers, from 'Pushkin on Literature' by Tatiana Wolff published by Methuen; The Bodley Head, from 'Lermontov' by Janko Lavrin, published by Bowes and Bowes; and also from 'Modern Russian Poetry, an Anthology', chosen and translated by Babette Deutsch and Avrahm Yarmolinsky, for their translation of 'The Captive Knight'; Cambridge University Press, from P. S. Squire's 'The Third Department'; Chatto and Windus from 'My Past and Thoughts': the Memories of Alexander Herzen, translated by C. Garnett, revised by Humphrey Higgens; and 'Tolstoy and the Novel' by John Bayley; Duke University Press from 'The Russian Army under Nicholas I 1825–1855' by John S. Curtiss, copyright 1965; Paul Elek from 'The Rebel on the Bridge' by Glyn Barratt; Faber and Faber from 'Poems from the Russian', chosen and translated by Frances Cornford and Esther Salaman; The Financial Times for Michael Coveney's review of 'Maskerade' which appeared on October 4, 1976; Hutchinson Publishing Group from 'The Marquis de Custine and his Russia', by George F. Kennan; Macmillan, London and Basingstoke, from 'A Book of Russian Verse', edited by C. M. Bowra; John Murray from 'The Russian Journal of Lady Londonderry' edited by W. A. L. Seaman and J. R. Sewell; and also the 'Sabres of Paradise' by Lesley Blanch; the New English Library from 'The Hero of our Time' (by M. Yu. Lermontov) translated by Philip Longworth; Peter Owen, London from 'Adventures in Tsarist Russia' by Alexandre Dumas translated by A. E. Murch; Oxford University Press from the 1972 Romanes Lecture of Sir Isaiah Berlin 'Fathers and Children'; Penguin Books from the 'Penguin Book of Russian Verse' translated by Dimitry Obolensky (revised edition 1965) pps. 159 and 160 Copyright Dimity Obolensky, 1962, 1965; RLT Ardis Publishers of Ann Arbor, Michigan, U.S.A. from 'A Journey to Arzrum' (translated by Birgitta Ingemanson) and from Helen Michailoff's 'The Death of Lermontov' Issue No. 10 of RLT; Southern Illinois University Press, from 'Mikhail Lermontov' by John Mersereau Jr.; C. E. L'Ami and University of Manitoba Press from 'Lermontov: Biography and Translation' by C. E. L'Ami and Alexander Welikotny; George Weidenfeld and Nicolson from 'Speak Memory' by V. Nabokov; University of Massachusetts Press, Amherst, from 'The Diary of a Russian Censor Aleksandr Nikitenko' abridged, edited and translated by Helen Saltz Jacobson.

Permission is also acknowledged in respect of illustrations to the Novosti Press Agency of Moscow, Leningrad and London; to Mrs Humphrey Brooke (General Benckendorff), University of Columbia (Varvara Lopukhina) and thanks to my Publishers for producing and editing a most useful map covering the Caucasus and Georgia in Lermontov's days.

Preface

The idea of this book was conceived during a journey which I made to the Caucasus and Georgia in 1971. I had received an invitation from the late W. E. D. Allen, the doyen of Georgian studies in England and Ireland, to join him on what proved to be his last visit to those fabulous mountains and homeric peoples, for he died in 1973 aged seventy.

Bill Allen, already in his lifetime, seemed to have inherited the laurels of a long line of European scholars, topographers, geologists, geographers, historians and artists fascinated by the Caucasus: Jules Klaproth, Dr Robert Lyall, Gamba, Hommaire de Hell, Dubois de Montpereux, and, within his lifetime, Freshfield and Baddeley. His standard *History of the Georgian People*, first published in 1932, had been complemented over the years by a series of learned articles, and in 1970 by *The Russian Embassies to the Georgian Kings*. It was with lively pleasure that I met him in Tiflis, where he was accompanied by his nephew Robin, and a writer, Michael Pereira, who has recorded our travels in a delightful travel book, *Across the Caucasus*, that came out in 1973. We all enjoyed the benefits of Bill's wry and racy humour, and his scholarship and learning so wittily and generously dispensed to us. There was another benefit too: an 'Open Door' policy for unusual expeditions arranged by the Georgian authorities, and similarly in Ossetia, north of the mountains in Vladikavkaz (now Ordjonikidze). Chief amongst our benefactors were Alexander Zjgenti, of the Georgian Friendship and Cultural Society, and Academician Abayev, himself a native of Kobi on the Georgian Military Highway.

Thanks to our itinerary, I was able to retrace Lermontov's steps – or more precisely perhaps those of his horses' hooves – from Pyatigorsk and the watering spas of Kabarda in the North, over the Great Military Highway through Georgia's ancient capital

Mtskheta, to Tiflis, and in the East, past Tsinandali, in t he fertile valley of the Alazan beneath the mountains of the Lesg h ian Line. Wherever we went, at the great feasts arranged by the local dignitaries with their ritual of speeches, songs and even poetry to meet the genial demands made on the guests by the *Tamada* or toast master appointed for the evening, I found a definite curiosity as to my own role in the retinue of the master: was I in some research collective, perhaps based in County Waterford, using the rich Allen library? It was certainly obvious that I was there to make use of my Russian, as *dragoman* for our party, rising to the heights of translating Bill's speeches after the tenth toast. I decided to strike boldly, and lost no time in explaining that there was a gap in English literature about Lermontov – there is still, as far as I know, no full-scale biography in English – and that I was hoping to use my Caucasian experiences as the starting point for a study of him. The idea, lightly put forward, soon hardened into resolution, my enthusiasm fed by the wealth of knowledge and scholarship vouchsafed to me by the Lermontov experts I kept meeting on my journey.

On return to London, however, I found that a well-known scholar, Philip Longworth, author of a translation of Lermontov's *Hero of our Time*, a life of Suvorov, and a history of the Cossacks, was already intending to fill a vital part of this gap. He wanted to describe Pushkin's adventures crossing the Caucasus which led to his *Journey to Erzerum* and to his famous poem 'The Caucasian Prisoner' of which Pushkin wrote, 'I wanted to exemplify in him that indifference to life and its pleasures, that premature ageing of the soul which have become characteristic of nineteenth-century youth. The Circassians, their customs and manners take up the larger and better part of my narrative . . . and serve as an *hors d'oeuvre*.'[1]

This would have been followed by a longer section describing Lermontov's impassioned entanglement with the Caucasus, lasting until his death there in 1841; and lastly Tolstoy's own pilgrimage as a very young man in 1851. The book would have been called in Byelinsky's appropriate phrase, 'The New Parnassus'.

At his kind suggestion, we agreed to collaborate, the central section on Lermontov falling to myself. He made available to me his notes, and gave me the benefit of his literary judgement and experience, for which I shall always be extremely grateful. But, to our mutual regret, other commitments prevented him from carrying out his project and thus there is still room for a full-scale treatment of the magnetic spell cast upon those two giants of Russian literature, Pushkin and Tolstoy, as well as on Bestujev–'Marlinsky', Griboyedov and a host of others, by the Caucasus. Meanwhile, it seemed to me that this study of Lermontov, with whose destiny, both as a poet and a man, the Caucasus was so inextricably entangled, could stand, as I had at first intended, on its own. Thanks to Philip Longworth, too, I was introduced to Professor V. A. Manuilov, of Puskhin House in Leningrad, whose years of scholarly dedication to establishing the truth about Lermontov's life and work have won him a worldwide reputation, and who gave me valuable, if not irreplaceable, books from his own personal library to help me.

There is hardly an edition of *Evgeny Onegin* that does not describe the enduring problem of translating Pushkin's verse, and it is a fact that there is no full anthology of his poetry in English. The same is true of Lermontov. Amongst the most dedicated of his translators must be ranked Alexander Welikotny and C. E. L'Ami in Canada who – in volume at least – attempted to translate more of his work than any other English admirers of Lermontov; and where they fail, the failure must be adjudged a noble one. As they write, no translation can reproduce the 'tonal music of the original, a great but not a total loss'.[2] And not all their translations follow the rhyming or metre of the originals, double and triple rhyming often occurring in Russian, which would strain the quality of any English version. Maurice Baring, in the introduction to his *Book of Russian Verse*, referred to the difficulty of translating Pushkin into English as as 'hopeless a task as it would be to try to transmute the melodies of Mozart into another medium, into colour or stone'.[3] This, too, applies to most translations of Lermontov, notably of the enchanting and at times overwhelming music of 'The Demon' or 'The Novice' quoted later in this book. Another translator of Lermontov (Mr John Pollen in his *Russian Songs and Lyrics*) has been criticised for his failure to observe

Lermontov's original metres, and phrasing. Madame Jarintzov
(a translator perhaps unknown to the general reader, and herself
Russian) rightly makes much of Lermontov's 'national state-
liness', and the artistic crime of disregarding 'the original swing'
of some of his poems (e.g. 'The Angel') where 'a gracefully grave
amphibrach is turned into a polka.'[4]

At all events, often caught between the Scylla of a trueborn
Russian's criticism of an English translation, and the Charybdis
of selecting the only translation available not by a Russian, I can
only plead the excuse that I have tried, in my selections, at least
to reproduce Lermontov's concision, 'the spirit, atmosphere,
colour and nature of sound' from the translations available, and
confess how tricky this problem of judgment has been.

There has also been the further problem of including poems and
ballads, loved by Russians since their childhood, showing – in
the words of a perceptive critic – 'a poetic genius such as rarely
graces any language' and yet which may not enhance any biographical narrative, and may even give the impression of having
been 'dragged in' somewhat awkwardly, to fit the chronology. To
overcome this problem, and to give the reader the chance to judge
for himself some of Lermontov's most attractive writings (for
example, 'The Sail', 'Borodino', 'My Country') I have included
these as Appendix II. There is still a need for a full edition of
Lermontov's poetic works translated into English by someone
uniting the talents of Baring, Bowra, and Bayley.

In trying to understand Lermontov through his own and his
contemporaries' written evidence, I must pay tribute to the loving
and enthusiastic work of Russian scholars, and Caucasian and
Georgian ones too, before and after the 1917 Revolution, whose
work now amounts almost to a major industry. Without access
to the archives, in Leningrad and Moscow, Pyatigorsk and Tiflis,
and elsewhere, it would be difficult for an outsider in the West to
lay claim to originality of research; so much has been destroyed,
even by Lermontov's contemporaries. Neither of his two closest
friends, Svyatoslav Rayevsky nor 'Mongo' Stolypin, left memoirs.
The archives of his Regiment disappeared during the First World
War; almost no official files remain about his second 'exile' to the
Caucasus; in the police archives of the Third Department there

were only three files on Pushkin and Lermontov. Almost every scrap of evidence published in Russia has been subjected to analysis by Soviet researchers, latter-day patristic scholars poring over the sacred texts of one of Russia's prophets.

Nevertheless, there have been opportunities for literary historians in the West, there for the taking. Until after the Second World War, there was a *cache* of albums, poems and drawings at the Schloss of Warthausen (near Stuttgart), belonging to the descendants of Alexandra Vereshchagina (a much loved cousin of Lermontov's), married to Baron Karl von Hügel, and retrieved by that Sherlock Holmes of Soviet Lermontov scholars Irakli Andronikov for Soviet collections. More of Alexandra's albums (sold by von Hügel descendants) ended up in the Library of Columbia University, New York, and have been admirably edited and analysed by Helen Michailoff.

Before the last war, there would have been a fascinating opportunity to unearth unknown Lermontov letters to his Stolypin and Filosofov relations in a villa in Normandy. To quote a letter to me from Monsieur Nicholas Rayevsky (of Vienna) whose family owned these, there were even *'pas mal de lettres.'* Alas, these were destroyed by the German occupying forces during their tenure of the villa in 1940–44. There are unpublished drawings of important figures of Lermontov's Caucasian and St. Petersburg life (General Yermolov for example), by the wife of the French Ambassador in St. Petersburg, and mother of the Ernest de Barante who fought a duel with Lermontov, still to be seen today at the Château de Barante in France.

I have been fortunate in obtaining new evidence from un-published sources through the kindness of Prince George Vassiltchikov, of Geneva. Prince Alexander Vassiltchikov, who was Lermontov's second at his fatal duel, was his great great uncle, and gave to his son Boris facts never publicly disclosed about the duel which Prince Boris wrote down as part of his memoirs, hitherto unpublished.[5] This material gives the last words of Lermontov before he fell dead to Major Martynov's bullet. Prince Alexander Vassiltchikov had, of course, given his official view of the duel in the journal *Russky Arkhiv* of 1872, some thirty years after the event, but *en famille,* as the text of the new evidence shows, he had a different story. Certainly the words so loudly and provocatively shouted at Martynov by Lermontov – if the new evidence is to be accepted – would account for Martynov's sudden fury, simplified in an instant of hatred, into the act of pulling the trigger. Much else, hitherto inexplicable, would fall psychologically into place. Speculation will continue, but that new evidence from a participant is now available is indisputable.

For the first time, to my knowledge at least, the opportunity arises in this book to publish in England, as illustrations to Lermontov's prose and poetry, his own paintings, acquarelles, and sketches. Pushkin, Jukovsky, Turgeniev, even Tolstoy were all dilettante artists who could try to do justice to the inevitable request of their admirers to dash off something for the souvenir album, as soon as they entered a drawing-room. Lermontov's soul was in his work. He started sketching before he was ten; took lessons from two minor professional painters, A. S. Solonitsky and P. E. Zabolotsky, and in 1840/41 worked with a close friend, Prince G. Gagarin, whose own vivid paintings and illustrated books about the Caucasian War and Georgia deserve warm praise in their own right. Much has been lost; but at least eleven oil paintings are known (nearly all in the Soviet Union), fifty-one acquarelles, fifty drawings, some seventy sketches or caricatures in the margin of manuscripts, and two albums with more than another two hundred drawings. Lermontov was an exceptionally fast worker, but there is a brilliance and mastery of movement in his drawings of horses that would not disgrace a Delacroix, mordant satire in the caricatures, and a warmth of colour in his Caucasian oil paintings that is the visual counterpart to his own rich colouring in the words of 'The Demon' or 'The Novice'.

Whilst Lermontov's talents as an artist can be illustrated in book-form, his influence on music cannot, and yet deserves mention. In Russia, verse and music appeared together, and the 'romance' as an art-song was an especially happy example of their interaction. Lermontov played the violin well enough to be praised for his performance in 1829 at Moscow University; he played the piano for himself and friends, and was an assiduous opera-goer. He used to sing these 'romances' with great feeling.

There is even evidence that he wrote his own music for the 'Cossack Cradle Song'. He believed passionately that music lifted the soul to the heavens, that the poet was gifted to hear it, and he endowed the fabled creations of his poetic world with song: the Angel, the Demon, the *russalka* or water-nymph, the fisher-girl, children, even snowstorms. He orchestrated sound and rhythm so that his verse should have, perhaps as its essence, the magic of music. And, not surprisingly, Russia's composers returned the compliment with enthusiasm. Rubinstein composed three operas; Glazunov the incidental music for *Masquerade*; Balakirev a symphonic poem 'Tamara'; Mussorgsky, Rimsky Korsakov and Glinka fell under the spell of his poetry to write music for it. So did Tchaikovsky. At least fifty-five of Lermontov's poems have been arranged for romances. Ivan Turgeniev taught Pauline Viardot a number of Lermontov's songs which she sang all over Europe with great success. Several western composers including Liszt took up the challenge, and, with Balakirev, could say 'I breathe through Lermontov'.

Whatever the limitations imposed upon a writer in the West, the key to understanding Lermontov's character is not to be found in biographical research, but in his ideas, in Byelinsky's phrase, 'presented in artistic form' – and for that, any edition of his works provides a lifetime's reward and fascination.

Taman

• Stavropol

• Anapa

Soundjouk,
Kale

• Fort Novorossisk

Georg

• Fort Kabardinskoye

Mt
Mashu

• Ghelendjik

Besh-Tau

Karras •

Pyati

• Fort Novotroitskoye

Kislovodsk •

• Fort Mikhailovskoye

Malka

• Fort Tenginskoye

Baksa

Fort Veliaminovskoye •

KA B A

Fort Lazarevskoye •

Fort Navaginskoye •

▲ Mt. Elborus
18470 ft

Pitsounda •

A B K H A Z I A

C A U C A S U S

Soukhoum Kale •

M T S

M I N G R E L I A

I M E R I

• Redout Kale

B L A C K   S E A

• Poti

K A R

Batoum •

P A S H A L I K   O F   A K H

P A S H A L I K   O F

P A S H A

E R Z E R U M

O F   K A

Cossack Line	xxxxxxxxxx
Advanced Cossack Line	– – – – – –
Chechniya advanced Line	··········
Georgian Military Highway	═══════

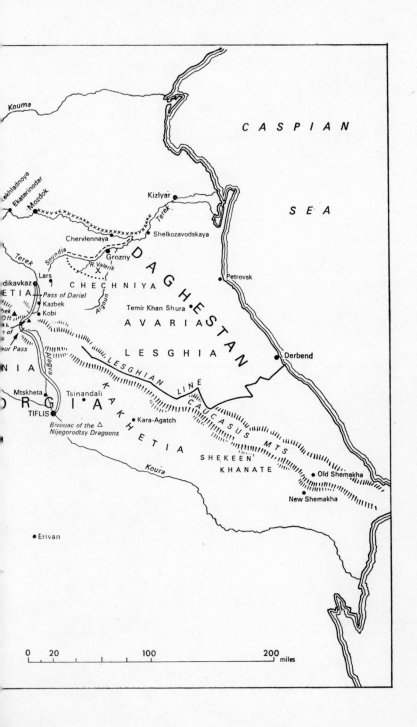

CASPIAN

SEA

Kouma

Vekhladnoye
Ekaterinodar
Mozdok
Kizlyar
Terek
Chervlennaya
Shelkozavodskaya
Soundja
Grozny
R. Valerik
Lars
CHECHNIYA
dikavkaz
ETIA
Pass of Dariel
Kazbek
hek
Oft
Kobi
Argoun
Temir Khan Shura
k
of
s
ur Pass
Petrovsk
DAGHESTAN
AVARIA
LESGHIA
Derbend
NIA
Aragva
Mtskheta
Tsinandali
ORGIA
TIFLIS
LESGHIAN
LINE
KAKHETIA
Bivouac of the
Nijegorodtsy Dragoons
Kara-Agatch
CAUCASUS
MTS
SHEKEEN
KHANATE
Old Shemakha
Koura
New Shemakha

Erivan

0   20   100   200 miles

Childhood in the Wild East

Mariya Arseniyeva was only seventeen when she fell in love with a neighbouring squire eight years her senior, Captain Yuri Lermontov. Dreamy, inexperienced, delicate, she seemed an incarnation of Pushkin's Tatiana. Her choice of suitor was a cheerful, handsome and passably elegant soldier, who had been invalided out of the infantry in 1811. His ancestors, not so grand nor so rich as her own clan of Arseniyevs and Stolypins, belonged to the landowning gentry in the Province of Tula, south of Moscow, having been ennobled as soldiers of fortune in 1621 by Tsar Michael Romanov. The Lermontovs claimed descent from the Learmonths in Scotland. Thomas the Rhymer, the twelfth-century bard, added an Ossianic lustre to their pedigree.

Married in 1812 against the wishes of Mariya's mother, the pair turned out to be ill-suited. The birth of their only son Mikhail in 1814[1] did not mend the marriage. The Captain turned to traditional distractions of serf-girls and drink. In February 1817, near Penza in Central Russia, at her mother's house of Tarkhany, Mariya died of consumption, a frail, disappointed and melancholic figure. Her marriage had lasted barely four years.

The Captain had been summoned from Moscow to be at his wife's side for her last weeks. Angry with his libertine ways, scornful of his poverty, his mother-in-law, Madame Arseniyeva, now made a formidable contestant for the possession of her little grandson. Yuri Lermontov already owed her twenty-five thousand roubles borrowed two years before. She turned the screw tighter and informed him that she would will all her serfs with their wives, serf children, and all her lands to her grandson if she had possession of him, and if the father abandoned his rights until the boy's majority. If the father reclaimed his son, all would go to her Stolypin cousins.[2] To show magnanimity she would even extend the 'loan' of 1815. He had no option but to accept. Father and son were separated, except for some holidays, for the rest of the former's life (he died aged forty in 1831). The Captain departed within days of the funeral to his modest estate and Mikhail entered, at the age of three, the gilded and luxurious cage lovingly prepared for him by his grandmother.

Elizabeth Arseniyeva was rich, aristocratic and formidable. Born a Stolypin, her relatives, though not titled, were very rich, and belonged to an inner cousinhood in St. Petersburg and Moscow, which expected Senatorships, Court appointments and nominations to the best Regiments as of right. A 'tall straight figure, leaning slightly on a cane, with an unhurried distinct way of speaking,'[3] she had undoubted charm for those she loved. Unfortunately her husband was not one of them. Eight years her junior, unhappily in love with a country neighbour, he had committed suicide in 1811 during a New Year's masquerade in their own house. His widow's only recorded comment was terse: 'a dog's death for a dog.'[4] From 1817 onwards she was to live only for her grandson. She was only forty-five years old.

Plunged into grief by the death of her daughter, and watching uneasily over the precarious health of little Mishka, Madame Arseniyeva was an object of sympathy and solicitude within her own large clan of sisters and brothers. One of these, also a widow, was Ekaterina Khastatova. She lived in the south and pressed her sister to bring her grandson into the dry warm sun of the Caucasian foothills to banish his rheumatic fevers, and the effects of a severe attack of measles.

She decided to accept, and on three occasions, in 1818, 1820 and 1825, her party of French tutor, German governess, French doctor and various cooks, servants, grooms and little Mishka set off in May or June from Tarkhany to the sunny northern flanks of the Caucasus.

Mishka was three, five and ten years old respectively on these three expeditions. To him they were the very stuff of adventure. The analogy of a young proper Bostonian or New Yorker spending his holidays within sight of the camp fires and tents of Sioux or Comanche chiefs in the 1820s would be an accurate one; for Mishka the Caucasus was the Wild East.

The perils of the thousand kilometre journey were considerable. It would be easy to assume that Madame Arseniyeva would have travelled in the cheerful and apparently comfortable style shown in nineteenth-century prints, a ruddy-cheeked coachman singing in a deep bass voice to the spirited horses, and beard streaming in the steppe wind, his whip urging the horses along a smooth road. And, as befitted her rank and means, she could well afford to travel in a comfortably appointed *landau* or *berline*, followed by a wagon for luggage, cooks, servants and tents. Experience showed, however, that their well-forged European axles, once snapped on the dreadfully rutted roads, could never be repaired by Cossack villagers. The very grand travelled with their own wheelwright. Prudence dictated the use of the *kibitka*, a large cart with a hood over the rear half in the style of Western wagons, or the uncovered *telega* whose wooden parts could all be quickly repaired or made afresh. If completely stuck, there was always the *tarantass*, described by that connoisseur of Caucasian travel Alexandre Dumas, as a vehicle that 'can go anywhere, like the boiler of a railway engine mounted on four wheels with a little window at the front and a door at the side; no springs and no seats, and floor covered with straw.'[5] The heavier the *équipage*, the greater the problem at fords or ferries across the Don, or the Terek. There were problems, too, of stampeding cattle, or bolting, exhausted or dead horses, of broken guide ropes or harnesses suddenly breaking at the gallop. Ice and snow formed deep sea waves and troughs that, after the spring thaw, simply turned into a sea of mud, a traveller's Passchendaele, whose ruts either made one vomit from travel sickness or inflicted skull-cracking bumps and crashes. Mud flew over the faces of the passengers. After an eight-hour stint in her *telega* another hardly middle-aged woman, Lady Londonderry, wrote in 1836 that despite bulky wrappings and bearskins, 'my face was cut to pieces; I was bruised all over and I could hardly stand.'[6]

Madame Arseniyeva, related to generals and well supplied with roubles, might have expected courteous treatment from the postmasters. In fact, all officials of the Empire, whether blue-coated Gendarmes, imperial couriers ('feld-jaegers'), perhaps escorting criminals to some secret destination, or epauletted general officers, took precedence over civilians in such matters as requisitioning fresh horses. A surly postmaster, unimpressed by your papers, might refuse to provide new horses at the relay; if he refused the hospitality of his house as well, you would be thrown into the company of the other travellers, chewing their melon and sunflower seeds in whatever flea-ridden hut there was available. Only the largest of the bribes then, to cure the 'galloping consumption' in the pockets of postmasters and Chief constables, could prevent you from being stranded for days in oriental resignation or western fury.

Once the party reached the Steppes, travel at last became easier; the horses could gallop full tilt on tracks as smooth as bowling greens decked in tulips. Beyond the Steppes of the Kuban the country began to change. The song of cicadas replaced that of the northern cuckoo. Bustards and vultures pecked at dead animals rotting in the dusty folds of the gentle foothills. Pelicans from the Sea of Azov flew over the convoy. The oppressive midday heat made the horses sweat. Instead of the monotonous grass plains of the Steppe, oaks and maples, feather grass, *fraxinella*, huge thistles, bell flowers and wormwood, reeds and marshes distracted the traveller's eye. The most thrilling moment – the official recognition of danger – came when the convoy entered the protection of the 'Line' to be met by Black Sea Cossacks, a troop of up to eight horsemen, in grey infantry coats of sheepskin wrappers, a musket slung over their shoulders with red lances. Nearer headquarters at Stavropol, these were replaced by the Grebentsy Cossacks, an altogether more warlike body of men eager for any fight with the Circassians sweeping down from the mountains.

The River Terek was a name famous throughout Russia as the natural frontier with the wild, murderous highlanders of the Caucasus. In the words of the most popular and widely read Russian writer about the Caucasus in Lermontov's childhood, Bestujev 'Marlinsky':

In the Caucasus, it must be confessed, there are no waters in which the mountains can worthily reflect themselves – those giants of creation. There are no gentle rivers, no vast lakes; but Terek receives in his stream the tribute of a thousand streamlets. Beneath the further Caucasus, where the mountains melt into the plain, he seems to flow calmly and gently, he wanders on in huge curves, depositing the pebbles he has brought down from the hills. Further on, bending to the north-west, the stream is still strong, but less noisy, as though wearied with its fierce strugglings. At length, embraced by the narrow gorge of Cape Maloi [Little Kabardi], the river, like a good Moslem, bending religiously to the east, and peacefully spreading over the hated shore, gliding sometimes over beds of stone, sometimes over banks of clay, falls, by Kizlar, into the basin of the Caspian. There alone does it deign to bear boats upon its waters, and, like a labourer, turn the huge wheels of floating mills. On its right bank, among hillocks and thickets, are scattered the villages [*aouls*] of the *Kabardinetzes*, a tribe which we confound under one name with the Tcherkess [Circassians], who dwell beyond the Kouban, and with the Tchechenetzes much lower by the sea. These villages on the bank are peaceful only in name, for in reality they are the haunts of brigands, who acknowledge the Russian government only as far as it suits their interest, capturing, as Russian subjects, from the mountaineers, the plunder they seize in the Russian frontier. Enjoying free passage on all sides, they inform those of the same religion and the same way of thinking, of the movement of our troops, and the conditions of our fortresses; conceal them among themselves when they are assembling for an incursion, buy their plunder at their return, furnish them with Russian salt and powder, and not rarely take themselves a part, secret or open, in their forays. It is exceedingly irritating to see, even in full view of these mountaineers, nations hostile to us boldly swim over the Terek, two, three, or five men at a time, and in broad day set to work to rob; it being useless to pursue them, as their dress has nothing to distinguish them from the friendly tribes. On the opposite bank, though apparently quite peaceable, and employing this as their excuse, they fall, when in force, upon travellers, carry off cattle and men when off their guard, slaughter them without mercy, or sell them into slavery at a distance. To tell the truth, their natural position, between two powerful neighbours, of necessity compels them to have recourse to these stratagems. Knowing that the Russians will not pass to the other side of the river to protect them from the revenge of the mountaineers, who melt away like snow at the approach of a strong force, they easily and habitually, as well as from inevitable circumstances, ally themselves to people of their own blood, while they affect to pay deference to the Russians, whom they fear.

Indeed, there exists among them certain persons really devoted to the Russians, but the greater number will betray even their own countrymen for a bribe.[7]

Along the Terek were spaced the Cossack lookouts, numerous airy stations slung on four high beams, reached only by a ladder, manned by an immobile, hawk-nosed Cossack, whose first duty on sighting a raiding party was to light a huge fire of faggots stacked under his tower. Perched too high for travellers galloping past even to admire his 'long mustachios', he had often been known to fall asleep from drink or exhaustion on duty, and had little to look forward to except death from a Circassian broadsword, or a Russian flogging for idleness. The fear of capture or death would now grip the convoy, an eleven-year-old boy scanning the horizon as closely as his escort. Was that party of mounted Circassians, fast catching them up at a gallop, friendly or not? If attacked, would their escort ever cut their carriage ropes in time, and who would vault onto the lead-horses to escape and warn the next fortress along the 'Line'? For poor Madame Arseniyeva, this was hardly a feasible escape; she and Mishka would be worth a rich ransom. And, indeed, were those shaggy Cossacks in the escort at all trustworthy? They were reputed often to desert to the hills, and to the newcomers, seemed indistinguishable from their enemies. Never would the shelter of the next fortress seem more desirable, even if it only consisted of simple earthen parapets, shallow ditches, an elementary barracks, a church, officers' mess, and two-pounder cannon.

Once within the fortress, excited questions would fly from

grandson to grandmother. What was that Tartar wearing as a kind of cloak? White or black, the 'felt-mantle', or *burka*, 'half an inch thick', covered in long hair, was the mountaineer's inseparable protection against the burning sun, the heavy rain, and could become his bed with plenty of straw underneath it. Who was that full blooded 'Prince', exchanging rye for salt or prisoners (two Russians for one Circassian)? Was he a Circassian? With a 'cupola formed leather cap, bordered with black sheep-skin, a dark striped surcoat, "coat of chain armour" covered with a white linen tunic, and on the arms steel armour silvered and gilt,' these Princes looked magnificent. 'His blue pantaloons were embroidered with silver, and bound at the knees by red leather garters and his boots, formed of red and yellow leather, were extremely long, sharp, pointed, and drawn close to the leg and foot by laces. In his right hand he held a Circassian whip whose handle was short and covered with leather, and instead of having a lash it ended in a heart red on one side, yellow on the other, admirably calculated for making a noise against the horse's side.'[8] His bow was ready for action, the quiver full of arrows, the sabre of Damascus workmanship with an ivory handle. The Prince was flanked by a Mullah (or priest) in white turban, wide flowing scarlet robe, yellow boots and also armed with a sabre. Patiently his grandmother or the Russian Commandant of the fort would seek to answer Mishka's questions.

South of Stavropol, night travel was out of the question, as the Circassians found the brushwood and thickets along the Terek to be their best cover for ambushes. The freemasonry induced by a siege mentality would thaw out differences of rank between Russians thrown together for the night in a post-station. High-ranking, arrogant officers would become sociable, courteous, and in their best St Petersburg French offer Madame Arseniyeva a pheasant, caviare, 'meat patties', and some Moët Chandon or Veuve Cliquot bought at Novo Tcherkassk. Those without champagne would console themselves with *Jonka*, a punch of rum and flaming lumps of sugar, and their first taste of pilaff, made up of rice, prawns, chicken and an atrociously over-peppered sauce.

From the fortress of Georgievsk to Vladikavkaz, and beyond

to Chervlennaya, and finally to the shelter of 'The Silk Factory' (Shelkozavodskaya) as the Khastatovs' estate was called, was a nerve-wracking final leg of the long journey, where the protection of a small troop of Cossacks was not enough, and the full panoply of that armed convoy (called the *okaziya*) was needed – formed twice weekly to protect the Tsar's mail and treasury to the Governor General of Tiflis on their journey through the gorges, defiles and mountain passes of the Georgian Military Highway. Madame Arseniyeva and her party would gratefully take their place in the motley cavalcade, escorted by perhaps seventy Cossacks in three parties, a three-pounder and powder magazine; there was the precious mail cart in the centre 'driven by a rude clumsy Russian female', and a hundred equipages: 'French *calashes*, Polish *britchkas*, Russian *Kibitkas* and *telegas*, Hungarian wagons, and Tartar *arbas* drawn by oxen'[9] nearly a mile long. Horses and herds of cattle completed the unwieldy convoy which the commanding lieutenant and his Cossacks tried to marshal into two lines. Another hazard was the crossing of the Terek, to be achieved by ferry to the accompaniment of much shouting, swearing, sweating and usually an accident or two. Twenty miles would take twelve hours.

The left bank of the Terek is covered with flourishing stanitzas of the *Kazaks* of the Line, the descendants of the famous *Zaporojetzes*. Among them is here and there a Christian village. These *Kazaks* are distinguished from the mountaineers only by their unshaven heads: their tools, dress, harness, manners – all are of the mountains. They like the almost ceaseless war with the mountaineers; it is not a battle, but a trial of arms, in which each party desires to gain glory by his superiority in strength, valour, and address. Two *Kazaks* would not fear to encounter four mountain horsemen, and with equal numbers they are invariably victors. Lastly, they speak the Tartar language; they are connected with the mountaineers by friendship and alliance, their women being mutually carried off into captivity; but in the field they are inflexible enemies. As it is not forbidden to make incursions on the mountain side of the Terek, the brigands frequently

Pyatigorsk, 1834. View of Nikolayevsky, Aleksandrovsky and Yermolov Baths. Lithograph from the drawing of I. Bernadazzi

Self-portrait in uniform of Nijegorodtsy Dragoon Regiment by Lermontov. Painted by Lermontov in 1837 as a gift for Varvara Lopukhina Bakhmetieva.

Varvara Alexandrovna Lopukhina, by Lermontov

(Above) *Nicholas I, Tsar of all the Russias, by Samsonov*
(Right above) *Count Aleksandr Christoforovich Benckendorff, Chef des gendarmes*
(Right below) *Grand Duke Mikhail Pavlovitch.*
Print from the painting by T. Cherikov

Portrait of Varvara Alexandrovna Lopukhina as a Spanish nun, by Lermontov

Elisaveta Alekseyevna Arseniyeva (born Stolypina). Artist unknown

View of Pyatigorsk and Mount Elborus, by Lermontov

*The headquarters of the Nijegorodtsy Dragoon Regiment
near Kara-Agatch, Kakhetia, by Prince G. G. Gagarin*

betake themselves thither by swimming the river, for the chase of various kinds of game. The mountain brigands, in their turn, frequently swim over the Terek at night, or cross it on *bourdouchs* [skins blown up], hide themselves in the reeds, or under a projection of the bank, thence gliding through the thickets to the road, to carry off unsuspecting travellers, or to seize a woman, as she is raking the hay. It sometimes happens that they will pass a day or two in the vineyards by the village, awaiting a favourable opportunity to fall upon it unexpectedly; and hence the *Kaẓak* of the Line never stirs over his threshold without his dagger, nor goes into the field without his gun at his back: he ploughs and sows completely armed.[10]

From Georgievsk onwards, little Lermontov beheld the grand chain of the Caucasus, the snowy triangle of Mount Kazbek nearest to him cleaving the skies, and in an uninterrupted, three-hundred-mile-long sweep of towering giants he would see the famous twin breasts of Mount Elborus, through which Noah's Ark was reputed to have passed to reach Mount Ararat. He abandoned himself, for the first but not the last time, to that mood of awe and reverence that gripped travellers, as they contemplated 'the whole chain of snow-capped mountains, raising their venerable heads to the clouds,' and reflecting the rays of the sun with all the colours of the rainbow. This was a sight 'to look through Nature up to Nature's God': the grandest view in Europe.[11] The thousand pointed peaks took shape as an eccentric procession of teeth, pillars, horns, cupolas, and pyramids. It was an incomparable impression. He wrote later:

Since childhood he had loved these things – to feel
The solemn glory of wild nature's scene;
The flood of sunset; icy peaks between
Shining against the blue far off and dim
Such things alone had never changed for him.[12]

At Vladikavkaz, the *okaẓiya* and the Arseniyeva party had to split up, the latter to be greeted now by the Khastatovs' own escort of mounted Cossacks, which brought them finally to their vineyards and plantations of red and white mulberry trees and of silkworms, where the five hundred Armenian, Georgian and Tartar serfs could straighten themselves from their work to wave dutifully to the safely arrived convoy. What a sense of relief Madame Arseniyeva must have felt!

But her sister, Ekaterina, displayed only stern feelings worthy of a Roman matron on the frontiers of darkest Scythia. She had been trained by doughty warriors. Her late husband, Akim, had been a veteran of Austerlitz, Borodino, and the fall of Paris in 1814. He had served under the great Suvorov at the bloody siege of Ismailia, chronicled by Byron in two Cantos of *Don Juan*.[13] Promoted to Major-General, he had been a crony of the Commander-in-Chief of the Independent Caucasian Corps, the ferocious General, Alexey Yermolov,[14] whose own fighting headquarters in a stone bunker were within fifty miles of them, at Fort Terrible (Grozny). It was not surprising that she treated night raiders with contempt. No crackle of hostile musketry would arouse her from a well-earned sleep. Her neighbours said that she would only move if the house itself were on fire.

There were two small cannons primed in front of the house. The remaining men in her family, her son and a son-in-law, Colonel Petrov, sported white panamas as they rode around the fields and plantations, scornful of the target they might present. To Mishka every day provided fresh examples of their sang-froid.

He began to learn about this new, wild, Eastern world, so different from the monotony and ageless routine of central Russia. Who were all these different tribes? He noted the shaven heads, small sparkling eyes, projecting cheek-bones and yellow-ness of the Nogay Tartars, whose ancestors had followed the Golden Horde. He discovered that the Ossetins had blue eyes, and red hair. He admired the svelte and noble figures of Kabardins, and their handsome aquiline noses. But it was the visit of occasional Chechens, Ingushi, Avars and Lesghi that caught his attentions. Swarthier and stockier than their western cousins, these tribesmen of the Eastern Caucasus had eyes that flashed with an unrivalled 'cunning and sanguinary spirit', and their jackal-like war cry, or dying chant to Allah, reminded all Russians that in the black, rocky fastnesses of Daghestan they faced tribes reared on the name of the Prophet, knowledgeable of their Koran and reminded of it by a line of warrior Sheikhs and Imams, Mansur, Kazi Mullah and Shamyl. General Khastatov, friend of General Yermolov, had never under-estimated these 'aborigines of the Caucasus'. They lived too close to him. Stories of prisoners buried alive or tortured by the horrible punishment of chopped horsehair inserted under the outer skin of their feet (which would then swell and make escape impossible) passed amongst the settlers.

These free men of the mountains, in contrast to the serfs of the plains, were mounted and bore arms: 'the Circassian is armed with a light gun, slung across the shoulder, and sabre suspended by a cord in the Turkish fashion; attached to the belt is a powder flask, and a small metal box containing flints, gun screws, oil, and not infrequently a small hatchet. . . . Sometimes he carries a javelin. The latter weapon is also used as a rest for the rifle. On either side of the breast of the coat are the *patron* pockets, made of morocco leather, usually containing twenty-four rounds of ball cartridge. Princes and nobles are alone entitled to the privilege of wearing red.'[15] It was Russian policy to allow them to ride singly in and out of the 'Line.' Lermontov's early observations, to be recorded in later years in oils, sketches and drawings, retained with precision their wild elegance and supple grace in saddle when mounted.

The Khastatovs, as befitted founder members of the local aristocracy, also had a summer house in the rapidly growing watering spa of Pyatigorsk, one hundred and fifty miles west towards Stavropol. The 'season' there would run from June to late September, when families from St Petersburg and Moscow, and indeed all over Russia, who had endured the long trek, came to cure themselves in the smelly and sulphurous baths, as did officers convalescing from their wounds. The Khastatov and Arseniyev families would make the journey once again along the most dangerous part of the 'Line' to be joined in Pyatigorsk by other cousins. There was a grandson of Ekaterina's, Akim Shan

Girey, who, though four years younger than Mishka, would do very well as a companion for him; and on the third of the summer holidays which Madame Arseniyeva spent in the Northern Caucasus Akim travelled with them.

The daily round at Pyatigorsk included picnics, and various expeditions adjudged safe and within sight of the Cossack pickets. During the Moslem feasts of Bairam, Lermontov was taken to the outlying villages of Nogay Tartars and Kalmucks near Pyatigorsk, where the descendants of the Golden Horde, tamed by three centuries of sly subservience to regular Russian troops and their Cossack satellites, lived, and where mountain tribesmen would ride in to buy war-stores, horses, and sunflower seeds, and gingerbread and lengths of cloth. Here he saw the *djigit*, a veteran of proven bravery, whose trophies included a score of heads or several hands tied to the saddle. He witnessed the *djigitovka*, that display of horsemanship by a clan's war braves which was the crowning glory of any Caucasian wedding or feast. After all, it was a form of battle training; there was often injury. Usually in two parts, there were acrobatic tricks of stunning versatility, involving total trust between rider and horse, the trust which in war could save a wounded man's life, and then a *feu de joie* of reckless bravado. There were camel fights. Wild gunplay was a standard feature.

Lermontov's life-long love of horses was born at this time. *En route* from the General's estate to Pyatigorsk, there was the magnificent sight of the finest stallions in the Caucasus of 'Sultan' Taw, the local stud-owner near Pyatigorsk, being driven down from the slopes of Mount Kazbek, some to the high reeds by the rivers, some to the corrals on the slopes of Mount Mashuk. These grey or bay thoroughbreds were highly valued across the Terek, throughout Kabarda, amongst the chiefs of the Black Sea Clans, and by Lesghian or Avar Beys from Daghestan. They were speedy, reliable, and beautiful. Ptolemy, a visitor centuries before, had called the five hills of Pyatigorsk the 'mountains of horses'.[16]

Later, Lermontov's poems would often pay some tribute to the horse. In his 'Circassian Song', the village minstrel gives advice, understood and accepted by any Circassian war brave:

In our hills the girls are plenty
Starry night is in their eyes.

Live with them – the choice may tempt ye:
Freedom's still the better prize,
O, be not so rash my lad!
Harkee, do not wed!
Better keep your cash, my lad,
And buy a horse instead.[17]

For the Russian on holiday or on cure at the Spa, the expedition to the Colony of Scots missionaries at Karras, two miles away from Pyatigorsk, was always a pleasant ride, skirting round the flanks of Mount Besh Tau on bridle paths through the profusion there of magnificent yellow azaleas and purple anemones. To Lermontov, aware of his Scots blood, it must have had a special interest. Plague, raids and time had decimated the original numbers of worthy Scotsmen to a mere handful, gallantly reinforced by greater numbers of Moravian Brothers from Germany whose practical skills in growing tobacco, potatoes and cabbages earned a good income for the community. Unfortunately, the original efforts of the Reverend Henry Brunton, transferred by the inscrutable ways of Providence from Sierra Leone to the Caucasus in the early 1800s, had not met with all the success they deserved. His fine *Tartar-Turkish New Testament*, printed in his own press in three thousand copies, and painstakingly translated by him, was used by Tartars and Kabardins merely as a binding for their own Korans, its sacred inside text being carelessly thrown away. Children, ransomed at great expense from their wretched Moslem parents to be brought up in the ways of the Lord, ran back to their parents. And the *Mullahs* and chiefs of the Tartars used the sophisticated argument that God gave each people their own way of communicating with Him and that that of the Koran suited them admirably. Poor Mr Brunton had died of melancholy, so it was reported, despite the 'relief of liberal potations.'[18] But the food was good there, the German *Fräuleins* were pretty, a relief from savage-eyed Moslem girls, and it was a novelty.

During the long summer evenings, there were not only the
military anecdotes of his uncles and their friends to be heard, but
those of a well-known local eccentric, Shora Nogmov, whose
folk tales and sayings were one of the attractions for literate
visitors to Pyatigorsk. Nogmov, once a *Mullah* (or Moslem
priest) had gone over to the more dashing life of an officer in
the Caucasian Highlands Guards Squadron. In St Petersburg
he had briefed Pushkin on the folklore and legends of the
Kabardin, Ossetian and Circassian peoples. He was a brilliant
linguist, master of Arabic, Turkish and Persian. As the boys sat
at his feet, he would regale them with tales of carnage and rapine,
of the law of revenge, 'the price of blood', the holiest writ in
the mountains, now beginning to involve the Northern Caucasus,
village by village, family by family, decade by decade, against the
Russians.

Shora Nogmov's stories and a hundred others would be
locked in Lermontov's memory as the Arseniyeva party rode
back to the north for the frozen rigours of the Russian winter.
The Caucasus had become for him a temple of liberty, decorated
with friezes of homeric heroes locked in mortal combat, Russian
against Circassian, Cossack against Chechen. But there was
another frieze, that of Nature, stronger in relief than that of
mortal heroes, a frieze of the animals and landscapes he had loved
there: the stag, 'Tsar of the forests', lying half asleep amidst
huge sunflowers; the snake, caught in the midday heat, its dis-
carded skin resembling a medieval coat of mail; the kite, eagle and
raven, circling a corpse; Moslem tombstones at grotesque angles,
half hidden by green juniper; the bloodied pheasant, iridescent
tail still quivering, shot by some Cossack poacher.

One other memory he recorded five years later. It was on his
last childhood visit to the Caucasus that he had the first ex-
experience of love. 'Who will believe me,' he wrote, 'when I say
that I knew what love was, at ten years of age?' It was a family
outing to the waters. The girl he loved was nine years old, playing
with her dolls, with fair hair and blue eyes. 'My heart began to
throb, my knees felt weak; I had no idea about anything at that
time. Nevertheless, it was passion, strong though childish, it was
real love. I still haven't looked like that since. They laughed at

me, teased me, for they noticed the emotion in my face. I would
weep silently without reason. I wanted to see her. The Caucasian mountains are sacred to me. And so early! At ten! Oh
that mystery, that lost paradise will claw at my mind until the
grave! Sometimes I feel strange, and I'm ready to laugh at this
passion! But more often to cry. They say, Byron did, that an
early passion is a sign of soul which will love the fine arts. I say
that there's music in such a soul!'[19]

Was it strange that he should link the ideal of this 'lost paradise'
with the mountains? Inaccessible, mysterious, pure, inviolate,
these were qualities with which he could endow both a girl and
the Caucasus; the rest of his life would be spent in the search
for them.

The Education of Cornet Lermontov

By late autumn of 1825 Lermontov and his grandmother had returned from their summer idyll in the Caucasus to Tarkhany. At the end of December, their sleepy, provincial society was electrified by the news that there had been a mutiny in St Petersburg on December 14th, crushed by the new Tsar, Nicholas I. Details of the astounding story began to trickle through to Central Russia.

The Tsar Alexander had died on 1st December 1825, in the far south, at Taganrog. In his will he had made the unexpected nomination of his younger brother, the Grand Duke Nicholas, not the elder Constantine, as his successor. Nicholas, hitherto a mere General of the Artillery Corps, had been warned by Alexander in 1819 that he might have power thrust on him, but neither date nor means had been spelt out to him by his mystical, irresolute, cryptic brother.

Three thousand soldiers of the Grenadier and Marine Guards, and the Moskovsky Regiment, however, refused to take the new oath to Nicholas: it meant treason to the 'true' Tsar, whom they thought was Constantine. Inveigled overnight by a number of their officers into marching onto the Senate Square in St Petersburg for the 'sake of the Constitution', most of the soldiers had no idea of the real aims of their officers, who had been conspiring actively for over five years to take power and reform the state, with or without a Tsar. Aristocratic almost to a man, 'liberal' veterans in some cases of the taking of Paris in 1814, the mood of these amateur plotters is echoed in the writings of Baron Andrei Rosen, possibly the best known of the Decembrists to have left his memoirs:

... the flower of the Guards, and especially the younger intellectuals, had attempted this master stroke of 1825. With youthful enthusiasm, they clung to a number of highly gifted but impractical leaders; many officers held it a point of honour to share danger and want with them whom they knew to be devoted, noble champions of modern thought, consciousness of working with the best of their time was more powerful than the fear of death or exile; for the first time they had come into contact with the Ideal, and they could not withstand the lustre of an enterprise which it appeared secured for every one who took part in it a place amongst the best and the very noblest of their fellows.'[1]

The night before the *coup*, the poet of the movement, Ryleyev, was speaking 'on his favourite theme, love of the Motherland', 'his jet black eyes lit up with an unearthly glow, his speech flowing as smoothly as molten lava'; it was not surprising that another of the conspirators (Prince Alexander Odoyevsky) should exclaim in exalted tones: 'We shall die, oh, how gloriously we shall die!'[2]

In the event the drawing-room leaders failed to match Nicholas' will power with an effective plan. As the day wore on, the mutinous infantry saw loyal batteries train their cannon onto them. Civilians, amazed and bewildered, surrounding them on every side of the Square, took no part. At dusk, Nicholas ended the deadlock with the order to his artillerymen to fire. Rank and file died on the Square, or were drowned in the Neva, whose thick ice was pounded by shot and opened. The rest were easily arrested as they fled. The leaders, officers and a few civilians, were rounded up. These were the 'Decembrists.'

By July 1826 sentences were executed on five ring-leaders, quartering was commuted by Imperial benevolence to hanging from makeshift gibbets on the ramparts of the Fortress of St Peter and Paul. A hundred and thirty others – '*les malheureux*' – began the long, fettered hobble to Siberia. An option Nicholas later gave them was to leave Siberia, and volunteer as privates in the Caucasian Independent Corps, and thus to rejoin friends and contemporaries serving as officers in the regiments there.

Mishka, now a twelve-year-old boy, saw his grandmother open every letter with anguish and talk to every courier from the capital with horror, for she knew that her brother, General Dmitry Stolypin, was a friend of Pavel Pestel, who, like Ryleyev, was to be hanged in 1826 as one of the leading conspirators. Her other brother, Arkady, a Prosecutor of the Senate, who had died the previous May, had been a close friend of the fiery Ryleyev, and indeed the latter had dedicated to him a funeral elegy, which young Lermontov learnt by heart.

Neighbours in the Province of Penza were interrogated, even arrested. The whole household heard, almost with relief, that the General had died in January in St Petersburg before he could be incriminated or interrogated by the dreaded Commission of Inquiry meeting over the cells in the fortress of St Peter and Paul where the fettered and manacled leaders lay awaiting their sentences.

As aristocratic families sought to pick up the pieces of their shattered world, and cast them into a conformist mould acceptable to the new ruler, Lermontov's grandmother turned to the serious subject of Mishka's education. She had already provided for him a series of foreign tutors, and as a result he read English and German, as well as French. Lord Byron became established as one of his literary heroes. He knew the 'Prisoner of Chillon' in Jukovsky's translations, and later – under an English tutor – read Walter Scott and Tom Moore, and tried his own hand at translating Byron. He wrote bardic stanzas called 'The Grave of Ossian.'

Now she arranged for him to attend the 'Noble Pension' in Moscow, the leading school for the children of the aristocracy. He was enrolled there in 1828, at the age of fifteen. On an impromptu visit to the school, the new Tsar found the pupils not only lacking in respect and discipline, but potential germ-carriers of 'liberal contraband', in whom 'an aftertaste of Decembrism of disastrous memory'[3*] had not been eradicated. In 1830, after this visit, he revoked its privileged status and downgraded it to a grammar school. In Lermontov's case an irascible temper, a rebellious nature, and a mischievous sense of humour made him a natural candidate for imperial suspicions of this kind.

* 'un arrière gout du dècabrisme de néfaste mémoire': French original.

Luckily for him a stinging poem, written at this time, was not discovered:

> The year shall come, the black year for Russia
> When the crown of the Tsar shall fall
> The rabble will forget its previous love
> And the food of many will be death or blood[4]

The poem was one of many written during his years at the Noble Pension, though no others were so apparently treasonable.

It was the Caucasus that continued to provide his chief source of inspiration. Some spirited verses (written 'under the oak at Tchembar') described the dawn raid of a Circassian prince seeking revenge on a Russian regiment for the capture of his brother. Some of the images are the staple diet of *Caucasica*, bold and simple as a primitive woodcut: a wolf loping along the rocks, a chamois skipping from pinnacle to pinnacle, a cawing flight of jackdaws wheeling over a bustling fortress, Russian infantrymen stiffly presenting arms on the parade ground, a wretched Cossack asleep in his guard tower, about to be knifed by a wily raider swimming the Terek, hardly distinguishable from the white foam of the waves. A more ambitious poem was Lermontov's version of Pushkin's *Caucasian Prisoner*, sufficiently changed in detail and plot to be stamped as the young poet's own. Chained in a mountain cave, his golden future reduced to a living death, a young Russian prisoner seeks consolation in Nature, in the sights of dazzling glacier corsetted by black lava, the fearsome majesty of an avalanche, the tamer beauties of the 'flowered carpet' of hills and dales, or the flight of an eagle and race of deer. But neither Nature nor the love of a young Circassian girl, who frees him at the risk of her own life out of hopeless passion for him, will save him from death. He is mown down by her father's bullet, within sight of the twinkling Russian and Cossack pickets, she is drowned in the pitiless waves of the Terek. 'The Caucasian Prisoner' is the first in the long line of Lermontov's heroes who fail to find happiness in love, either through tragedy or because they deliberately reject it. It was a pessimistic, though suitably romantic, philosophy to adopt so young.

Opposite the first page of Lermontov's poem, written in the neat copperplate of a student, he has sketched his own frontispiece. It shows the prisoner's captor, the Caucasian prince, Girei, dragging him lassoed behind his horse to his lair in the black woods and foothills of his native mountains. Lermontov had begun the practice, which would continue all his life, of illustrating his own work.

In September 1830, Lermontov left school and was enrolled into Moscow University. He had scarcely begun his student life when he found himself swept up – as an extra medical orderly – in fighting the horrors of the great cholera epidemic of that year. He survived unscathed and celebrated the victory of life over death in drink, in parties at Moscow's Assembly of the Nobility, waltzing with his pretty cousins and their debutante friends, in exercising his sharp tongue and caustic wit at others' expense, in opening his mind to new ideas and friendships among fellow students, his acquaintances including Ivan Turgeniev and Alexander Herzen, already something of a stormy petrel as an undergraduate.

To his cousin, Akim Shan Girey, Lermontov appeared as 'the most cheerful of companions.'[5] But in heart-searching letters to his closest female confidantes, such as Mariya Lopukhina, Lermontov confessed to a melancholy that was more than a fashionably romantic pose. Behind the masque of social gaiety there was a young man still in his teens, perplexed and unsure, 'unfit for society', 'seeking impressions, any impressions', tortured by the secret consciousness that 'I shall end life as a contemptible person', aware that life was no mere dream but a reality of 'compelling emptiness'.[6] He had yet to dismantle those inner reserves created to overcome childhood and adolescent griefs, chief among them the estrangement from his father imposed by his grandmother, and his father's death in 1831, virtually a stranger to his own son.

His nostalgia for the South, perhaps to some extent allaying these tensions, continued during the University years. He continued, too, to write about it. A crisper, sharper style developed, worthy of those *Mullahs* and story-tellers he had so keenly observed in 1825, lazily puffing at their long curled hubble-bubbles, sitting on their Persian carpets in the villages near Pyatigorsk, and holding enthralled a cross-legged audience, half-hidden in wreaths of Turkish smoke, with tales of their brothers,

> Seeking the loot by which they live
> And terror everywhere they wreak
> Nothing to them to steal and cheat
> Honey and wine their daggers seek
> Pay with a bullet for their wheat. . . .[7]

Poems and ballads re-echoed his love for the Caucasus: 'Blue mountains of Caucasus, I greet you! You fostered me in childhood'; 'I love you, chain of blue peaks'; 'In the north, that country alien to you, I am yours in heart, forever and always.'[8]

Such personal enthusiasms, culminating in the claim that the beauties of nature in valley and mountain had consoled him for the loss of a mother, were complemented by more general themes, which would recur in his Caucasian writings until his death. First, there was the proposition that the wind-swept peaks, inaccessible and incorruptible as the coruscating snows that covered them, stood for freedom which 'neither the glory of the Tsars nor their deadly infamy' could ever tarnish or destroy. Secondly, that those who have chosen freedom need show no other form of patriotism: where it is, there is their spiritual and moral country. And thirdly, that the present Lords of these peaks, namely the Caucasian tribes, so far 'free as the winds', must expect the 'clank of gold and chains' to din in their ears, bloody wars to be waged on them by the 'sons of autocracy', and finally their freedom to be extinguished.

This last theme, with all that it implied of blood and conflict, was expressed magnificently in Lermontov's poem 'Ismail Bey.' The story was based on one that he had heard as a boy from Shora Nogmov. It was a tale of divided loyalties. Three generations of a princely dynasty, the Atajouka-Khamourzins, had successively served as officers in Russian regiments, only to revert to the life of their clansmen, rejecting the honours of their adopted country. Ismail Bey, like Atajouka, has been surrendered

by his father as a hostage, brought up as a Russian aristocrat and
given a Russian commission. But he has abandoned rank and
honour to return to the mountains; he has seen the destruction
wrought by the Russians on his countrymen, the smoking
villages left behind them:

> The village where his youth was spent,
> The mosques, the peaceful roofs, all rent
> And ruined by the Russians are.[9]

Ismail wages murderous war against the Russians, only to be
treacherously shot down in battle by his own brother, distrustful
of his Russian past. On being stripped for burial a lock of golden
hair is found upon his breast, and within it the white cross of St
George, the coveted Russian award for gallantry. 'Accursed
Giaour, let him die, as he lived, alone,' cries his brother.

The character of Ismail Bey, though displaying to the full the
exaggerations and contradictions of a romantic hero, was more
than a Byronic copy. Lermontov knew the realities involved in
the Caucasian war: the Eastern setting of his poem (in contrast
to the imagined East of *Lalla Rookh* or Hugo's *Les Orientales*)
was based on personal observations, and so, too, was his knowledge of the insoluble conflict of loyalties which his hero faced.
Ismail dies, a failure, betrayed by the very tribesmen for whom
he fought: a lonely, futile sacrifice, for nothing can prevent the
eventual triumph of Russian imperialism:

> Yield thee Tcherkess! For soon the East and West
> May share your fate, perhaps and call it blest!
> For comes an hour when you yourself shall cry
> 'Slave though I be, I serve a prince most high,
> King of the world?' – a new stern Rome comes forth,
> A new Augustus rises from out the North![10]

Lermontov's prophecy would have given pleasure to the
authorities, but there were other passages in the poem which
were less acceptable. It was dangerous for Lermontov in these,
his salad days and still a student, to imply, as he does in 'Ismail

Bey', that the official propaganda justifying the war as a Christian crusade was a lie. Romantic convention gives way to unpalatable truth. (When 'Ismail Bey' was first published, posthumously in 1843, huge cuts were made by the Censors.)

But the Caucasus was far, far away; his poems were still written only for himself; the certainties and confidence he sought must be found not in some distant Paradise but there and then, at Moscow University. Perhaps the miracle would come through love. He scribbled dedications and impromptu verses to any beauty with whom he had danced the night before. But there was one above all others, Varvara Lopukhina.

He had first met Varvara in 1827. He was still a precocious thirteen-year-old at the Noble Pension, she was the daughter of family friends. They continued to see one another during his years at the University. It was an attraction that developed during long summer walks in cousins' parks, family pilgrimages to the famous shrine of Zagorsk, all in the tight-knit world of old Moscow families, chaperoned by aunts and his grandmother. Varvara had a 'passionate and poetic nature', she was 'pleasant, clever, bright as the day and ravishing.'[11] Lermontov sketched her once as a nun with a cross on her breast, her enormous dark eyes cast down; another time wrapped in furs, her abundant hair coiled and plaited. He sent her early poems such as 'The Sail', and dedicated the first drafts of the ballad 'The Demon' to her (in 1831) with the line, 'Receive my gift, my Madonna.' His time in Moscow, he wrote later, was 'happy beyond all bounds.'

But for a hundred and one reasons – lack of self-confidence, inexperience due to extreme youth, curiosity about other girls, introspective doubts – the romance hung fire. He pursued others.

Lermontov hardly attended the Spring term of 1832 at the University. He was impertinent to various Professors. Disenchantment led to a formal departure in June 1832. He sought to enrol this time into the University of St Petersburg. An ever indulgent grandmother agreed. To his surprise, however, the authorities there refused to allow him the two years' seniority to be carried over from Moscow; he would have to start again. Despite the chorus of disapproval and anxiety from loving aunts

and cousins, he now got his grandmother to agree to his enlist-
ment as an officer cadet in the '*Junker*' School in St Petersburg.
After two years he hoped to emerge as a cavalry cornet in the
Regiment of the Life Guards Hussars. To Varvara's sister,
Mariya Lopukhina, he sought to explain this about-turn: 'Until
now I had lived for a literary career, and now I am to become a
warrior. Perhaps this is the shortest way. If it does not lead me
to achieve my first aim, perhaps it will be the final solution.'
A leaden bullet was better than the 'slow agony' of an old man.
The paths of 'vice and silliness' also had to be explored.[12]

During the next two years of military training, the secret fires
of his soul were dampened down by the crude demands of
barrack-room life, of irate riding masters, of tipsy Uhlan and
Hussar officers. He suffered from a lack of privacy in which to
write. Escapes, spiritually and emotionally, to the Caucasian
shrines of his childhood became fewer and fewer.* Varvara, too,
was half-forgotten on some shelf of his Moscow memories, a
love revived in his letters to her sister, but playing, so it seemed,
no role in his daily life. In May of 1835 he was thunder-struck
to hear of her wedding to Nicholas Bakhmetiev, a rich, portly
man twelve years her senior. Had she despaired of him, the
heartless Onegin forgetful of his Moscow Tatiana? Had she been
urged into this conventionally safe marriage by her parents?
His reactions were bitter. He ridiculed her and the very idea of
happiness in his play *Masquerade*, and a short story never
finished, 'The Princess Ligovskaya.'

And this bitterness, dyed with a sense of almost hysterical
disappointment, was worked up by him into a 'drama of five
acts', called *The Two Brothers*, which today would be considered
a fine pastiche of the tawdriest Romantic melodrama. A dying father
welcomed home his son Yuri, just back from the wars. Another
brother, Alexander, interested only in gratifying his lusts and in
his prospective inheritance, keeps importuning the poor old man
to sign papers making over his money. The soldier-brother learns
that his former mistress, Vera, has married a rich Prince who rents
part of their palace when in Moscow, and, undeterred, declares

---

* With the exception of 'Ismail Bey', finished in 1833.

afresh to her his undying passion. In a *coup de théâtre*, brother
Alexander tells him – before their father – that he, too, seduced
weak Vera. The old man dies, and the curtain falls on Yuri's despair. As in so much that Lermontov wrote, this can be seen as a
barometer to his mood in those months after Varvara's marriage;
and his feelings about her can be gauged from Yuri's declaration:
'Of her at this moment there is left for me only the name, which in
moments of anguish I pronounce as if it were a prayer. It is
mine – I keep it like an icon, like a mother's blessing – as a
Tartar keeps his talisman from the tomb of the Prophet.' 'She
asked no promise when I held her in my arms. . . . But she herself
voluntarily made vows . . . to love me forever.'[13]

But if *The Two Brothers* is unplayable by today's standards,
Masquerade was produced in Glasgow as late as 1976 and is very
much a repertory piece in the Soviet Union. Set in worldly St
Petersburg, with a cast of hard-faced gamblers and corrupt
baronesses, pursuing pleasure at the famous Lenten Carnivals
where masked balls allowed every licence, the plot traces the
moral downfall and damnation of Arbenin, who, Othello-like,
poisons his wife in an obsessive and misplaced mood of jealousy.
Lermontov seasoned the play with many a dash of social satire
unacceptable to the Censors, which smacked of *lèse-majesté*. It
was well known that even Nicholas took advantage of masked
balls (often at the Engelhardts' house) to seduce his prettier
subjects. Other quips on current *mores* were also unfunny;
an inadmissible attack on existing morality which the duelling
laws enshrined:
  'If he's angry, there's no great harm in that either; a pair of
  pistols from Lepage's, and thirty two paces should settle the
  business;'
or a joke about the grave threat of:
  'drawing-room socialism; just a fashion like having their
  adenoids out.'
or the substitution of the fear of God by the philosophy of
fatalism:
  'Life is a bank; fate is the dealer; I am the player, and the rules
  of the game I apply to my fellow men.'
The Censors never approved the play as it stood.

The interest of the play lies in Arbenin's confessions, before the demons of doubt and despair overwhelm his reason and turn him into a *Grand Guignol* monster, for Lermontov once again discloses his feelings for Varvara as he had in *The Two Brothers*:

> I saw the mark of perdition printed firmly on my life, and I closed my heart to emotion and the years went by. When you came along, I didn't realise your value; but gradually you peeled away the hard shell from me and showed me a new world, and I was resurrected to a new life. . . . But even now sometimes, there is a malignant spirit that draws me back to the turbulence, the poisoned restlessness of those early days. . . .[14]

In August of that year he got his commission. Would life now be – despite the loss of Varvara – 'poetry drowned in Champagne'?* The pessimist in him thought otherwise. 'The time of my dreams is past,' he wrote to Mariya. 'I need material pleasures, a tangible happiness, one that can be bought with gold.'[15]

And indeed he set out, then and the next year, to seek just that. A costly flat was furnished in St Petersburg; an elegant carriage purchased; his grandmother arrived to entertain; he bought a fearfully expensive horse from a General. Social life took off.

As one of the Tsar's 'military friends', he was formally presented to Nicholas by his Colonel, the Grand Duke Michael. To be sure, Lermontov, merely a young man seen at parties of his cousins, chasing some ballerina paid for by an older, richer man, or hearing the melancholic songs of the gypsies at Pavlovsk, was not taken seriously by the grandest circles. He was not an 'elder' son, heir to innumerable souls, though he was on a footing of perfect equality with such young men in his own Regiment, and the other Guards Regiments. They bore distinguished names: they included the brothers Trubetsky, Sergei Golitsyn, and other princes, and their amusements, innocent sounding

---

* *'de la poésie noyée dans du champagne?'*: French original.

enough, were drawing, singing, drinking, charades and 'gymnas-
tics.' In daily propinquity to Lermontov was the good-
looking if somewhat oafish 'Mongo' Stolypin, one of his cousins
(so called after a favourite Newfoundland dog), his other cousin,
Akim Shan Girey, and the highly intelligent Svyatoslav
Rayevsky, son of one of his grandmother's friends, with whom
he collaborated on *Masquerade,* and who lived at his grandmother's as a paying guest. The latter's modest frock coat as a
civil servant contrasted pathetically with the glittering red and
gold uniforms of his Life Guard friends.

But social successes in a minor key did not satisfy him. After
all, St Petersburg society was – as he put it – a French garden,
'suitably narrow and simple',* where all individuality was lost,
and where, as between one tree and another, the clippers of the
master had reduced all to uniformity. Irresistibly, irony would
take over just when some pleasure or other 'in the society of
gentlemen'** should be satisfying him as it did his cousins and
contemporaries. To compete with the world 'where everybody
had their pedestal, position, name, title', might be gratifying to
his vanity, but where was his lost soul, 'as I once was, trusting,
generous in affection and loyalty'?[15]***

And looking around society, how could he – or any intelligent
observer – pretend to themselves that all was for the best in this,
post-Decembrist Russia? There had been the contagious and
disturbing examples of the French Revolution of 1830 and of the
Polish uprising. Lermontov had certainly praised these 'proud
ones', for 'once again rising' for the independence of their
country, and now once again 'before you the sons of autocracy
have fallen.'[16] Had he in mind, too, the freedom fighters in
the Caucasus?

Can it be shown that Lermontov was, as it were, an honorary
'Decembrist without December'? Did he even know all their
aims? There is no evidence that he would have been a regicide,
ready to see the death of the Tsar and the whole of the Imperial

* *'bien étroit et simple'*
** *'dans la bonne société'*
*** *'tel que j'étais autrefois, confiant, riche d'amour et de dévouement'*
all French originals.

family, as Pestel had contemplated. He wrote nothing directly about the abolition of serfdom, which had been a cardinal aim uniting all the Decembrists. His grandmother's revenues came from the land, and when his turn came, he spent his income from it, as had his forefathers, without undue guilt. Certainly he tried to be a good landlord, and personally intervened to have stone houses built for serfs at Tarkhany. But it was not a cause that caught his imagination, nor his sustained and concentrated attention. Of the Decembrist programme, there were two issues that did, however, call forth his support.

The first issue was the resentment amongst the old Russian aristocracy of the Baltic and neo-Prussian Praetorian Guard, whose senior members had pinned down key positions at Court, in the Army, or in the bureaucracy since the days of Catherine, and whose numbers had increased with the general expansion of Nicholas' civil service. It was hardly wise, with a tribe of Benckendorffs, Lievens, Adlerbergs and Korffs about the Tsar himself, with a Nesselrode as Foreign Minister, and others of their ilk in his own Regiment, to write:

> Heart of a scoundrel, hid in uniform,
> Toadying for rank, enduring men's disdain,
> Bowing at last to Germans like a worm. . . .
>
> Wherein's a German better than a Slav?
> It is not, that whatever fate we have,
> He'll find himself, in any land or place,
> Fatherland and potatoes . . . what a race!
> Rules without talent, always to be bought,
> Fawning on all, and beaten, caring naught.[17]

Though Lermontov could hardly have known it, one of the reasons for Yermolov's disgrace in 1828, and removal as Viceroy of the Caucasus, had been his contempt for the 'German' party. Once waiting to see the Tsar, he had cast a contemptuous eye over the goldfrocked assembly of generals in the anteroom, and asked which of the 'gentlemen spoke Russian.'[18] Lermontov and Yermolov both shared a dangerous attitude of patriotic Russians about the inner establishment at Court.

And secondly, there was the issue of daily importance, for a budding poet and writer – of the Censorship and the Censors. Every poem, every short story, which appeared in print had to go before them before it was published. As Byelinsky, the critic, reprovingly wrote to Gogol: 'You do not, I see, quite understand the Russian public. Its character is determined by the condition of Russian society, which contains, imprisoned within it, fresh forces seething and bursting to break out, but crushed by heavy repression and unable to escape, they produce gloom, bitter depression, apathy. Only in literature, in spite of our Tartar censorship, there is still some life and forward movement. This is why the writer's calling enjoys such respect among us, why literary success is so easy here when there is little talent. This is why so much attention is paid in the whole of our society to every manifestation of any so-called liberal trend . . . no matter how poor the writer's gifts. . . . The public . . . see in Russian writers its only leaders, defenders and saviours from autocracy, Orthodoxy and the national way of life.'[19]

Lermontov's first taste of the Censors was in 1836 when his play *Masquerade* had been rejected. In bitterness and disgust, he set it aside; he would never write another play.[20] But he had learnt at first hand how under Nicholas the censorship had widened its powers, so that all criticism, direct or indirect, of those socially important or in authority could be stifled before it appeared in print. A new staff of efficient majors and colonels, supervised by the foxy-faced, clever General Dubbelt,* had come in with the new Tsar in a greatly expanded Third Depart-

---

* Lermontov's grandmother and Dubbelt were indirectly related through her brother, Senator A. A. Stolypin, who had married Vera Mordvinova, daughter of the famous Admiral N. S. Mordvinov. Vera's aunt (the Admiral's sister) was herself mother of Dubbelt's wife, Anna (1800–1853) and Dubbelt's own son of this marriage was to marry Natalie, Pushkin's daughter. So both through Dubbelt and the respected Mordvinov, Madame Arseniyeva was exceptionally well placed to influence Benckendorff, who was to remain sympathetic about Lermontov's scrapes (at least until 1838) and could hardly escape any pressure brought to bear upon him by Dubbelt.

ment, with a newly constituted *Corps de Gendarmes* as its executive branch. An active and vigilant Censorship, directly answerable to its chief director, Count Benckendorff, and through him to the Tsar, was one of the by-products of the Decembrists' failure. On this issue certainly, for freedom of publication had been a Decembrist and liberal aim, Lermontov could be classified as a Decembrist in spirit.

At all events, Alexander Herzen described[21] for himself and the rest of his generation their predicament after 1825: 'the moral level of society sank; development was interrupted; everything progressive and energetic was struck out of life. Those who remained – frightened, weak and bewildered – were petty and insignificant. The trash of the generation of [Tsar] Alexander occupied the foremost place.' And he pointed out how the facts of life destroyed the idealism of the young: A 'young man had either to dehumanise himself ... or ask himself: but is it absolutely essential to go into service?' ... For some, the weaker, there followed the 'idle existence of a cornet on the retired list, the sloth of the country, the dressing gown, eccentricities, cards, wine.' For others, 'we were dreaming how to get up a new league in Russia, on the pattern of the Decembrists, and looked upon learning as a means to our end. The Government did its best to strengthen our revolutionary tendencies.'[22] And with fervour Herzen summed up Lermontov's and his own heritage from the Decembrists: 'the awakened feeling of human dignity, the striving for independence, the hatred of slavery, the respect for Western Europe, and for the [French] Revolution, the faith in the possibility of an upheaval in Russia, the passionate desire to take part in it.'[23] He concluded: 'What has our generation bequeathed to the coming age? Nihilism.'[24]

Herzen's description of this apparent desert in Russia's moral life rang true for another reason. Despite the colossal efforts of Peter the Great and Catherine to 'open windows on the West', Russia remained isolated in her heart from the post-Napoleonic values of a bourgeois Europe, values so brilliantly exposed as predatory, mercenary and corrupt by Dickens, Balzac and Thackeray. The siren appeals of material self-improvement, aided by reason of man's perfectibility, optimistically announced by the new European prophets on all sides, had as yet no place in the sombre analysis of Russian society offered by Herzen.

The years 1835–36 had been fraught with depression and disillusionment for Lermontov. What writing he had achieved was – as usual – autobiographical, and in a letter in 1836 he confessed to Rayevsky a certain sense of failure about his work. After all, in the years 1833–36, Pushkin had published *Evgeny Onegin*, *The Queen of Spades* and other masterpieces. Nevertheless there is a long poem of over 1700 lines which ranks amongst the best work he ever wrote, and it was probably finished in those two years. *Sashka*, a 'Moral Tale', at first sight seems to be Lermontov's attempt to mock himself, and in a cheerful self-indulgent mood of sensuality, to drown the memory of Varvara in drink and the kisses of warm-hearted courtesans. Lermontov begins his 'moral' tale of immorality with some fun at the expense of gloomy romantics:

> This being a pitiable and silly age,
> They write of tales of chains and executions,
> Of exiles, dark emotions, panics, rage,
> And miseries and woes and dissolutions.
>
> ... I've grown more wise and mellow;
> I laugh and sing; my hero's a good fellow.[25]

There is virtually no plot. Without any of Onegin's St Petersburg hauteurs:

> My hero was of Moscow. That is why
> I scorn the Neva's fog, and hate and mock it[26]

Sashka visits two 'beauties' (sisters in body and soul of Harriet Wilson) to find his beloved Tirza, daughter of a Jew from Prague and a Polish mother, fortune-telling with her friend Varyushka. After a voluptuous encounter, in the best erotic traditions of the eighteenth century (and usually censored in Tsarist editions), he falls asleep by Tirza's side, and the Narrator is free to digress on Sashka's education, and fall from grace. At fourteen, he chances upon his father 'Shameless, the aged libertine embracing one of his serf girls underneath a blossoming cherry tree, but all in vain.'

Adjusting his dress, the old gentleman leaves

> The cheated lass,
> Like Ariadne, unassuaged and cross

for Sashka to take his chance. A passionate affair ensues, more opportunity for erotic verses. Sashka's 'sapless', pedantic French tutor catches them; his mistress is condemned to marry a serf:

> But kiss my breast, my eyes, or soul's delight
> Kiss where you wish for this the last, last night.'
> At dawn in a *kibitka* I must go
> Off to a distant farm, where I shall know
> Both torture and a peasant's shaggy beard.[27]

Sashka's progress through Pension, University and Moscow society follows in the Narrator's mocking asides, on education, on worldly values and on friendship. Lermontov seems to be asking himself whether the 'wise and mellow' ways of the world would not resolve his problems, and form a passable enough philosophy for the time being.

But here and there in the 'Tale', whilst Sashka's powers are allowed to revive before another delightful bout with the girls, Lermontov, the cheerful cynic, a libertine belonging properly to the eighteenth century, is stalked by Lermontov the brooding post-1789 poet of the Romantic Revolution. Passable philosophies would not do. The familiar old frustrations of Russia after 1825 drive him to other questions:

> We reason in accordance with our creed:
> Unto what end this life? Of that perforce
> 'Tis not for our poor wisdoms to discourse,
> Though save the few short days of childhood's trance,
> Beyond debate, 'tis foul inheritance.[28]

Just as Lermontov used the same image or symbol repeatedly, from childhood to maturity – the Caucasian peaks, a sail, waves and the sea: freedom, if not anarchy, and defiance of man-made artifices; rocks, rivers and trees, above all stars: God's unchanging values – so the same questions begin now to reappear in some form in his serious work: What of the after life? What should be the poet's relationship to God? What can Nature offer us?

Eternity, o eternity! What is there
Beyond the celestial boundary of the world?
Tossed boundless ocean where the ages bear
No names or numbers; where lost stars are hurled
Aimless towards other stars . . .[29]

'*Sashka*', after all, had turned out to be a 'Moral Tale.' And '*Sashka*' is Lermontov's first long poem in which a usually libertine and sensuous Lermontov listens avidly to his *alter ego*, a restless, metaphysical, searching Lermontov whose themes would – in the words of Byelinsky – henceforth encompass:

invincible spiritual power; subdued complaints; the fragrant incense of prayer; flaming, stormy inspiration, silent sadness; gentle pensiveness; cries of proud suffering, moans of despair; mysterious tenderness of feeling; indomitable outbursts of daring desires; chaste purity; infirmities of modern society; pictures from the life of the universe; intoxicating lures of existence; pangs of conscience; sweet remorse; sobs of passion; quiet tears of a heart that has been tamed in the storms of life; joy of love; trembling of separation; gladness of meeting; emotions of a mother; contempt for the prose of life; mad thirst for ecstasies; completeness of spirit that rejoices over the luxuries of existence; burning faith; pains of soul's emptiness; outcry of a life that shuns itself; poison of negation; chill of doubt; struggle between fullness of experience and destructive reflection; angel fallen from heaven; proud demon and innocent child; impetuous bacchante and pure maiden.[30]

In the last six months of 1836 and January 1837, the family drama that culminated in Pushkin's death was to take place. Within hours of this, Lermontov, still a mere cavalry cornet, and unknown as a poet, had rocketed into fame with his elegy on the death of Pushkin. 'The Death of a Poet' would mark publicly Lermontov's poetic coming of age, and bring about, as a direct consequence, his return, this time as an exile, to the Caucasus he had loved since childhood.

Lermontov had never met Pushkin, though he had long been an ardent admirer of his genius, nor, still diffident about his own work, had he come in contact with Pushkin's literary circle, almost all of them contributors to his newly launched journal, *The Contemporary*, with the exception of Andrei Krayevsky, Pushkin's able young editorial assistant. But as a young Guards officer he must have seen Pushkin at numerous functions, a familiar and unmistakable figure, with his crinkly African hair, dark skin and scowling face, trapped in the uniform of a Gentleman of the Chamber and the mindless routine of official fixtures, and Natalie, his wife, considered the reigning beauty of Nicholas' Court. As the autumn of 1836 slipped into winter, he must also have heard the innuendoes about Pushkin's marriage which were circulating in St Petersburg society.

Natalie had hitherto avoided adultery though not flirtation. But a new, attractive and persistent claimant, Baron George D'Anthes, the adopted son of the Dutch Ambassador, Van Heeckeren, was rumoured to have won her heart, although, out of caution, or perhaps loyalty to her husband, she refused to become his mistress. Pushkin, jealous, embittered, and deeply possessive, derived some consolation from conducting an affair in his own house with Natalie's younger sister. And Ekaterina, Natalie's elder sister, was herself dumbly in love with the dashing D'Anthes. Society, in the shape of friends, gossips and the homosexual circle surrounding Van Heeckeren, stoked the fires of slander and an anonymous denunciation poured on Pushkin's head. An infuriated Vulcan next to an irresponsible Venus, he could stand the diet of almost daily humiliations at Court and in Society no longer. In November 1836 he challenged D'Anthes to a duel, but since he was on guard duty it was the Ambassador who received the challenge.

Scandal and a duel were just averted. Through the intervention of the Tsar, a face-saving marriage was arranged – to the surprise of all St Petersburg – between Ekaterina and D'Anthes. The wedding took place on January 10, 1837. Almost immediately D'Anthes resumed his blatant attentions to Natalie under cover of his new status as her brother-in-law. Pushkin refused to speak to him or to receive him in their house. On January 25 Natalie was trapped into a meeting alone with D'Anthes at the house of a conniving girlfriend. Dismayed, she fled, but an anonymous note reached Pushkin that same day, telling him of the meeting. Was Van Heeckeren the author? Probably not, but Pushkin undoubtedly thought so. Infuriated beyond recall, Pushkin despatched a stinging letter challenging him to a duel. D'Anthes, a crack shot, took up the challenge on behalf of his adoptive father. The duel took place on January 27th. Pushkin was mortally wounded, and on January 29th, after prolonged agonies, he died.

Outside Pushkin's house a silent crowd of more than fifty thousand Russians gathered in homage. Fearing demonstrations, the Tsar had his body removed at night by Gendarmes, not to Saint Isaac's, the new national Pantheon, but to the small Court church. In print there appeared eulogies calling Pushkin the 'sun of our poetry, our joy, our people's glory.'

Even as Pushkin lay dying, Lermontov had reacted with all the indignation and passion that a true-born Russian could feel at the callous destruction of his country's greatest poet. Written in a day, the fifty-six verses of his elegy, 'The Death of a Poet', were headed 'Revenge, Sire, Revenge'. They rang in the ears of his hearers with the two themes of wrath and sorrow – wrath poured contemptuously, furiously upon the murderer, a sneering fugitive seeking fortune and rank in Russia who had brazenly despised the elementary laws of his adopted country; sorrow lamenting the divine music of genius now silenced, the 'prophet's lips sealed,' and the tragedy for Pushkin himself, dying a victim of slander, crowned not with laurels but thorns.

The verses were immediately copied by hand around St

Petersburg. Lermontov himself read them to a friend, Andrei Muraviev, who was not only a writer but had strong connections with the Third Department, and received his approval. Nicholas' son, the future Alexander II, was shown them by Jukovsky, his tutor and the Court poet, with obvious admiration. His Colonel, the Grand Duke Michael, struck by his young cornet's talent, forecast that 'there would be a fine harvest from the budding poet.'[31]

But the ranks of the cold-blooded 'egoistic and soulless' beau-monde supporting D'Anthes began to close. More gossip and scandal about Pushkin was circulated. Lermontov's grandmother, to his indignation, repeated society's view that D'Anthes had behaved as a man of the world should, in defence of his 'honour.' Other stories suggested D'Anthes had been the pawn of the highest dignataries of the Empire, and had been unofficially encouraged to kill Pushkin. The effect of such distortions, hypocrisies and rumours on Lermontov's nerves and health led to a fever. By February 7th the Court doctor, Arendt, was summoned by his grandmother and prescribed a dose of valerian to calm his nerves; a further remedy lay in his minute-by-minute eye witness description of Pushkin's last days. Lermontov, with tearful avidity, heard every last word spoken by his dying hero.

Within minutes of the doctor's departure, a cousin, Nicholas Stolypin, a smart young diplomat serving in the Foreign Ministry of von Nesselrode, appeared. He also took the party line that Pushkin had failed to behave as a gentleman. He heard and praised Lermontov's poem, but repeated that D'Anthes had to protect his reputation: '*Honneur oblige.*' Lermontov blazed up; irrespective of honour, any true Russian would have accepted whatever insult Pushkin proffered, for the glory of Russia. At white heat, using up half a dozen pencils, with hardly a correction, Lermontov then wrote the following postscript:

And you, the proud and shameless progeny
Of fathers famous for their infamy,
You, who with servile heel have trampled down,
The fragments of great names laid low by chance,

You, hungry crowd that swarms about the throne,*
Butchers of freedom, and genius, and glory,
You hide behind the shelter of the law,
Before you, right and justice must be dumb!
But, parasites of vice, there's God assize;
There is an awful court of law that waits.
You cannot reach it with the sound of gold;
It knows your thoughts beforehand and your deeds;
And vainly you shall call the lying witness;
That shall not help you any more;
And not with all the filth of all your gore,
Shall you wash out the poet's righteous blood.[32]

Observing Lermontov's pencil-chewing composition, his cousin smiled patronisingly and said, 'The muse of poetry is giving birth.'** Lermontov's anger boiled over; he addressed Stolypin: 'You, sir, are the antithesis of Pushkin, and if you do not leave this second, I will not answer for my actions.' Stolypin at this left hurriedly, muttering, 'He is mad enough to be locked up.'***[33]

The witness to this scene, a regimental brother officer, then took five or six copies of the postscript; these flew round the town and even reached Moscow. Russians have long practice in breaking the censorship, and this is an early and honourable case of *samizdat* or do-it-yourself publication. Lermontov's grandmother, terrified of the consequences, tried to reclaim the copies. It was too late. They had reached Pushkin's closest friends, such as the historian Karamzin's daughters, by February 10th. Andrei Krayevsky saw to it that they reached even Jukovsky.

Sofiiya Karamzina wrote to her brother with the latest news: 'I cannot tell you what a gloomy impression Ekaterina's [D'Anthes] *salon* made on me on that first Sunday when I called there again [after the funeral]; there was nobody from the Pushkin

---

* Rigoletto's line (Act II) flaying the Duke's courtiers, '*Cortigiani, vil Razza damnata,*' echoes Lermontov fourteen years later.
** '*la poésie enfant*'
*** '*Mais il est fou à lier*'
    French originals.

family – always there before – and I thought I heard the ringing, silvery laugh of Pushkin. Here are the verses written on the death of Pushkin by a certain Mr Lermontov, a hussar officer. They are so good from their truthfulness and from their feelings that I should like you to know them.'[34] And she quoted 'The Death of the Poet'; a copy would go to Natalie, 'who reads avidly anything written or said about her husband', and to the critic A. I. Turgeniev, who had the melancholy duty of taking Pushkin's corpse, by night, to its final country grave. 'Beautiful verses,' he wrote in his diary.[35]

Benckendorff, on reading the first verses of 'The Death of the Poet', had turned to his Chief-of-Staff, General Dubbelt, remarking that it would be better to overlook such irresponsible outpourings. The Grand Duke Michael thought that Lermontov had gone too far, and probably advised Benckendorff to keep the poem from the eyes of the Tsar. Fortunately they did not see the original itself. There, in the margin, were the enormous moustaches and sunken eyes of Dubbelt himself, caricatured by Lermontov. However, at a reception at the Austrian Embassy soon after, Anna Khitrova, known as the 'leper of society' and a daughter of old Field-Marshal Kutuzov, publicly stopped Benckendorff and asked him:[36] 'No doubt you have read, Count Alexander Christoforovitch, what Lermontov has written about us? About the *crème de la noblesse*?' The scandal was out in the open. Benckendorff, perhaps burdened with his own responsibility for Pushkin's death, sought to evade the question, and denied knowledge of the verses. In fact, he had not yet seen Lermontov's damning postscript. But the matter had become sufficiently serious for the Chief of Gendarmes to make inquiries about this young officer.

With a creased and tired face, renowned for his absent-mindedness, and 'immoderate devotion to women',[37] Benckendorff habitually sought to evade trouble as much as possible, and delegate all he could to General Dubbelt and his staff. He was constantly being button-holed by desperate anxious mothers and aunts, and fawning fathers of those in trouble, whose entreaties he countered with his 'deceptively good-natured expression ... often found in evasive and apathetic people',[38] and 'his bittersweet smile, like that of a man who had bitten a lemon.' On this occasion, he had to move swiftly. The Tsar was following every detail of Pushkin's death. But it was too late. The Sovereign had already had his own copy sent anonymously through the town post, and headed 'A Call to Revolution.'

'Pleasant verses indeed,' he wrote in the margin of Benckendorff's report.[39] 'I have sent [General] Weimarn to seize them. I have also ordered that the senior medical officer of the Guards Division inspect this gentleman to see if he is demented; and then we shall deal with him according to the law.' Benckendorff tried to play down the offending verses, calling them 'shameless free-thinking' rather than 'criminal.' But to no avail. Neither he nor Lermontov had bargained with the implacable vindictiveness of Nicholas on any issue touching security. Lermontov's protestations of loyalty might be pleaded before the bar of public opinion, but it was Nicholas' definition of it that would settle his fate 'according to the law.' Lermontov might arraign those around his Sovereign:

Why did he walk with them, with false and worthless
   slanderers?
Why take for truth the words of fawning, lying panderers?

But he could not know of Nicholas' own involvement in the chain of murky events leading to the fatal duel. And he had no personal experience of the Tsar, that Germanic grand inquisitor, who used his commanding height of six foot two, stentorian voice, and eyes 'with the power of a rattlesnake'[40] to keep a whole Empire in step. What chance stood a cavalry cornet in these circumstances when – as de Custine once remarked – 'a fly that flew off course in the Imperial Palace during a ceremony humiliates the Emperor ... He is a military chief and every one of his days is a day of battle'?[41] In this battle Lermontov was destined to lose. His flat at Tsarskoye Selo was searched. He was confined to barracks and his papers were impounded. The investigation into the 'Case of the Impermissible Verses' had to take place.

Lermontov, in his own 'Apologia' for the Elegy, and under

interrogation by the universally disliked General Kleinmichel,
pleaded the vileness of character-attacks being made on Pushkin,
'struck down by the hand of God,' dying, innocent and incapable
of defending himself; and his horror at this being increased by
his own 'nerves aggravated by my illness.' Even after his death,
he wrote, 'highly placed families' continued to slander Pushkin.
So all the 'bitterness of his heart' spilt onto paper. 'The truth has
always been sacred to me and now in offering my guilty head for
judgment, I have recourse to the truth with firmness as the only
protector of an honest man before the Tsar and before God.'[42]

There was a side issue to the interrogation, where Kleinmichel showed experienced claws, doubtless sharpened on many
an earlier candidate for Siberia or disgrace. Lermontov was
threatened with degradation to the ranks, which entailed automatic loss of status as a noble, the risk of corporal punishment
and other frightening penalties, if he did not disclose the name
of his accomplice in getting 'The Death of a Poet' copied and
distributed. For fear of the effect on his grandmother, he gave
way. To be sure, Rayevsky understood – as soon as Lermontov
could tell him of the odious blackmail – and forgave his friend;
but it must have been for one so young, so proud, and so secretly
tormented as Lermontov a crisis of self-doubt achieving self-
knowledge dearly bought.

Rayevsky, who was to be punished with Lermontov, also
had to make a statement. He described how Lermontov's indignation had been aroused by the knowledge of the anonymous letter
sent to Pushkin. The main poem had been composed the day
Pushkin died. He had thought that no harm could come of the
offending postscript; the Emperor had shown magnanimity to
Pushkin's widow. Lermontov had signed his name quite openly,
the 'highest Censorship' would have stopped their circulation
if there had been the slightest objection. 'We had no political
ideas . . . we are both Russians and totally loyal.'[43]

The reaction amongst the young reading Lermontov's poem
was enough to justify the authorities' alarm. ' "The Death of a
Poet" ', wrote V. Stasov, a student then, 'which was secretly
smuggled into the school almost immediately in manuscript
form, as it was distributed everywhere, profoundly excited us,

and we read and recited it with boundless gusto during the breaks between classes. Although we did not really know, and there was none from whom we could find out, to whom applied the words of the stanza: 'You, hungry crowd that swarms about the throne . . .' we were nevertheless affected. Our hearts swelled with profound indignation, with heroic enthusiasms; we were probably ready for anything, so greatly were we uplifted by the power of Lermontov's verses, so contagious was the zeal permeating these verses. It is doubtful whether such a tremendous and universal impression had ever been created by verses in Russia.'[44]*

On 20th February Lermontov was placed under house arrest in the General staff headquarters. Sentence came on 25th February. Rayevsky was exiled to a minor Government job in 'some cold province' and Cornet Lermontov was transferred in the same rank to the Nijegorodtsy Dragoon Regiment in the Caucasus. His brother officers were not allowed to throw a farewell dinner party for him.

---

* They were first published in London, by Herzen in his *Polar Star* in 1856.

C

The Grand Tour

'Farewell, my friend,' wrote Lermontov to Rayevsky on the eve of his departure. 'I shall write to you about the country of marvels, the East. Napoleon's words console me: "*Les grand noms se font à l'Orient.*" As you can see I still write nonsense!'[1]

A self-portrait of him at this moment in watercolours survives. Smartly kitted out by St Petersburg's military tailors in his new uniform as a Nijegorodtsy Dragoon, he shows himself gripping a Circassian sword tightly, waist high. Half his body is wrapped in the *Bourka* or fleecy Caucasian cloak, black as the Daghestan rocks behind; the gilt cartridge cases of the Nijegorodtsy uniform, also worn by every warrior from the mountains, are on his breast, and one epaulette and red uniform collar peeps out to remind the painter, and others, that he was still an officer. His dark eyes are fixed and pensive. There is a wistful softness about the whole face, a resigned melancholy upon setting out for the wars – an only son, an only grandson, and unmarried. The last of the Lermontovs.

In fact, the situation was not altogether depressing. He had escaped degradation to the ranks, he adored the Caucasus, and the prospect of action was one publicly desired by half the 'lions' in the Guards who were his friends; it would, at the very least, offer a spice of danger to his palate, and he and his grandmother had enough friends and family who could make periods of leave more pleasant in Pyatigorsk, Vladikavkaz, Kizlyar and the other frontier towns. The Khastatovs were pillars of the Establishment in the deep South. It would be a pleasure to see them again.

His childhood mentor and relative, Paul Petrov, now promoted from being Colonel of the Mosdok Cossacks to Major-General, was Chief-of-Staff of the whole 'Line' Command at Stavropol where, in common with all officers entering the Caucasian area of operations, he would have to report. Another

General, Vladmir Volkhovsky (a reformed Decembrist), replied soothingly to a colleague's letter interceding for him (inspired naturally by his grandmother) that two or three months with an expedition against the mountaineers might be the best way for Lermontov to efface all memories of his *faux pas*: 'it would be *calmant* . . . Besides, the Sovereign is so merciful.'[2]

In tune with Volkhovsky's suggestion, General Petrov obligingly did his best to get Lermontov included in the only genuinely military manoeuvre of the summer. It was to be commanded by the leading general of repute in the Caucasus since Yermolov, Aleksey Veliaminov. He used his brain as well as brute force to strike terror into his foes and to keep discipline among his own men, and had served with Madame Arseniyeva's brother in the 1812 War. Lermontov carried letters of introduction to him. But Veliaminov's expedition was delayed, and Lermontov, in any case, proved unable to join him. On the long journey south he had caught a serious cold, perhaps even influenza, which was rapidly followed by a violent attack of rheumatism, and after a spell in Stavropol hospital he was transferred with full medical honours to Pyatigorsk, where he was carried into the Military Hospital on a stretcher.

'Pyatigorsk is the most invigorating of the Caucasian mineral waters,' wrote Baron Rosen, the Decembrist. 'A little outside the town innumerable sulphur springs of various temperatures [from 21 to 37 degrees *Réaumur*] issue from a mountain. So full of sulphur are these springs that the air is impregnated with the smell and almost every piece of metal carried round by people becomes tarnished; the silver epaulettes and ornaments of officers who come here annually turn quite yellow after a time and almost all coins do the same. The regular course is for bathers, who arrive in April, to leave Pyatigorsk in late June, and then go to the iron springs of Zheleznovodsk nearby, or to the chalybeate springs of Kislovodsk, or to the akali and soda springs of Sentuki.'[3]

Lermontov's cure lasted from his arrival at the end of May until early August, and he took no less than sixty of the health restoring baths, ruefully describing his life as 'fit for a duck.' The waters themselves, so beneficial to Lermontov as a child, had been approved and analysed by painstaking German chemists. They came out piping hot, their smell of 'sulphorous hydrogen' causing many an aristocratic nostril to twitch uncontrollably.

Lermontov joined the other patients, military and civilian, in following the doctor's routine. The first patients arrived at the springs as early as five o'clock in the morning, some in carriages, others on horseback or on foot. These morning hours were the most disagreeable of the day; patients were duty-bound to swallow several large glasses of nauseous water, straight from the springs, at hourly intervals. About noon, everybody dispersed, some to the baths, others home, where a glass of coffee and a bun awaited them; lunch followed soon: not much more than a bowl of watery gruel, and two soft-boiled eggs with spinach. At five in the afternoon the patients were back at the springs, their glasses in their hands. The sexes were mixed, the more elegant ladies dipping in wicker-covered glasses attached to white strings; moustachioed cossacks, with long whips slung across their backs and swearing as they tried to gulp down the foul-smelling water, reminded civilians vividly of the close proximity of the war. In the evening, from five to seven, healthy Guards officers on leave with eye-glasses appraised the visiting beauties – their day's cure over – as they strolled along the boulevard to the sounds of regimental music. 'Thus must the day end for the ailing,' writes a contemporary observer. 'But it is not always so. How many often spend the whole night playing cards and drag themselves like shadows straight from the card tables to the watering places; after which these people shamelessly converse about the futility of the local remedial treatment.'[4]

Lermontov – who normally enjoyed gambling with his close friends – was little tempted to join the other officers in the cardroom at the military hospital which was known as '*la chambre infernale*.' Before long he had rented some rooms and was sufficiently fit to go for long walks, to ride a little, and to enjoy his favourite distraction of painting. A landscape in oils, painted during these months, has survived. Rocky brown mountains frame Pyatigorsk's only little street, with its blue, raspberry and red brown roofs; blue-green foothills roll back to snow-topped mountains in the distance; a Circassian, on a sprightly horse, and

a Russian gentleman, strolling in a top hat, enliven the foreground. It is a charming and elegant scene.

And indeed Pyatigorsk in 1837 had been transformed from
the elementary, Russianised Tartar village of Lermontov's youth.
Not only was it popular as a spa, proud possessor of its baths,
but standing athwart the main communications between Stavropol,
the GHQ and distant Petrovsk on the Caspian, it had a strategic
importance, which warranted the appointment of a military
Commandant. In 1830–31 two gifted Italian architects, the
Bernadazzi brothers, had begun the transformation of Pyatigorsk's
miserable bath house, which could take no more than twelve
patients, flanked by wretched wooden hovels, into a fashionable
watering place. They laid out Empire colonnaded and porticoed
houses on the main boulevard; an alley of aromatic lime trees;
a Grotto of Diana for romantic trysts; a smart new Bath House
and Gallery by the springs. Building speculators and tradesmen
had moved in, and in their wake an enterprising Armenian called
Naitaki had opened an hotel. The Cossack's sentry post on the
rocky spur above the Khastatovs' house had been replaced by a
stone pavilion, with tinkling bells attached to a weather-vane,
from which ladies could inspect Mount Elborus through a
telescope.

There remained, however, a need for patrols and sentries to
dispel the fear of attack from brigands, highwaymen, outlaws
and 'unpeaceful highlanders' (as the phrase went amongst visiting
Russians). The fair sex, riding to some tryst or picnic, were especially apprehensive whenever they saw a troop of mounted
Circassians approaching them; a kidnapping followed by – at
best – a ransom was an expensive experience. When the principal
character of *A Hero of our Time* mock-ambushes Princess Mary
dressed with 'just the right amount of lace, costly weapons in
simple settings, the fur on the cap neither too long nor too short,
a long white tunic and a dark brown Circassian coat', the Princess
exclaims, '*Mon Dieu, un Circassien!*'[5] with genuine terror. And
another lady, wife of the French geologist Xavier Hommaire de
Hell, who visited Pyatigorsk in the 1840s, likewise ran into some
'terrible Circassians' at whom she screamed. Never would she
forget their glances, nor their hatred of her escort of Cossacks.

'They were all fully armed. Their pistols and their damasked poniards glittered from beneath their black *bourkas*. . . .' Seen through the mist, they reminded her 'of Ossian's heroes.'[6] It was wise always to travel with an escort.

Another passage from Lermontov's novel, *A Hero of our Time* gives an exultant description of the town and its surroundings:

Yesterday I arrived in Pyatigorsk and rented rooms on the outskirts of the town, at its highest part, at the foot of Mount Mashuk. When there is a storm, the clouds will come right down to my roof. Just now, at five o'clock in the morning, when I opened my window my room was filled with the scent of flowers which grew in the modest little front garden. Boughs of flowering cherry look in at me through the window and from time to time the wind scatters their white petals over my writing table. I have a marvellous view in three directions. To the west, five-peaked Beshtu rises up like a shaggy Persian cap and covers the entire northern part of the horizon. In the east, the outlook is more cheerful: down below me is the trim, spotless, colourful little town and the noise from the medicinal springs, the chatter of the polyglot crowd. Farther away the mountains became darker and mistier, rising in a semi-circle. And, at the very edge of the horizon, there stretches the silver chain of snowy peaks which starts at Kazbek and ends at Elborus with its twin summits.

What a joy it is to live in such a land! A kind of comforting feeling runs right through my veins. The air is clean and fresh as the kiss of a child; the sun is bright, the sky clear blue – what more could one ask for? Why should passions, ambitions and regrets exist here? But it is time for me to get on. I am going to the Elizavyetinski spring: they say that all the spa's society meets there in the morning.[7]

As soon as he felt well enough, Lermontov began to see the more interesting visitors to the Waters. In a gay and chatty letter to his ever faithful confidante, Varvara's sister, he struck a characteristic pose. 'I expect to be pretty bored . . . though it's very easy to strike up acquaintances here, I'm trying to avoid them.'[8]

Even had he truly wished to shun society, however, he would have found it hard to do so. With a growing literary reputation, armed with his quiverful of introductions and family connections, it was almost impossible for Lermontov to go into splendid isolation in such a tiny place. His fame as the author of 'The Death of a Poet' had been further increased by the publication in May of his ballad 'Borodino' in *The Contemporary*, the journal founded by Pushkin and still run by his friends. The poem, destined to become a classic, a recitation piece for generations of Russian schoolboys, paid tribute with sincerity, humanity, and perfect artistry to the ordinary Russian infantryman and artillery man whose bravery had saved their country in 1812. It made an immediate impression.

In any case, there were rewarding friendships to pursue. There was his former school-fellow from the Noble Pension, Nicholas Satin, whose name was bracketed with that of Alexander Herzen, now notorious as a publicist and 'revolutionary.' They had been arrested together in 1835 and now Lermontov found him in Pyatigorsk, an agreeable enough companion. And it was with Satin that he saw again the sallow, consumptive-looking Vissarion Byelinsky for the first time since they had been together at Moscow University. They both came from the same part of Russia, Tchembar. Byelinsky's reputation as a fearless and distinguished critic – 'the Savonarola of his generation'* – was already established with literary circles in Moscow, and in St Petersburg. They had not been friends then, Byelinsky being somewhat humourless and serious, Lermontov, sarcastic and apparently insouciant; time had already deepened these contrasts in them. Their meeting took an unfortunate turn. Byelinsky picked up a copy of Diderot's essays, lying on the table, and began to extol the French Encyclopaedists, and, above all, Voltaire. The more portentous Byelinsky's pronouncements the more flippantly Lermontov responded. 'As for your famous Voltaire,' he concluded, 'if he were to appear now in Tchembar,

---

* Sir Isaiah Berlin's phrase.

not one decent household would take him on as tutor.'[9] In silent fury Byelinsky grabbed his cap and strode out of the room to the sound of Lermontov's laughter. For some time after the disgruntled Byelinsky would dismiss 'The Death of a Poet' as 'a few lucky verses', and its author as a '*Poshlyak*', a cross between a vulgar fellow and a cad. It would be another two years before the two men could exchange literary views without their different natures clashing.

A more satisfying relationship, and indeed friendship, developed for Lermontov with Nicholas Maier, a doctor with practices in Pyatigorsk and Stavropol. The doctor was very ugly, with one leg shorter than the other and a large head set on a small thin body. But he was kind, extremely well-read, a first-class talker, a liberal, and probably a freemason. The Decembrists exiled in the Caucasus loved him as a brother, and commanding generals and colonels, turning a blind eye to any unsuitable connections, were also his friends.* He embodied the tradition – active since General Yermolov extended his protection to the Caucasian Decembrists of the 1820s – whereby the Caucasus continued to be 'the home of Russian freedom of thought' at least in private.

He lent Lermontov such dangerous reading, from a censor's standpoint, as de Tocqueville's *Democracy in America* and Guizot's *History of the English Revolution*. The doctor's acquaintance may be made by any reader of *A Hero of our Time*, for he entered its pages as Doctor Werner:

> Werner is a remarkable man in many ways. Like almost all medical men he is a sceptic and materialist, but he is a poet as well, seriously – always a poet in deeds and often in words, though he has not written two verses in his life. He has

---

* Even in Siberia the Decembrists had had privileges unimaginable in the world of *Gulag*. 'Of one accord we subscribed to the most noteworthy political and literary works of the time, through our ladies . . . as also to the finest periodicals, Russian and foreign alike. Everything at all remarkable then being written and published in Russia, everything being printed abroad and worth reading whether in periodicals or monographs, we received without exception'.[10]

studied the whole gamut of the human heart, as people study the veins of a corpse. But just as a distinguished anatomist cannot cure a fever, he has never been able to make use of his knowledge! Werner usually laughs at his patients on the sly, but I once saw him weep over a dying soldier . . .[11]

Through Maier, Lermontov saw much of the Decembrists, transferred from Siberia to the Caucasus, nearly all of them serving in the ranks. The attitude of Nicholas and officialdom towards them can be gauged from this Order of the Minister of War of June 21, 1837:

> State convicts Naryshkin, Lorer, Likharyov, Nazimov, Fohkt and Rosen, all presently in settlements, are to be made privates in the Caucasian Corps . . . in such a way that they discharge normal infantry service, with no mitigations what-soever.

Their relationship to Lermontov was by no means easy. He treated many of the issues that had caused their sufferings with apparent cynicism. There was a generation gap, pointed up in the story of one of the Decembrists, Mikhail Nazimov (who was very fond of him), whose earnest questions about con-temporary youth and its inclinations received the answer – delivered in a rhetorical and mock-heroic manner – that 'we have no purpose, we just meet, go on sprees, follow some sort of career and chase women.' This was 'the blustering of vice';* Nazimov was rather shocked.[12]

To these veterans Lermontov's sense of humour and his so-called practical jokes were also unendearing – pranks, which might be acceptable from a Hussar cadet, seemed unfunnily immature from the author of 'The Death of a Poet', in disgrace for his subversive verses. He had been known, for instance, to eat the whole of a picnic lunch, amidst shouts of laughter, leaving nothing for the other guests. And there had been the unfortunate case of a would-be poet who visited him, and was invited to recite his verses, while Lermontov ate half his hamper

---

* *'la fanfaronnade du vice'* : French original.

of freshly salted cucumbers – always a treat – and then scampered away, in mid-recitation with the other half stuffed into his pockets. Nor did he make a pleasant first impression on strangers. 'You have not even started talking to him,' wrote one acquaintance, 'but he has already seen through you; he notices everything; his glance is heavy and it is tiring to feel this gaze upon oneself. His presence was unpleasant for the first minutes. But at the same time I understand the only reason for such a strong effect was only mere curiosity . . . this man never listens to what you are telling him; he is listening to you yourself, and is observing you. You remain an exterior force to his life, having no right to change anything in it.'[13]

Of all the Decembrists serving in the Caucasus, the best known and one of the most attractive to Lermontov was one he was never to meet; and who had died that June on one of those senseless and brutal skirmishes so typical of the times. Alexander Bestujev, whose *nom de plume* was 'Marlinsky', was the brother of Nicholas Bestujev who had led the Marine Guards on to the Senate Square. Condemned to exile in Siberia, Marlinsky's sentence was later commuted to active service in the Caucasus, where his gallantry won him a recommendation for the St George's Cross. Shortly afterwards, however, his young mistress, whether through suicide or accident, was found shot dead in his bed. In the resulting scandal the decoration was cancelled and the disgraced Marlinsky sought and found death in action.[14]

His importance to Lermontov was not so much as a Byronic figure, satanically attractive to women, nor as a political martyr, but as a poet, novelist and populariser of the Caucasus, the setting for most of his works. Lermontov drew illustrations for *Ammalat Bek*, one of Bestujev's most succesful novels, a typical sketch depicting two Russian officers toying with the *kinjal*, the Caucasian dagger, with a title beneath, 'Be slow to take offence, be speedy in revenge.' He took the opening lines of his own enchanted poem 'The Sail' from one by Marlinsky. Marlinsky's claim 'we have sown, others will reap' would come true, though with an unexpected twist. After initial plagiarism Lermontov would use Marlinsky as a foil for his own almost diametrically different point of view. In the 1820s the gallant, good-looking

Grushnitsky, from *A Hero of our Time*, with his Byronic airs, would have been a Marlinsky hero. In the 1830s Lermontov deliberately makes of him a rhetorical ass, 'with pompous phrases ready for all occasions, not touched by beauty, but cloaking himself solemnly in unusual feelings, lofty passions, and exclusive sufferings'[15] whose unthinking heroics lead to tragedy.

By August 1837 a cured, fit Lermontov was ready for some fighting. It seemed as though the delayed expedition of General Veliaminov might still take place. Its starting point would be at Anapa on the Black Sea coast. On his way there Lermontov was held up at the fishing village of Taman (the scene later on for the 'Taman' episode in *A Hero of our Time*). Meanwhile orders and counter-orders, involving the movements of the Nijegorodtsy Regiment and the impending visit of Nicholas I to Georgia, brought pleasant consequences. The Veliaminov expedition was finally cancelled. Lermontov was ordered to return from the Black Sea ports to Stavropol and thence rejoin his dragoons in Kakhetia. He was able to spend October in a leisurely peregrination crossing the great mountains.

'Ever since I left Russia,' he wrote to Rayevsky, 'believe me I've been travelling continually, now by post chaise, now on horseback. I've ridden the whole length of the line from Kizlyar to Taman, crossed the mountains, was in Shuma, in Kuba, in Shemakha, in Kakhetia, dressed as a Circassian, with a rifle at my back. I've spent nights in the open, fallen asleep to the cries of jackals, eaten *Tchurek* [flat cakes of bread], even drunk Kakhetian wine . . .'[16]

Travellers crossing the mountains usually survived on rancid butter, dried fish, old eggs and soup drunk from pan lids. Only coarse brown bread and cheese could be bought along the way; you did all your own cooking in bivouac. Lermontov, in *A Hero of our Time*, speaks of a cast-iron kettle as his 'only comfort.' As for the Kakhetian wine, the gourds of goat or ox-skin in which it was kept gave a flavour of tar to an otherwise excellent *vin du pays*, Burgundian in taste.

Lermontov took discomforts in his stride in the exhilaration of the journey. 'As I careered up and down the mountains in

Georgia I abandoned the cart and took to horseback; I've climbed the snowy mountain of the Cross to the very top which isn't altogether easy; from it, one can see half Georgia as though it were on a saucer, truly I don't mind explaining that amazing feeling; for me the mountain air is balm; the blues go to the devil, the heart thumps, the breast breathes high; nothing is wanted at such a moment; I could have sat and looked for the rest of my life.'[17]

He carried with him a portfolio which he filled with sketches of the breathtaking views spread before him. Eight have survived. Carefully topographical at the early stages of the Georgian Military Highway, they become looser, more Ossianic, as he moves further into the mountains. Basalt rocks rise in soaring pinnacles; bridges arch over uncontrolled torrents in ways that defy the laws of engineering; the conical towers of Sioni point menacingly to Mount Kasbek, to whose icy sides Prometheus was chained eternally; clouds swirl round the base of peaks as pointed as sharks' teeth; black granite and white snow provide the dominant colours.

There are countless travellers' descriptions of the stupefying grandeur of the Dariál Gorge:

We left Vladikavkaz on November 6 and journeyed along the left bank of the broad and peaceful stream of the Terek, penetrating further into the country. The road wound up and down hills all the way, and as we heard the mountains in the evening, a singular spectacle was presented to our eyes: fires without number blazed on every side. ... On the right was this sea of fire, on the left, the foaming Terek which seethed faster every minute. ...

Along the left bank of this river, an excellent road takes the traveller into the interior between rocks of a giddy height. Beneath us foamed the raging mountain torrent, whilst above us the rocks seemed so close together that only a streak of sky was visible in the pass of Dariál. Here and there the path was barred by fallen boulders, or stopped by sudden twists in the river. In spite of the burning air, the air we breathed in the defile was cool, aromatic and invigorating.[18]

Such was Baron Rosen's impression.

An extract from Bestujev's *Ammalat Bek* is as purple a passage as one could hope to find in the school of 'romantic' Caucasian writers:

Wildly beautiful is the resounding Terek in the mountains of Darial. There, like a genie borrowing his strength from Heaven, he wrestles with Nature. There, bright and shining as steel, cutting through the overshadowing cliff, he gleams among the rocks. There blackening with rage, he bellows and sounds like a wild beast, among the imprisoning cliffs; he bursts, otherthrows and rolls afar their broken fragments. On a stormy night, when the belated traveller enveloped in his furry *burka*, gazing fearfully around him, travels along the bank which hangs over the torrent of Terek, all is terror such as only a vivid imagination can conceive. ... Suddenly the lightning flashes before his eyes ... before him the roaring Terek. At one moment he sees its wild and troubled waves raging like infernal spirits chased by the archangel's brand. After them with a shout as of laughter, roll the huge stones. ... Then bursts the thunder crash, jarring the foundations of the rocks, as though a thousand mountains were dashed against each other ... then a long protracted growl as of massive oaks plucked up by their roots. ...[19]

Another traveller described the disturbing, if not terrifying, experience of a summer storm in the high mountains. First, an extraordinary stillness and gloomy twilight fell over the peaks. The sun's rays, broken by the rocky spires, probed the massed clouds. Shattering explosions then broke the silence, their echo to roll away. Clouds blacker than ink, 'edged with a blood-red border, sped fleetly past.' Spectral shapes of mist were in continual metamorphosis. The forked lighting was blue and red over the snowy slopes. Lastly, a measure of peace returned to the traveller with the appearance of 'double' rainbows and a silvery moon.' Certainly the times were ripe for the wondrous colours of a Turner, or the dazzling fireworks of Lermontov's poetry. Lermontov's prose also reflected the wonders of this journey, and passages from *A Hero of our Time* look back to his travels through the mountains:

> Coming closer to nature we cannot help becoming children. . . . Mists glide, whirling and winding like snakes down the furrows of nearby precipices. . . . Below us lay the Kayshaur Valley, crossed by the Aragva and by another river, like two silver threads; a pale bluish haze glided over it, heading for the neighbouring ravines, away from the warm rays of morning; right and left rose the crests of mountains, each higher than the next . . . and all these snows burned with a ruddy glow, so merrily, so brightly[20]

– these were the famous 'blood snows' of the Caucasus, their colour due to oxides of iron bearing rock tingeing the glaciers.

For an unaccompanied traveller the only safe alternative to crossing the mountains with a convoy or an official escort was to throw oneself upon the hospitality of the Ossetians living in the poor villages dotted along the Military Highway. This would confer on the traveller, albeit temporarily, the friendship of some wily, red-haired Ossetian hunter, whose other moments might be spent in relieving the unprotected of their purses or even lives; but once again, the protection of the status of *kunak* or friend would be sacred. In a smoky mountain hut, full of sheep and ferocious dogs, the favoured traveller would sit by a fire, smoking a pipe, drinking tea, or – if he were lucky – a strong local beer, or some vodka from his own coat pocket, and hearing the legends of the mountains.

One such legend, which Lermontov doubtless heard in this way, was the tale of Tamara, the fabled siren of the Dariál Gorge, based, with scant regard for history, or memories of the thirteenth-century Queen Tamara, the ruins of whose medieval castle still clung to the crags above the gorge. In the legend, and in the ballad which Lermontov later wrote from it, Tamara is an enchantress, who lures unsuspecting travellers to her tower on its black cliff for a night of drunkenness and wild, voluptuous delights. She is an angel of beauty, with a demon's heart; come

the dawn, her all too human lovers pay the price of death, and
are cast into the foaming waters of the Terek:

> Lo! a lifeless corpse is carried,
> Sounds of moaning voices swell,
> From the tower a white gleam shimmers,
> Comes a distant cry, 'Farewell.'[21]

Lermontov's journey south, though it brought him no such
adventures, was not without its whiff of danger. 'I've only heard
one or two shots,' he told Rayevsky, 'but I've shot my way out of
trouble twice in my journeyings. Once at night three of us rode
out of Kuba,* myself, an officer in our regiment, and a Circassian
(a friendly one, of course) and very nearly ran into a gang of
Lesghians.'[22] A painting, soon after this near fatal encounter,
shows a caravan wending its way through the sabre-toothed
crags and crannies: two camels, a horse, three armed Lesghians
and a veiled woman on one of the camels. Were they returning
from some skirmish, disgraced by the loss of two horses? His
favourite Caucasian colours dominate: copper and brown for the
nearby rocks, grey blue for the middle ground, the peaks dazzling
white under a pale gold sky.

Lermontov found the headquarters of his regiment at Kara-
Agatch, well to the East of Tiflis. It was early October by this
time; and he reported to his new colonel, whom he found to be a
friendly, cheerful veteran, a crony of the Grand Duke Constantine. The Dragoons were the only regular and trustworthy
cavalry that the Tsar could rely upon, stationed south of the
great mountain chain, to keep Kakhetia and Georgia safe for him.
Their role was to defend the 'Lesghian Line' below that ice-blue
mountain chain separating the sunny vineyards and lazy winding
river Alazan from the incursions of hard-riding bands of Avars
and 'unsubmissive' beys sweeping down from their granite
fastnesses to loot, maim or abduct. That the regiment was in hostile
ground was proved by the long line of hay and barley wagons
that stood by the tents. Two squadrons were away quelling

---

* In Eastern Georgia, famous for its rugs.

trouble down by Baku. Lermontov's fellow officers were laconic
about their military duties, describing them as pure guerilla
warfare against 'mountaineers as brave as steel'. For the few
weeks that Lermontov was to be with them, however, his duties
were to be of the lightest.

The officers' mess was very hospitable. An English military
visitor, passing through only a few days before Lermontov's
arrival, wrote of trestle tables groaning with a 'long array of
empty champagne bottles',[23] after a birthday party for the
colonel. Kakhetia was famous for its champagne:

> Sweet wine in foaming rills
> Upon his patterned pantaloons
> The drowsy Georgian spills[24]

wrote Lermontov in 'Ismail Bey.'

Lermontov's fellow officers were an interesting and mixed
collection. There were Russians of distinguished families,
temporarily in disgrace, a Shuvalov, a Jerve, cooling their heels.
There were princely Georgians of wit and education, foreign
mercenaries, and locals with little or no private means, who
'could hardly support the character of a gentleman',[25] depending
for their horses on the colonel's generosity.

Outside the mess the dragoons were fortunate in their social
life, for one of their etstwhile senior majors was none other than
Major-General Prince Alexander Chavchavadze, whose rambling
country house at Tsinandali – the name of Kakhetia's most
famous sparkling champagne – stood close to their quarters. It
was open to all officers from the regiment.

The General had met Pushkin on his famous journey to
Erzerum in 1829. He had translated his poetry into Georgian,
and wrote elegantly himself. His daughter Nina had married
Alexander Griboyedov, the author of *Woe from Wit*, who had
been Nicholas' ambassador to the Shah of Persia and had been
assassinated in Persia; the beautiful widow and her two sisters
graced their father's parties.

The General's political role had been intriguing. Fearful of
the Persians, he had been prepared to accept a Russian general's

epaulettes, and in 1825, and again in 1830 when there had been a chance for the disaffected Georgian aristocracy to recover some of its earlier powers, he had refused to give a disloyal lead to up-country die-hards against the Tsar. Despite this, however, Nicholas had summoned him to St Petersburg, placing him under surveillance there from 1832 to 1836. During this time the General had rented an apartment from Lermontov's aunt, Praskoviya Akhverdova, the widow of a former Governor of Georgia.

For Lermontov this was a ready-made link with Tsinandali, and its open-handed hospitality, where everyday amusements were mixed with specifically Georgian entertainments – the *djigitovka*, for instance, the wild display of horsemanship which Lermontov had known from childhood. Russians and Georgians vied with one another, parading in a circle, showing off their arms, daggers and short sabres, the Dragoons on Kabardin horses and the Georgians on superb Karabakh mares, astride Persian saddle cloths, embroidered with silk and adorned with gold metal plates that tinkled at the slightest movement.

While Lermontov was settling into this pleasant round of regimental life, decisions affecting his immediate future were being taken – without his knowledge – by the Tsar, now close at hand in the capital of Georgia, Tiflis. In early October, Nicholas had descended like a Jovian thunderbolt upon his corrupt and sleepy proconsuls in Armenia and Georgia. Lermontov's grandmother had already heard (through a niece, married to one of the Tsar's aides-de-camp) that 'Count Orlov told me that Mikhail Yurievitch will probably be pardoned during the Sovereign's stay at Anapa, that Count Benckendorff wrote about it to him twice and the second time entreated him to report to the Sovereign that he will consider a pardon to this young man as a personal reward to himself.' Pushkin's friend, Jukovsky – in attendance to the Imperial suite as tutor to the Tsarevitch – reinforced Benckendorff's plea to the Tsar, calling Lermontov 'the hope of Russian literature.'[26]

Installed in the Governor-General's palace, Nicholas and his suite were attempting to recover from their journey. There had been the horrors of the axle-deep muds of Mingrelia, the attentions of mosquitoes and fleas which dared to attack the Tsar in his carriage overnight, and the infuriating misunderstanding when, on arrival in Tiflis, the Tsar had sought forthwith to worship in the Cathedral of Sion and had found the doors locked, while the Patriarch took his post-prandial rest. His aides-de-camp unpacked their kashmir dressing gowns and English silver travelling sets; one was posted at the gate to receive innumerable complaints; and the forbidding Baron Hahn, a Baltic German civil servant, compiling a huge dossier of abuses and necessary reforms, was ushered in to make the case for the removal of the Governor-General, Baron Rosen.* The latter's French chef, as if to underline his master's incompetence, was more often drunk than not, and meals in the palace suffered accordingly. To Rosen's consternation, the Prophet Shamyl, leader of the warring Daghestan tribes, had just sent an impudent message refusing to pledge his submission to Nicholas, which unfortunately Rosen had promised to his master. The atmosphere did not look promising for pardons.

Fears as to Nicholas' mood were quickly realised. Within days the Governor-General saw his son-in-law (the hereditary Prince of Mingrelia) publicly degraded for alleged misdemeanours, his epaulettes stripped off on parade in front of all the troops and despatched to Siberia. At another military review on October 10th a colonel, whose battalion had marched indifferently, was summarily removed from his command. However, at this same review four squadrons of Lermontov's own regiment won the Tsar's warm approbation as they marched past first at the walk, then at the trot – as irregular cavalry they were not fully bitted for a gallop. Lermontov was not among them, but the Tsar's approval for his regiment may have had something to do with one of the first acts of clemency on this stormy visit – the issue of an order on October 11th for Lermontov's transfer to the Grodnensky Hussar Guards regiment, stationed near Pskov – in other words, a pardon, and an end of exile.

Lermontov did not hear the news until six weeks later. The Imperial order had to be duly processed through the War

* Lermontov was a friend of his son, Dmitry.

Ministry in St Petersburg, and travel by courier back to Kakhetia before he could be told. He was not overjoyed and admitted to Rayevsky that, were it not for his grandmother, he would have far preferred to have stayed in the south; the Grodnensky Regiment was garrisoning the gloomy Military Settlements near Pskov, founded under Alexander I by the tyrannic General Arakcheyev, and was a byword for useless parades, soulless drinking and occasional bouts of vicious discipline inflicted on hapless military veterans forced to till the soil under military orders. 'I've already made plans to travel to Mecca, to Persia,' he informed Rayevsky airily. 'It only remains for me to ask to join the expedition to Khiva with Perovsky.'[27] The remark can only have been made for effect, to distract poor Rayevsky, languishing in his cold province in the North. Even the most optimistic spirit could scarcely expect that, having just received his pardon from Nicholas and Benckendorff, he would as a further favour be given passports to leave the Empire. Mecca was well known to be forbidden to *Giaours*, nor were Russians encouraged to practise tourism in Persia, until very recently at war with the Tsar. As for the expedition to Khiva under General Perovsky, nearly all its members were to perish in the pitiless steppes of Central Asia: it was one of the Tsar's least successful imperial adventures. But the freebooting world of Kakhetia and Georgia seemed made to encourage Eastern fantasies, and it was with reluctance and a head full of escapist dreams that Lermontov set off on the long journey back to Russia.

He arrived in Tiflis at the end of November, confirming his reluctance to hurry home by staying there for several weeks. An oil painting, dating from this visit, gives his impression of the view on entering Tiflis from the east. In the foreground the swirling yellow-blue waters of the Kura wind a serpentine way between high chalky cliffs, covered by the bazaars of the Persians, Georgians and Armenians; water wheels, worked off the river, supply the vineyards. Here and there, squat domes of churches, mosques and balconies offer shade to cool Russian soldiers exhausted by the heat, under orders to keep their uniforms buttoned up. A few minarets rise above the cypresses. Moulding the rocky crest overlooking the town stands the massive fort of Narikala, old as Alexander and Ptolemy, crowned by fairytale towers. Blue mountains rise behind fortress, town and river, their contours softened in the light of the setting sun.

> Beyond the wooded mountain now
> The evening sun declines,
> And scarcely murmuring in its flow
> The warm spring gently shines;
> Gardens with living fragrance blow,
> Scenting the air around;
> Tiflis in silence basks below.[28]

begins a ballad of Lermontov's where he casts himself as the jealous and impatient lover, kept waiting by a Georgian girl.

> And now in pairs with timourous feet,
> A white parade of mirth,
> From bath houses on every street,
> Good Georgian wives come forth.

Night falls. A chill Eastern wind accompanies the merchants as their caravans wind out from the city. Still no tryst! Perhaps she has dropped him for

> ... a Tartar brave,
> 'Tis not for naught he preens and struts
> Before your door, indeed;

He resolves to kill the Tartar, or possibly indeed the treacherous lady. But she just redeems herself before he rises to the ambush:

> Hark! Do I hear a trampling near?
> 'Tis thee, thou wicked one![29]

Hidden in the old city were new Russian barracks, the Governor-General's palace and a hospital for veterans of the Chechen and Daghestan campaigns. The whole town, much rebuilt since the disastrous rapine of 1795, when it was sacked by the Persians, had just been repainted for the Tsar's visit. The hierarchical roll-call (itemised by Klaproth) was a 'Georgian patriarch, a Georgian metropolitan, 55 Georgian priests, a Greek *archerei*; three Greek archimandrites, one Armenian archbishop, 73 Armenian priests, 8 Armenian *archereis*, 4 Catholic fathers, one tartar *effendi*, 160 Georgian princes, 16 Georgian gentlemen, 1983 bourgeois, 25 peasants, 426 slaves and 3684 private houses.'[30] Probably there were 20,000 people at any given moment, excluding the Russian garrison.

One of the leading Decembrists, Baron Andrey Rosen, was also – as the phrase then ran, coined by Nicholas – 'finding his way back to Russia through the Caucasus' – and was on his way to his Regiment a few days before the Tsar's visit. His impressions emphasised the Asiatic character of Tiflis:

> Next day as soon as I woke up I walked over to my window, and perceived that in Tiflis every face and object has a quite un-European stamp: the houses with flat roofs, Armenians with loaded camels, Georgians with their bullock carts, the women veiled, the asses with bundles of firewood, the horses with rawhide waterskins on their backs. . . . Persians led the splendid Persian stallions by my windows, gifts from the Shah to the Emperor. . . . The bazaar and the renowned baths were still on a completely Asiatic plan, and were served only by orientals.[31]

For Lermontov, this muddle of ranks, races, titles, faiths and armies, provided a feast of contrasts: mountain chiefs, proudly riding through in their Circassian felt mantles; a Persian headsman, half-hidden under his lambskin hat and kashmir cloak; Tartars in fur cloaks and red silk trousers; princes from Imeritia or Kakhetia in close fitting tunics of rich brocade, with short sleeves, loose silk Eastern trousers, black boots and lambskin capes; the Patriarch in his robes, sporting the broad ribbon of Saint Stanislaus; Georgian generals in the uniform of the Erevan or Mingrelian regiments; Georgian ladies, attended by their servants, their white veils tactically deployed (depending on age and beauty) to show their dark eyes and long black tresses held by velvet headbands. Jostled by all, he made his way to the very centre of the town, to the covered bazaars and the *Maidan* (market place) his nostrils assaulted by the smells of roasting sheep, garlic and herbs, camel and goat dung. The renowned silver, gold and gunsmiths of the town spread out their tempting wares; and there were none – save perhaps at Kubachi in Daghestan – to match the local swordsmiths.

Lermontov's aunt, Madame Akhverdova, divided her time between Tiflis and St Petersburg. In Tiflis, the Chavchavadzes, to whom she had let her apartment in St Petersburg, had taken a wing of her house for the season. Lermontov, who doubtless stayed with her, was able to meet his friends once again: Nina Griboyedova-Chavchavadze, her sisters and other sloe-eyed princesses from Georgian families – among them two sisters, Sopiko and Maiko Orbeliani. Lermontov seems to have been especially drawn to Maiko, and her name has been found scribbled in the back of his valedictory poem 'Hurrying northwards from afar', which he wrote on leaving Tiflis.

The girls of the Chavchavadze circle provided amusing and attractive company, but Georgian women in general may have been a disappointment. Few of them, Lermontov complained, could speak a word of Russian. Western visitors of the period, condemned their low foreheads, henna-stained eyebrows, painted faces, and immodestly low-cut dresses. But Circassian costumes and dances were picturesque, and Lermontov sketched a dancing girl with tambourine and swirling veil, watched by her family, from grandmother to baby son, on the roof of a flat-topped Tiflis house.* He preserved a still more pleasing impression of Georgian dancing in his poem 'The Demon':

---

* Alexander Dumas' descriptions of a Georgian dancer produced for him in 1858 by the officers of Lermontov's Regiment bears quoting:

Leila was in full evening dress. On her head she wore a little gold-embroidered cap from which a long gossamer veil floated to her knees. Her gown of black satin and gold braid had wide slashed sleeves that hung far below her hands, and over it she wore a tight-fitting tunic of silk,

Tamara takes her tambourine,
And nimbly shakes it o'er her head;
With fleeting motion
Now trips it lighter than a bird,
Now holds a-sudden in her dance,
And casts a shining roguish glance
From underneath the jealous lashes. . . .[32]

Lermontov had no time nor indication to learn much Georgian. His forces, linguistically, were poised to crack the nut of 'Tatar – ' in other words Azeri Turkish.[33] He agreed with Bestujev that this was the *lingua franca* of the mountains, the French of the East, and engaged as a tutor the same man who had taught Bestujev, Mirza Fet Ali, a skilled translator, and chronicler of Azerbaidjani tales. From him Lermontov gathered the themes for several ballads in the Eastern genre. The closest in mood to an oriental folktale, doubtless picked up from Ali, if not direct from the Tiflis bazaar, was his *Turkish Tale*, in prose, whose hero Ashik Kerib, a poor balalaika player, falls in love with the daughter of a rich Tiflis merchant, is transported by a wizard on a magical white horse from Erzerum to Tiflis, and finally wins his bride in the teeth of countless obstacles.

Tiflis, so full of the smells and colours of the East, had not yet acquired all the comforts or sophistication of the West. The best hotel was a 'miserable tavern kept by a Jew.'[34] There were no public libraries, and no bookshop for Europeans. The *Petersburg Gazette*, weeks late, and mainly consisting of Government propaganda, was the only newspaper obtainable. European cooking was almost non-existent: apart from the Governor's French chef, the only other exponent of the French cuisine was a certain Jean-Paul, an ex-veteran of the Napoleonic army,

white and pink, which emphasised her waist and the curves of her thighs. From her silver belt hung a little curved dagger, its ivory hilt inlaid with gold. A pocket on the outside of its sheath contained a tiny knife of exquisite workmanship. As a finishing touch, she had little pointed slippers of cherry-coloured velvet trimmed with gold, which now and then peeped out to reveal a very pretty foot, but were generally concealed by the folds of her black satin dress.

whose cooking 'savoured more of the barrack than of the Palais Royal.'[35] Gambling was one form of escapism. The other stand-by, shared by Georgians and Russians alike, was drinking: seven and a half million bottles of wine were consumed each year in Tiflis.

The greatest luxury Tiflis could afford was, without doubt, its marble-lined and vaulted bath house. Lermontov, subject to attacks of rheumatism, and with arthritis in his knee joints, badly crushed some years before in the military riding school of St Petersburg, plunged with delight into a course of baths. Taking a bath was a delightful process.* Attendants would scrub your body with goatshair gloves, and then with tubfuls of soapy water, pressing, squeezing and kneading your body, and finally, if you wished, would walk over you, in the Japanese fashion,

---

* Pushkin's experience was even more delightful. As he wrote in *The Journey to Erzerum*:

At the entrance to the bathroom sat the owner, an elderly Persian. He opened the door for me, I went into a spacious room, and what did I see? More than fifty women, young and old, half-dressed and completely undressed, sitting and standing, were undressing and dressing on the benches which were placed along the walls. I stopped. 'Come on, come on,' said the owner to me, 'today is Tuesday: Women's Day. It doesn't matter, no harm.' – 'Of course no harm,' I answered him, 'on the contrary.' The appearance of men produced no impression. They continued to laugh and talk among themselves. Not one hurried to cover herself with her yashmak; not one stopped undressing. It seemed that I had entered like an invisible being. Many of them were genuinely beautiful, and justified the imagination of T. Moore:

A lovely Georgian maid,
With all the bloom, the freshen'd glow
Of her own country maiden's looks,
When warm they rise from Teflis' brooks. [*Lalla Rookh*]

On the other hand I know nothing more repulsive than the old women in Georgia – they are witches.

The Persian took me into the baths: a hot, iron-sulphurous spring was pouring into a deep tub hewn out of the cliff. Never in my life have I encountered either in Russia or in Turkey anything more luxurious than the Tiflis baths.

giving you 'the exquisite sensation of cracking all over the joints',[36] and then, ablutions and massage completed, would signal you to enter the warm and soothing waters of the bath for as long as you wished.

The baths at Tiflis provided the starting point for a tantalising draft of a short story, found among Lermontov's papers:

I follow a Georgian girl to the baths; she makes a sign but does not enter as it is a Saturday. Leaving, she makes another sign. To amuse her I draw with charcoal a Tatar on the wall, and mark him with a devil on his back. I follow her. She agrees ... provided I swear to obey her: a corpse must be disposed of. I carry it away and throw it into the Kura. I am arrested. I can't remember the house. We decide to find it. I pull out a dagger [*kinjal*] as evidence, from the corpse and we take it to Geurg who made it for a Russian officer. We ask Achmet to identify the owner; apparently it was a Russian officer who, according to his orderly, long frequented the neighbourhood, visiting an old woman and her daughter. The latter got married. And within a week the officer was killed. We discover where the girl lives, now married; Achmet hears that a man has crawled out of the window. The husband immediately asks the household awkward questions. At night, in the caravanserai, we see the girl walking with a man; they halt and the girl points to me.[37]

There is a *dénouement* on the bridge, the narrator is attacked by the avenging husband. The world of old Tiflis, of swordsmiths and intrigues in the bathhouse, and in a Moslem home, leading to murder and revenge, provided imaginative stimulants in plenty.

But sadly, the weeks in Tiflis had to end, the journey home must be resumed. What would he find there? An anxious note sounds in his farewell poem, 'Hurrying northwards from afar':

O, since that day of banishment,
Am I forgotten quite at home?

Shall I meet there the old kind eyes?
The old kind welcome greet my ears?
Shall friends and brothers recognise
The wanderer after many years?[38]

His vagabond life in fact had lasted for less than a year.

Lermontov left Tiflis by post-chaise, his only luggage a smallish trunk, packed half-full with travel notes. The road up to the mountain passes went past the monastery and fortress of Mtskheta, where the rushing green waters of the river Aragvi met the more placid yellow swell of the Kura. The place was a melancholy pleasure of ruins, round which huddled a miserable village. It had known glory in the past, for Mtskheta had been the capital of Georgia until it was sacked by Tamerlane, and superseded by Tiflis. But its eleventh-century cathedral, though crumbling and smothered by ivy and yew, still had the presence and nobility that had justified its use as the last resting place of the kings of Georgia. In the dank body of the church, beneath the central dome, Lermontov could see the tombstones of departed kings and captains, and read the inscription that commemorated the last of them:

> Here lieth the Tsar Irakli (Hercules), born in 1716, who ascended the Kakhetian throne in 1744, that of Georgia in 1762 and died in 1798. To mark his distinguished reign, in the memory of his descendants, this monument was erected by order of the Tsar, Alexander I in 1812, by the General Officer Commanding in Georgia, the Marquis Paulluci.[39]

So, by the hand of a foreign mercenary, at the order of a Russian Tsar, was the last king of Georgia honoured. Outside the cathedral there was a view of other, still more ancient shrines, crowning the surrounding mountain tops, and here, as he stood to admire them, Lermontov was greeted by a group of old men, monks who had survived the fall of their kingdom, the invasions of the Persians, and the incessant passage of Russian troops, and from one of them heard the tale of the Georgian novice (Mtsyri), which would become the basis of his poem 'The Novice', his first major work to have a Georgian setting.

The story of 'The Novice' is that of a captured orphan, abandoned at the gates of the Mtskheta monastery at the age of six by the Russians, and brought up by the monks to become one of them. But he rejects his vows, and the enclosed life they offer,* to search for freedom among his own people, setting out through the mountains, with their mists, dark ravines, rugged rocks and fresh green meadows, on a journey that will end in death. The poem is musical, voluptuous, a hymn of praise to the Caucasus, steeped with the love of nature, from awesome crags to the smallest rustle in the meadow grass:

> And on God's world there lay the deep
> And heavy spell of utter sleep,
> Although the landrail called, and I
> Could hear the trill of the dragon fly
> Or else the lisping of the stream ...
> Only a snake, with a yellow gleam
> Like golden lettering inlaid
> From hilt to tip upon a blade
> Was rustling, for the grass was dry
> And in the loose sand cautiously
> It slid out and then began to spring
> And roll itself into a ring,
> Then, as though struck by sudden fear
> Made haste to dart and disappear.[40]

The novice seems so much a child of the Caucasian mountains, and his rejection of the monastery, with its fettering security, for the freedom of a noble savage, so much an echo of local legend, that it needs scholars to remind the reader that Lermontov had already toyed with just such a theme in earlier poems, written before his year of travel. In his poem, 'Boyar Orsha', men awaiting death are offered the chance to confess and repent, and defiantly decline it, preferring freedom in death to life in spiritual chains. Lermontov usually wrote extempore and with very few corrections; but the path of his creative journey is

---

* Some interpret the 'Monastery' as meaning Russia herself.

scattered with the skeletons of earlier experiments. 'The Novice', in which 'rhythm, phrasing and diction are saturated with an unflagging dynamism, from the first line to the last',[41] combined the freshness of immediate perceptions with a long and deeply thought gestation.

It is easy to read symbolic meanings into 'The Novice.' Lermontov himself gave as the heading

> I have barely tasted the honey;
> And I must die

from the Book of Kings. Nature herself was free from the taint of original sin. Her denizens 'cry like children' and he, the novice, fights like a beast, despite his civilised training received at the hands of the 'monks', who speak for authority and man-made traditions. The Novice has one strength, in contrast to other heroes of the Lermontov pantheon – he knows no doubt. He would rather die than live out his life in the monastery. The only valid alternative would be the return to the peaks

> Where in my youth I loved to range –
> All heaven and time would I exchange.[42]

Leaving Mtskheta, the road north led up to the Kaiyshaur Pass, flanked by the mountain of the Cross, to the main highway past towering Mount Kazbek, and the Dariál Gorge. The opening pages of 'Bela' in *A Hero of our Time* describe a chilling, even frightening journey which may well have been based on Lermontov's own experiences. But he dismissed it elsewhere in the book in the best anti-Marlinsky style:

> I galloped briskly through the Terek and Darial passes, lunched at Kazbek, had tea in Lars and reached Vladikavkaz in time for supper.[43]

It was there, with the worst of his journey over, that a fellow officer, years later, recalled seeing him. He was sitting at a table in the primitive posting house, wearing a military frock coat, accompanied by an unidentified civilian, a Frenchman. They were both painting; and Lermontov was singing full-throatedly, '*A moi la vie! A moi la vie, à moi la liberté!*'[44]

On arrival in Stavropol, in full swing for its winter season, he whiled away as much of December as he dared with his friends – guards officers, exiled Decembrists, Doctor Maier. His kinsman, General Petrov, he felt, could fend off awkward questions from St Petersburg as to why he was not 'hurrying homewards' faster.

He arrived in Moscow on January 3rd, 1838, and within days was seeing family and friends in St Petersburg where he was to spend the customary leave allowed to officers returning from the Caucasus. He found his grandmother busily intriguing for his transfer back to his old regiment there, the Life Guards Hussars, and, in the hope of this, eager to dissuade him from any attempt to leave the service. Lermontov resigned himself, not too unwillingly, to a continuing existence as a cavalry lieutenant, and for the time being, to his transfer, on the Tsar's orders, to his new regiment, the Grodno Hussars near Novgorod. He joined them at the end of February, drowning the sour taste of the military settlement with champagne parties, flirtations with regimental wives, and, less obtrusively, with work, in particular with drawing and painting Caucasian scenes.

Meanwhile his grandmother was continuing her pleas to those in authority, harrying Benckendorff until he agreed to make a further personal intervention with the Tsar, which was successful. The Tsar, after consultation with the Grand Duke Michael, gave his consent to Lermontov's reinstatement with the Life Guards Hussars as a final pardon to be made in honour of Easter. On April 9th, after only two months at the Military Settlement, Lermontov received his transfer back to St Petersburg.

The Rise and Fall of a Society Lion

Lermontov's period of banishment was over. Now, with only the lightest of military duties to distract him, it was time to reap the fruits of his Caucasian experiences in literary work. He was able to meet the leading literary figures of the day in the family circle of the historian Karamsin. There his widow Ekaterina entertained for her unmarried daughters Sofiya and Lisa, and Lermontov became a welcome guest. Such arbiters of taste as Jukovsky, the Vyazemskys, the inveterate gossip, ladies' man and diarist, A. I. Turgeniev, were familiar figures at the readings, name-day parties, and frequent lunches, dinners and evening charades given by Madame Karamsina to amuse the young. Lermontov might have made his way with them on sulky charm alone, but he had earned the sincere enthusiasm of these, Pushkin's friends, for his poem 'Borodino'. Over the next few years their journal, *The Contemporary*, provided an important outlet for his work, Jukovsky, the editor, more than once using his influence to push his poems past the Censors.

Another friendship, renewed at this time and equally important in literary terms, was that with Andrei Krayevsky, editor of the newly founded journal *Notes of the Fatherland*. Krayevsky, four years older than Lermontov, and as suave and tactful as Lermontov was not, had taken particular care to cultivate individuals on the Committee of Censors; and the Censors, taking personal responsibility for what they approved, were often academics of integrity and moral courage. Nikitenko, the son of a serf, who as Censor passed several of Lermontov's submissions, despaired more than once of the 'miserable conditions of writers'. In 1831 he commiserated with Pletnev: 'We talked about our literature, that is, we bewailed its ruin.' Krayevsky's diplomacy with them did much to ensure that Lermontov found a reading public.

Surprisingly, Lermontov's first poem to appear on his return had nothing to do with the Caucasus, though it had probably been written while he was there. A romantic ballad, 'The Song of the Tsar Ivan Vasilievitch, the Opritchnik (the Young Body-guard) and the bold Merchant Kalashnikov', it was published unsigned, as befitted the work of one recently exiled. A second poem, which he showed to Jukovsky (who had steered the first one past the Censors and the Minister of Education personally), shortly after his return, was his tale of 'The Tambov Treasurer's Wife.' This, too, was not Caucasian. Pushkinian in its stanzaic form, but thoroughly Lermontovian in its ironies and black humour, it gave a witty picture of the strait-jacketed life of Russian provincial towns, the arrogant vanities of officers, their fawning civilian contemporaries, merchants, landlords and miserable mayors, where wives are sold off to pay gambling debts. It was published by Jukovsky in the *Contemporary*.

But it was the Caucasus, and Lermontov's experience there, which would dominate his two most substantial literary achievements during this period in St Petersburg, his novel *A Hero of our Time*, and his poem 'The Demon.' Both were deeply self-revealing: the conflicts and contradictions in Lermontov's character, and his passionate desire for freedom come to life most vividly against the savagery and splendour of a Caucasian background.

A Hero of our Time was Lermontov's first and only novel, though he had sketched out drafts for other, uncompleted works. Till now, Bestujev 'Marlinsky' had monopolised and, perhaps in the end, made ridiculous, the genre of blood and thunder novels with Caucasian settings. Pushkin had parodied noble savages, romantic maidens and disillusioned young heroes in his *Journal to Erzerum* published in 1836. Lermontov picked up the challenge to infuse new interest into this well-tried form.

He finished the novel in 1839 and it appeared first in instalments in Krayevsky's *Notes of the Fatherland* and then as a complete novel in April 1840. *A Hero of our Time* consists in fact of five short stories, each self-contained, but each revealing, either through hearsay ('eavesdropping' as Nabokov calls it), eye-witnesses, or autobiographically, the character and soul of

Grigory Pechorin, a rich, worldly and possibly disgraced young officer in the Caucasus.

The psychological disclosure begins in the 'most vile' Black Sea port of Taman, where Pechorin is bewitched by a gipsy girl, a decoy for ruthless gun-runners and smugglers beating the Russian blockade of the Black Sea, and is nearly drowned by her ('Taman'). A water colour by Lermontov records the hut, where the *undina* or combination of mermaid, gipsy, sorceress and smuggler seduced Pechorin into a madcap fishing expedition in her rowing boat. A brother-officer of Lermontov's stayed in this very hut the next year and confirmed the presence of a beautiful girl, a blind ten-year old boy, and a ruffianly old Crimean smuggler. The cast of 'Taman' was still there. Chekhov qualified 'Taman' as the perfect short story: 'I don't know a use of language better than Lermontov's. Here's what I would do: Take his story and analyse it, the way we analyse stories in school, by sentences, by phrases, by clauses. That way, one would learn how to write.'[1]

Pechorin then enters the watering spa life of Pyatigorsk, where his cool sarcasm and cynical courtship of a young Muscovite Princess lead him into a duel, in which he kills a fatuous and pathetic rival, also an officer ('Princess Mary'). Ordered to a lonely border Fort as punishment, he dispels his *ennui* by kidnapping and then seducing a chief's daughter, the sloe-eyed Bela, but, in a brutal murder of revenge, she is killed ('Bela'). Pechorin is released back to St Petersburg. As a short interlude in the Bela drama, he visits a Terek settlement where Russian officers speculate whether freewill or predestination rules their lives, and he escapes once again with his own life by heroically capturing a Cossack murderer ('The Fatalist'). Four years later, Pechorin meets his former nominal superior in the 'Bela' Fort, the grizzled, warm-hearted and somewhat naive old veteran, Captain Maxym Maxymych at Vladikavkaz, to tell him laconically that he is off to Persia, and he casually gives him his 'Journal' ('Maxym Maxymych') A year or so later, his death is reported, and the narrators (that is, the Captain and Lermontov himself, as the Captain's questioner and fellow-traveller across the mountains), feel free to publish Pechorin's most intimate revelations.

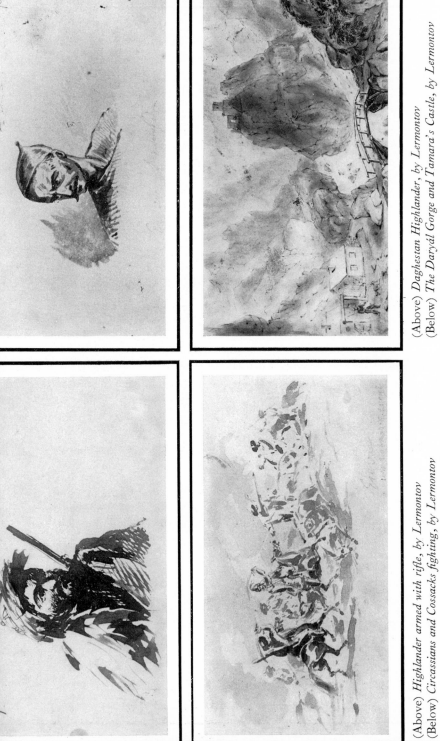

(Above) *Highlander armed with rifle, by Lermontov*
(Below) *Circassians and Cossacks fighting, by Lermontov*

(Above) *Daghestan Highlander, by Lermontov*
(Below) *The Daryál Gorge and Tamara's Castle, by Lermontov*

Left above) *Two Russians firing at Highlander. Copy of Lermontov's drawing by Prince G. G. Gagarin*

Left below) *Illustration by Lermontov for A. Bestujev Marlinsky's 'Ammalat Bek'*

Above) *View of Tiflis, by Lermontov*

Resting Room at the Baths of Shemakha, by Prince G. G. Gagarin

'Djigitovka' or Tournament, by Prince G. G. Gagarin

Feast at Mtskheta, Georgia, by Prince G. G. Gagarin

The novel, purely in literary form, was remarkable for the subtlety of its technique. Pechorin is presented to the reader, first by Maxym Maxymych, by the 'Author', and by himself. There is the silhouette of him as the dashing, bored romantic youth pitted against the noble savages of the Caucasus; outwitted by the true hero of 'Taman', Yanko the smuggler; triumphing over a parody of himself in the portly shape of Grushnitsky, the 'rival' in 'Princess Mary'; and, after these Herculean trials, of him measuring his will, the key to his character, against Fate itself in the 'Fatalist.' Lermontov uses these different cameras in logical sequence to focus on the human heart. It is a brilliant anticipation of flashback from the world of television or cinema.

In his Foreword to the Second Edition (of 1841), Lermontov sought to disarm those critics who would claim that the author 'had drawn portraits of himself and his friends', warning them that *A Hero of our Time* is simply a portrait – but not of a particular man; it is a portrait made up of the fully developed vices of our generation.[2]

Such a disclaimer is misleading. There was much of Pechorin in Lermontov. To begin with the outward man, descriptions of Lermontov by his contemporaries closely follow his own of Pechorin. Like Lermontov, Pechorin had broad shoulders, and a constitution able to withstand hardships. He sits down as though he 'hadn't a bone in his back.'[3] His smile is childlike. His eyes never laugh but shine with a phosphorescent glitter, 'like that of smooth steel, dazzling but cold.'[4] His smile has the 'disagreeable effect of an indiscreet question, almost insolent.'[5] You might think he was twenty-three but, says the narrator, one was 'prepared to give him thirty.' Pechorin often yawns. 'Time to be off, Maxym Maxymych', he says, 'bored to death.' It might have been Lermontov speaking.

Lermontov identifies with Pechorin, too, to the extent that Pechorin is an artist, and an author, who one day may even seek publication, though for the present his diaries are purely private confessions.

In experience the parallels are equally close. Pechorin's journal from time to time makes poignant references to his lonely childhood, his early loves and present unhappiness. His good

D

instincts, thwarted in childhood – 'I was modest, they accused me
of being crafty, I became secretive,'[6] or 'I was gloomy, other
children were merry and talkative' – turn to jealousy, moodiness
and the habit of suspicion. His 'unfortunate disposition' is a cause
of unhappiness for others. Plain for all to sympathize with – who
have a knowledge of Lermontov's childhood – was a soul bereft
of a mother's love, estranged from a father, and hemmed in by a
grandmother's possessiveness. If reasons for the poet's sense of
alienation have to be found, these are sufficient; so was solitude
born and unhappiness encouraged to dominate the nobler feelings, perhaps of Lermontov, and certainly of Pechorin. Thus were
the super-egoists developed.

But how to find a cure for unhappiness? Leaving childhood
for the pleasures of youth it seems that to Pechorin women were
attractive but relationships with them fail to give fulfilment; a
proposition so far true enough for Lermontov as well. Study
provides no substitute for happiness. Of what value were the
sharper emotions generated in the face of danger, the prospect of
death by a Chechen bullet? 'In vain,' says Pechorin, 'after one
month I got so used to their buzzing that really I paid no more
attention to them than mosquitoes.'[7] For Lermontov, though not
for Pechorin, such sang-froid was premature – Lermontov had
not yet seen active service. Travel? Pechorin, admitting a 'restless
fancy and insatiable heart', seeks the great escapist cure of travel,
to America, to India, to Arabia. This had clearly been Lermontov's own diversionary tactic, in putting off the difficult moment
of coming to terms with his own role in society; he, after all,
had had madcap plans of visiting Mecca, Persia, and the East.
Pechorin's malady is given different names: 'disillusionment', the
English sickness learnt so well from Byron's heroes; 'cold
despair', masked behind outward amiability, which no sudden
impulses – headlong gallops, duels, fatalistic gambling – can
conjure away.

So far, there is nothing in Pechorin which Lermontov, at
some time or other, must not have felt, sometimes passionately.
But Lermontov went further in creating Pechorin, and it is here
that one must tread warily in attributing to the former characteristics of the latter. The distinction was clearly drawn by Akim

Shan Girey, his cousin, who knew him so well. It was not his fault, he wrote in the 1860s, that many construed a satire into an apologia, and attributed to Lermontov the 'grand dandyism' and 'misunderstood anglomania' of Pechorin in which it was good form to be surprised by nothing and to be above everything, where, in Pechorin's words, 'In my early youth, I was a dreamer. ... What did it leave me with? ... Only a weariness. ... I entered on this life having already lived it in my thoughts, and I became bored and disgusted, like one who reads a poor imitation of a book he has known for a long time.'[8]

Lermontov could understand and enter into the sins of Pechorin: his almost irredeemable selfishness, his callous seduction of Princess Maria, his contempt for human life, displayed in the duel with Grushnitsky – but from there to behaving similarly himself is a very different matter. Pechorin feels himself 'a moral cripple', despising himself, doubting the meaning of his life, but asserting his confident will deliberately and monstrously, at the expense of other. His future is empty, life has no answers and no obligations, and can be gambled away on a futile point of honour. As the Captain says to poor Grushnitsky at the last moment before his duel with Pechorin, 'nothing has any significance in the world. Nature's a simpleton, fate is a goose, and life is worth but a brass farthing.'[9]

Such a philosophy was obviously that of the post-Decembrist generation, frustrated and, when frustrated, destructive. There is a curious review of Lermontov's book by the Tsar Nicholas himself, in the form of a long letter to his wife, where he refused to recognise – in Pechorin – one of the faces of the society which he himself had so resolutely fashioned since his stormy accession in 1825:

I have now read and finished the 'Hero'. I find the second volume odious and quite worthy to be fashionable [*à la mode*] as it is the same gallery of despicable, exaggerated characters that one finds in fashionable foreign novels. It is such novels that debauch morals and distort character, and whilst one hears such caterwauling with disgust, it always leaves one painfully half-convinced that the world is only composed of such people whose best actions apparently are inspired only by abominable or impure motives. What then is the result? Contempt or hatred of humanity. Is that the aim of our life on earth? One is only too disposed to be hypochondriac or misanthropic. So what is the use, by painting such portraits, of encouraging these tendencies? I therefore repeat my view that the author suffers from a most depraved spirit, and his talents are pathetic. The Captain's character is nicely sketched. In beginning to read the story I had hoped, and was rejoicing, that he was the Hero of our Times. In his class there are indeed many more truly worthy of this title than those too commonly dignified with it. The (Independent) Caucasian Corps must surely number many of them, whom one gets to know only too rarely, but such a hope is not to be fulfilled in this book, and M. Lermontov was unable to develop the noble and simple character (of the Captain). He is replaced by wretched and uninteresting people, who – proving to be tiresome – would have been far better ignored and thus not provoke one's disgust.[10]

Lermontov was not, of course, to know that the Tsar's hard gaze would focus so precisely on him – the letter was dated June 1840 – but he realised in presenting Pechorin to the tiny, worldly reading public of St Petersburg and Moscow that he should set a distance between himself and his hero. In his 'Author's Note to Pechorin's Journal' he made the following comment:

Perhaps some readers would like to know my opinion of Pechorin's character. My answer is the title of this book. 'But that's a wicked irony,' they will say. I do not know.[11]

Pechorin had, without doubt, been endowed with some devilish characteristics. His 'chief satisfaction' had been to subject those around him to his will. He had defined happiness, in a chilling phrase, as 'satiated pride.' Vera, his mistress, says to him that in no one else is 'evil so attractive.' Part of his philosophy is that 'the idea of evil cannot enter a man's head without his wanting

to put it into practice.' In his outlook there was even something
of the great gothic tradition when he confesses 'there are moments when I understand the Vampire.'[12] To many of Lermontov's readers, Nicholas included, it was obvious such a monster
was not 'the Hero' of their times. But in his 'Author's Note'
Lermontov had hoped to separate the obvious attacks on himself
as author from those awaiting the doomed Pechorin. Lermontov
appealed to his audience: 'If you admire far more unattractive
and abnormal characters in fiction, whey then do you show my
hero less mercy?'[13] He had written a moral tale, 'bitter medicine'
perhaps, but he would not become a preacher, and try to put
'human vices to right'.

Pechorin and Lermontov, created and creator, become one
again in the noble and redeeming words of Pechorin's, which
must have represented Lermontov's philosophy at that time:
'I became convinced of the innocence of the man who brought
his own weaknesses and vices so mercilessly to light.'[14]

At the same time as he was completing *A Hero of our Time*,
Lermontov was pursuing other major themes in his poem 'The
Demon', which allowed him, perhaps because it was a fantasy,
to express emotional truths still closer to his heart. Pechorin,
after all, 'had never given up anything for those he loved.' In
'The Demon', with its story of passion and despair, Lermontov
dropped his mask of fatalistic cynicism and laid bare his own
experience of unhappy love.

Any regrets which he had felt about losing Varvara Lopukhina,
now Madame Bakhmetieva, had been sharply revived when in June
1838, barely six seeks after his return to St Petersburg, he and
his cousin Shan Girey met Varvara and her stuffy husband on
their way to take the waters at Reval on the Baltic. She had
just lost a baby. White as a sheet, thin as a nail, she was a shadow
of her former self. The sight of this ghost of his dreams, in whose
eyes only there flashed the sparkle and the gentleness of the old
Varvara, deeply moved Lermontov. Later that year, he sent the
sixth draft of his poem to her, wondering whether its 'long
familiar music' would still cast a spell on her; he had dedicated
his first draft to her as long ago as 1831.

Does it awake regret for all the past?
Or through the tiresome pages do you steal
Only dead empty phrases at the last
Laying upon it like heavy seal?

Seeing no more in it the simple theme
Of grief, of my poor brain so many years
Unhappy? And lightly, as a play or dream
Taking my soul's delirium and its tears?[15]

Ever 'seeking the fantastic since childhood', Lermontov had
been obsessed with the theme of Miltonic Satans from the age of
fifteen. In 'Cain' Byron had popularised an updated version of
the Fallen Angel, 'excluded from human society by having
dared to know too much, and regarding remorse stoically as an
aspect of wisdom', and indeed – to some – this was Byron's
'most important single contribution' to the culture of his time.[16]

There was in him a vital scorn of all,
　　As if the worst had fall'n which could befall,
He stood a stranger in this breathing world,
　　An erring spirit from another hurl'd.[17]

Earlier drafts of 'The Demon' were thus rich in echoes of
Byron's 'Cain' and 'Heaven and Earth', Vigny's 'Eloa', and Tom
Moore's 'The Loves of the Angels.' But it was his experience of
the Caucasus in 1837 which had finally fixed the setting for the
poem; as for the details, they were to come from Georgian and
Ossetian folklore, topography and legend.

The poetry of 'The Demon' is essentially musical. 'I have
always thought,' wrote Shan Girey, 'that "The Demon" was
like an opera with the most enchanting music'.[18]* The overture
of the opera-ballad heralds a swoop by the Demon, the 'spirit of
exile' upon the Caucasus:

---

*　Not surprisingly, it has become an opera by A. Rubinstein, and also by a
Georgian Tsintsadse, to Tchabukiani's libretto. E. F. Napravnik also called
his third Symphony 'The Demon.'

Now o'er the Caucasus, on high,
Was Eden's outcast flying by.
Kazbek, beneath, with diamond light
Of everlasting snow shines blinding;
And deep below, a streak of night,
Like some dark cleft, the snake's delight,
In endless curves the Daryal's winding
And Terek like a lion springing,
With bristling mane in fury roars. . . .[19]

In the verdant valley, sheltered by these mountains, an earthly paradise where nightingales sing, the Demon sees Tamara, a Georgian princess, as she dances in her father's castle before her wedding. He falls fatally in love. Gudal, the prince of Sinodal, Tamara's bridegroom, is murdered by a mountain bandit's shot as he rides with his lordly caravan to meet her. The arrival of his bloodied body turns the wedding into a wake. Tamara, inconsolable, withdraws to a convent. Here the Demon, gripped by passion and the inexplicable hope that human love will free him from his burden of pride, despair and loneliness, follows her, trusting that with time her nature will rebel against the chastity and solitude of the convent. Finally, entering her cell, he pleads with her to yield to him, and to save him from eternal solitude. Tamara, terrified, objects that a power stronger than them both will judge them:

Demon: We are alone.
Tamara: And God?
Demon: His glance on us will never dwell,
His realm is Heaven,
He scarce can spare for Earth a thought.[20]

And in a magnificent declamation he declares his love: will she be his companion in eternal damnation?

Torn by compassion and desire, Tamara yields to him, but in the moment of her yielding and the Demon's triumph she dies. She is buried by her grieving father, who builds a chapel on the granite rocks, which only vultures haunt.

Gloomy that castle now, its story
Hid in the annals of the past,
Like some old man, enfeebled, hoary,
Doomed all his dear ones to outlast.
By day its denizens are hidden,
But when the moonbeam glads the night
They hum, and creep, and fly unchidden,
And take their freedom and delight.
Grey hermit spiders there are weaving
Their webs for silly flies' deceiving,
And sportively the lizards green
Play on the ruined roof unheeding,
And wily snake from hole unseen
Crawls down the crumbling staircase leading
To where a lofty hall had been,
Slow wriggling o'er the steps between
Garret and basement, or extended
With long striped body stretched outright,
Like sword, abandoned after flight
By warrior slain, whose wars are ended.

And massive icebergs without number
Tower sombre frowning over all,
As if the frost had charmed to slumber
A vast cascade in headlong fall.
And there the blizzard never weary
Whirls snow, like dust, from those gray walls,
Or, howling dirges long and dreary,
The ice-bound guards to duty calls.
Soon as that summons calls to rally,
That lonely temple's worshippers,
From bleakest east continually
Cloud and with hurricane concurs.
None venture here with fearful tread
To mourn Gudal, Tamara dead.
Kazbek's grim barrier guards for ever
The secret of its icy breast,
And busy hum of men may never
Break through their everlasting rest.[21]

In the sixth draft of 'The Demon,' Lermontov had ended with Tamara doomed, defiant and irredeemable, the willing victim of the Demon. But the poem, though unprinted, was read and circulated in copies through St Petersburg. Unexpectedly, Lermontov learned that 'the highest circles' at court (in effect the Empress and her daughters) had expressed interest in the poem and wished to read it. Lermontov drafted two further versions, in which, perhaps bearing the imperial susceptibilities and his own somewhat shaky position in mind, he brought the ending more into line with conventional orthodoxy. He may well have intended to revise it further to pass the Censors. In the last extant version, written in early 1839, Tamara's somewhat bullying guardian angel announces that she has won redemption through her death. She is saved, her soul will be borne to heaven. As for the Demon, he

> Again, as formerly was left,
> Of hope, of love, of paradise bereft
> Unpitied and alone in space.[22]

The Demon, despite his titanic egoism, despite his powers, despite his exercise of a will regardless of the consequences for others, has a human nature. And being human, he is unhappy, disillusioned and can only find redemption through love. Such a surrender to love – the Demon to Tamara, Lermontov to Varvara, is in no way a surrender to the conformist philistine values of the herd. Alas, like Pechorin, like Ismail Bey, like all Lermontov's other heroes, however, the Demon, and, dare one draw the conclusion, his creator, lose their gamble for salvation through love.

Lermontov was exploring through the Demon other problems too, more perplexing, even agonising than those that had beset the amoral, cynical and fundamentally agnostic Pechorin. The age-old dilemma of the necessity of evil in a world created by an all good, all-powerful God had been set out for him in Byron's *Cain*, crying to Lucifer:

> Why do I exist?
> Why art thou wretched? Why are all things so?

To Byron the answer was clear that

> Evil and good are things in their own essence
> And not made good by the giver.

There was only one consolation, arid enough:

> One good gift has the fatal apple given
> Your reason.[23]

Lermontov, in his short life, was never to reach such clear-cut answers in favour only of rationalism or scepticism. Byelinsky caught him once in a serious mood: 'I argued that I was delighted to see in his rational, cold and outraged outlook on life and people the seeds of a deep faith; he smiled and said, "God grant it may be so".'[24]

The conclusion which Lermontov had reached was that in an ignoble society and time the honourable man would earn salvation, if such a thing existed, by protest and independence, truer principles to live by, and if necessary to die with, than the submissive humility recommended by orthodox religion, or indeed to accept mindless passivity; such is the fate of Pushkin's Tatiana in her marriage: Onegin is reduced to compliance. Gogol burnt the second part of *Dead Souls* in a fit of humility understandable only to a Russian. Tolstoy preached non-resistance to evil. In the pantheon of his country's great writers, Lermontov stands very much alone, a disquieting reminder to all Russians, and others willing to listen, as the poet of freedom, moral, political and social. The Demon would not compromise; nor would his creator.

Lermontov's literary position was now firmly established. The editors of the *Russian Veteran*, *The Contemporary*, and from 1839 onwards the *Notes of the Fatherland*, all wanted to publish the new star who in Sofiya Karamsina's phrase 'glitters on our literary horizon, otherwise so sombre.' Socially, too, he seemed to be accepted in 1838–9 where he before was unknown. Ivan Turgeniev, the novelist, described a meeting:

At Princess Sh[akhovaska]ya I was observing the poet who had rapidly become famous. He sat down on a low stool in front of a sofa on which, attired in a black dress, sat the blonde countess M[usina]- P[ushkina], one of the beauties of that time in the metropolis, a really charming creature. Lermontov was dressed in the uniform of an Hussar regiment of the Life Guards; he did not take off either the sabre, or the gloves, and hunching his shoulders and frowning, glanced morosely at the Countess from time to time. She did not talk much with him and more often addressed herself to Count Sh[uvalov], also a hussar, who was sitting next to him. There was something sinister and tragic in Lermontov's appearance; a certain gloomy and unkind force, pensive disdain and passion emanated from his swarthy countenance, from his large and steady eyes. Their heavy gaze strangely disagreed with the expression of his almost childishly tender and protruding lips. His whole figure, squat, bow-legged, with a large head and wide stooping shoulders, roused an unpleasant feeling; but all who met him were immediately conscious of his inherent strength. It is known that to a certain extent he portrayed himself in Pechorin. The words 'When he laughed, his eyes were not laughing' could really be applied to him.[25]

An ex-mistress of Pushkin, Elisabeth Khitrovo, now fifty years old, took a liking to him. One of her daughters, Catherine Tiesenhausen, was in the Empress' set of intimates, another, Dolly Ficquelmont, was one of the best informed women in St Petersburg, and married to the Austrian Ambassador. These were powers in the 'swinish' social life of the capital, who opened to him most doors, including those of foreign embassies.

But such social successes were hollow. Lermontov, with his pitiless powers of self-analysis, was no dupe of flattery. His Aunt Vereshchagina valued bluntly his chances of marriage. 'These people catch either rich ones or persons of rank, and Misha is too poor for them. What is his income of twenty thousand, a hundred thousand is too little, they call it *"une petite fortune"*. The old woman [Lermontov's grandmother] is distressed and frightened.'[26]

And Lermontov knew that even if he were as desirable as a Grand Duke, something of his own character would find the victory short-lived, and the satisfaction evanescent. As he wrote to Varvara's sister Mariya, still his confidante towards the end of 1838:

I must tell you that I am the most miserable of all men, and you will believe me when you learn that I attend balls daily. I threw myself into the high society. A whole month I was in vogue, I was torn to pieces. This, at least, is candid. All this society, which I insulted in my poetry, is delighted to lavish flattery on me; the most beautiful women beg verses from me and boast about them as about a victory.

And he continued then with a confession worthy of Pechorin:

May be it will seem strange to you that one can seek amusements to be bored, that one haunts *salons* when there is nothing interesting there? Very well, I shall reveal to you my reasons – You know that my principal shortcomings are vanity and egotism (*amour propre*). There was a time when I longed to be accepted in this society as a new recruit. . . . I did not succeed, the aristocratic portals were closed to me. But now I am admitted into the same society not as a petitioner, but as a man who is there by right of conquest. I excite curiosity. I am being solicited, I am invited everywhere, and I never give any indication that I desire this; ladies who must, without fail, establish the most fashionable *salon*, wish me to visit them, because I am also a society lion; yes, I, your Michel, a good fellow, whom you never suspected to have a lion's mane. Do agree that all this can turn one's head! Fortunately my innate laziness gains the upper hand – and, little by little, I am beginning to find it all extremely intolerable. However, this new experience has been good for me, because it placed in my hands weapons against society, and should society ever persecute me with its calumnies (and this will happen), I shall at least have the means of revenge; undoubtedly nowhere else is there so much that is vile and ludicrous.[27]

The constraints of society in St Petersburg had within a few months turned his homecoming and reunion with his grandmother – his only reason for putting up with the Life Guards again – into a claustrophobic and intolerable situation. Ivan Turgeniev had found the right words. Describing Lermontov in society, he wrote, 'he was suffocating in the crowded circle into which fate pushed him.'[28] Lermontov had compared St Petersburg to a 'very narrow garden', and now, uncontrollably, out of malice, boredom or anger, he was to jump on the larger social sunflowers and military tulips in its flower-beds. The most infuriating aspect of the whole black comedy was that he knew where he wanted to be – on his own terms – and he could not be there. Byelinsky had recognised that the 'exile' of 1837 had changed Lermontov into the poet who

> upon the inaccessible heights of the Caucasus crowned with eternal love [finds] his Parnassus ... in its raging Terek, its mountain torrents, and its healing springs, he finds his Castalian spring, his Hippocrene. ... Strangely the Caucasus has somehow been destined to be the cradle of our poetic talents.[29]

Byelinsky was right, for the 'healing' memory of the Caucasus combined with Lermontov's tender love for children inspired him to write for his cousin Alexandra Vereshchagina's new-born child the most famous of all lullabies probably ever written in Russian, the 'Cossack Cradle Song.' His grandmother, in a covering letter to her niece, excused Misha's failure to send it himself. 'You know how lazy he is':

Softly, pretty baby, sleeping,
　Bayushki-bayu,
Quiet moon bright watch is keeping
　On your crib for you.
I shall tell you tales past number,
　Sing you ditties too.
Close your tender eyes in slumber,
　Bayushki-bayu.

Terek on his stones is fretting
  With a troubled roar;
Wild Chechen, his dagger whetting,
  Crawls along the shore.
But your father knows war's riot,
  Knows what he must do.
Sleep, my darling, sleep in quiet,
  Bayushki-bayu.[30]

And Lermontov now knew that Byelinsky's insight had been right. He wrote bitterly to Mariya Lopukhina (at the end of his self-indictment as a creature of 'vanity and *amour propre*'): 'I asked to go to the Caucasus – they refused me. They won't even let me be killed.'[31] In fact, 'they' would not even let him go to Moscow on leave – which he had requested three times.

How indeed could life in St Petersburg be a substitute for the fighting, travel, the mountains, adventures with brigands, and, in Lermontov's case, for the marvels of Nature? There had proved to be no real substitutes in love to the ideal of Varvara

We parted, but my heart still wears
Thine image, gracious yet,
Pale token of those better years,
I never can forget.
What though new passions rule my will?
Deserted and untrod
The temple is a temple still,
The idol still a god.[32]

He paid court to the adorable, recently widowed Princess Shcherbatova,* whose beauty was 'out of a fairy tale':

---

* According to Ekaterina Sushkova (herself a victim of Lermontov's insincere attentions in 1834–35), Lermontov was actually 'engaged' but – to avoid marriage – begged his grandmother to refuse her permission. If true, a case of having his cake and eating it, but Ekaterina herself may not be the most trustworthy of sources.

As the Ukrainian nights glitter to stars that never set
So the words of her scented lips
Are filled with mysteries
Her eyes are transparent and blue
As the skies of those lands,
As the winds of the desert,
Her caresses are tender and loving. . . .[33]

But all to no avail. In these days of resignation, he wrote a lament ('Duma') for his own generation which even received the Censors' approval to be published in the *Patriotic Notes* of January 1, 1839:

Sadly I contemplate our generation:
Its future is either empty or dark
Meanwhile, under the burden of knowledge or doubt,
    It will grow old in activity. . . .
Life wears us out, like an even road with no destination . . .
As forced fruit, ripe before its time,

That pleases neither taste nor eye,
Hangs amid blossoms, an alien orphan –
And the hour of its beauty is the hour of its fall . . .
And we hasten towards our coffin without happiness or glory,
    Looking derisively behind.

A cheerless throng and soon to be forgotten
We shall pass over this earth without sound or trace,
And shall leave to ages neither fertile notion
Nor any work begun with genius;
And our ashes . . .
They will mock in a contemptuous rhyme,
The bitter mockery of a disappointed son
    For a prodigal father.[34]

This requiem echoes the doleful cadences, which Lermontov must have known from the 'Philosophical Letter' published in the Moscow *Telescope* of 1836, written by the notorious P. Ya

Chaadeyev. Ever since its publication, the latter had been under virtual house arrest in Moscow, adjudged 'mad' by the authorities. Chaadeyev had described Russia's bloody history and arrested development in phrases which are the mirror, in prose, reflecting Lermontov's 'Duma':

> But I ask you: where do you find our sages, where do you find our thinkers? And yet, placed as we are between the two great divisions of the world, between the Orient and the West, touching at one end on China and at the other on Germany, we ought to have united in ourselves the two great principles of intelligent nature: imagination and reason, and in this way, united within our civilisation the histories of the entire globe. But this is not at all the role that Providence has allotted to us. Far from it: Providence does not seem to have occupied itself with our fate at all. . . . One would say, to look at us, that the general law of humanity had been revoked in our case. . . . We have given nothing to the world, we have learned nothing from the world; we have contributed nothing to the human spirit; and all that has come to us of its progress we have disfigured. . . .
>
> We grow but we do not mature. We advance, but only obliquely, along a line that does not lead us to our goal. We are like infants . . . whose entire knowledge is on the surface of their being, whose entire soul is outside themselves. . . .[35]

The similarity in ideas and content is remarkable. 'Duma' impressed, too, Byelinsky, who felt that he would 're-echo' this cry:

> These verses are written in blood. . . . They come from the depth of an outraged soul. It is a cry, the moan of a man for whom the absence of an inner life is an evil a thousand times more horrible than physical death. And who of the new generations of men will not find an answering chord in his own weary soul, in his apathy, in his inner emptiness, and will not re-cho this cry and this moan?[36]

All in all, it was extraordinary that the Censors had allowed 'Duma' to be published.

Furthermore, that remarkable Censor, Nikitenko, in February of 1839, continued to show extraordinary moral courage and discerning literary judgment by allowing another of Lermontov's heady declarations of artistic integrity to be published in the *Notes of the Fatherland*. The Poet, declared Lermontov, was like his rusty old Caucasian dagger – the *kinjal* – hanging harmlessly from a wall as a fashionable form of interior decoration; in other times, poet and dagger had wielded powers of life and death:

> The time was when the cadenced sound of thy mighty words
>> Nerved the warrior to the fight;
> When thy song was as needful to the people, as the goblet to
>> a feast,
>> Or as incense in the hour of prayer.
> Like God's sweet air, thou breathed over them,
>> And called forth high and noble thoughts;
> Even as the bell within the guildhall's tower
>> Mingles its sound with the people's joy or sorrow.
> But the simple and proud notes now weary us,
>> And in tinsel and deceiving flattery we find delight;
> Like some old beauty, our old world has learned
>> To hide its wrinkles beneath a layer of rouge.
> Wilt thou awake once more, thou despised prophet,
>> Or wilt thou never again, in answer to the cry for revenge.
> Pluck forth from its gilded sheath thy blade
>> Now covered thick with rust of contempt?[37]

With Lermontov, irritation could turn to anger, frustration to resentment, and disappointment to sarcasm all too quickly. It was difficult to shake off a childhood spent as his grandmother's darling. And never had there been such an irritating and frustrating way of spending the day as on parade under the Grand Duke Michael's eye, or confined to the Imperial barracks at Tsarskoge Selo. In this mood of crystallised bad temper, Lermontov was clearly vulnerable to trouble with his military superiors.

Soon the storms broke about his devil-may-care head – not once but four times.

The first irritant, angering his Colonel, the Grand Duke Michael (who cared passionately for military punctilio), was his appearance on parade with a toy sword instead of his cavalry sabre; this childish gesture earned him twenty-one days under arrest.

The second was his membership of the so-called 'Circle of Sixteen', a convivial cigar-smoking club of young lions who used to gather together to discuss freely their fancies, political, social, amorous. Its members had hardly the neo-Decembrist* stamp of Herzen's set in the mild 1830s who had all been exiled, but its existence smacked of presumption to Benckendorff, the Grand Duke Michael and Nicholas. Lermontov was the cleverest and wildest amongst them, but the others were of note: Prince Lobanov-Rostovsky, Prince Grigory Gagarin, an artist of real talent, Baron Dmitry Fredericks, the dashing and good-looking Prince Sergey Trubetskoy, Nicholai Jerve, the young sons of the President of Nicholas' Council, and of the Minister of Finance, Vasiltchikov and Kankrin, and the Shuvalovs, 'Mongo' Stolypin – a roll-call of the most favoured of that generation (Ivan Turgeniev later admitted taking the complacent 'Mongo' Stolypin as his type for Paul Kirsanov and 'similar ex-lions' in his *Fathers and Sons*). The Grand Duke Michael disliked such signs of independence; he let it be known he would destroy the 'nest' of these young officers.

Thirdly, the 'Circle of Sixteen' were too close to the Empress for Benckendorff's peace of mind. Her flirtations with these young men nettled the Tsar himself, well aware of her weaknesses. She was approaching forty. A Hohenzollern Princess, married since 1817, daughter of King Frederick William III of Prussia, and the famous Queen Louise, she was highly strung, still attractive, but exhausted by pregnancies. She had lost Nicholas to one of her Ladies-in-Waiting, and he had many other brief encounters. She was prey to migraines, and took frequent cures at Ems and other German spas. She found what emotional consolations she

---

* Sometimes cruelly described as 'Decembrists without December.'

could, but there was a cumulative price to pay in nervous pros-
tration and indiscretions. More than once she tried, tearfully, to
get Nicholas to rescind some order transferring her favourite
young men to the Caucasus. She participated in 'masquerades',
flirted with 'Mongo' Stolypin's brother, and the handsome
Sergey Trubetskoy. Lermontov was enmeshed by close friendship
with the Empress' friends; Nicholas knew of it and disapproved.

The Empress' escapism also showed itself in a thirst for
literature. Her daughters called the Journal *Contemporary* 'our
Contemporary', and discussed with Pletnev, its editor, the contents. In 1838 Lermontov's 'Tambov Treasurer's Wife' had
appeared there, with its ribald echoes of hussar feasts and provincial seduction.

In February 1838, Lermontov's hand-copied and edited
'Demon' had been privately read to the Empress. It had apparently enchanted her. Nicholas must also have heard this
version, as he is reputed to have said: 'Why can't he write
everything in the style of "Borodino"?' And the Grand Duke
Michael had remarked: 'We had the Italian Beelzebub, the
English Lucifer, the German Mephistopheles, now the Russian
Demon; in other words, the Unclean Spirit has arrived. But I
can't decide who created whom: Lermontov the Evil Spirit, or
the Evil Spirit Lermontov.'[38] The Empress wrote down lines
from Lermontov's 'Prayer' in her intimate diary; and her Court
composer, Theophilus Tolstoy, set it to music. All this was
enough to disturb Benckendorff, whose duties included the protection of the Empress' reputation, and the discreet control of her
amusements.

In this hothouse atmosphere of the Empress Alexandra's set,
Lermontov now committed a foolish and strangely ill-bred act,
proving how far recklessness could lead him. He had been at the
ball on New Year's Eve 1840 of the Assembly of the Nobility,
where he had behaved imprudently – what words were exchanged
is not known – with two ladies disguised in rose-coloured
dominoes. It seems possible one of them was the Empress herself.
Benckendorff was rapidly apprised of the incident. His views
veered sharply from earlier indulgence to a firm conviction that
Lermontov had become an irredeemable troublemaker. His

conviction hardened, shortly after, with the publication of a stinging poem 'The First of January', which denounced the company that evening, and the ladies in particular, with cold-eyed scorn:

When I am surrounded by a motley crowd
And figures of soulless people, genteely grimacing masques,
Flit before my eyes as in a dream,
To the sound of music and dancing,
And to the absurd whispering of speeches learnt by heart;
When the hands of town beauties
Which have long ceased to tremble,
Touch my cold hands with loveless audacity –
How often then, outwardly absolved in their glitter and vanity,
Do I cherish in my soul an old Dream,
And the sacred sounds of bygone years.

And if in some way I succeed in losing myself in a reverie
I fly in my memory like a free bird
Back to the recent past.
I see myself a child again.
All around me are familiar places.
The tall manor-house, and the garden with the broken down
    conservatory,
The sleeping pond is filmed with a green network of grass
And in the distance the mist is lifting from the fields. . . .

Oh, how I long to disturb their gaiety and to cast insolently
In their faces iron verses, steeped in bitterness and fury![39]

The fourth and final storm blew up entirely unexpectedly. Prosper de Barante, the French Ambassador in St Petersburg since 1835, was a distinguished man. A *Préfet* at twenty-five under Napoleon, it was rumoured a one-time lover of the ageing Madame de Staël, and now a somewhat pompous Academician, historian, and friend of the Imperial family, he took a close interest in the Russian literary scene. He had known Pushkin well, and had attended his deathbed and funeral in 1837. He had sent his First Secretary, Baron d'André, to inquire from Lermontov's friend, A. I. Turgeniev, if Lermontov's strictures on d'Anthes in 'The Death of a Poet' had been directed against all Frenchmen, or just against d'Anthes. Lermontov forwarded a copy of the poem for de Barante to form his own judgment. He presumably found it harmless. On 14th January 1840, at all events, Lermontov found himself invited to a ball of the de Barantes, as a literary curiosity. He enjoyed the party. In fact, Lermontov was passionately interested in French politics, and wrote a sweeping indictment (whilst under arrest later) of Louis Philippe's showmanship, in organising the 'Return of the Ashes' of Napoleon to a bourgeois France that had betrayed him.

The Ambassador's twenty-one-year-old son, Ernest, an *Attaché* on his father's staff, was handsome, spoilt, and was reputed to be a poor loser to Lermontov in pursuing the beautiful Princess Maria Shcherbatova. Both he and Lermontov were also admirers of a very lively and attractive thirty-six-year-old coquette and blue-stocking, Teresa von Bacherach. On February 16th, at another ball, Ernest took Lermontov aside and accused him of disobliging slanders repeated to a third party – presumably to either Maria or Teresa. The 'slanders' may have been simply Lermontov's condemnation of foreigners in 'The Death of a Poet' considered insulting by the son, if not the father.* Lermontov denied them; then refused to add to his brief remarks. At which:

Ernest: 'If I were in my own country, I would know how this matter would end.'
Lermontov: 'In Russia the laws of honour are observed as strictly as anywhere. And less than others, do we allow ourselves to be insulted without redress.'[40]

And on February 18th they fought at the same place, knee-deep

---

* P. A. Viskovatov, Lermontov's first biographer, thought Teresa was the cause – Shan Girey thought that it was Princess Shcherbatova. Evdokiya Rostopchina told Alexandre Dumas the duel was over 'The Death of a Poet.'

in snow, as Pushkin had done. Ernest, for ten minutes, half-heartedly sought to run Lermontov through with '*l'épée française*' (in which he was well skilled), whilst Lermontov was only trained to handle a cavalry sabre. Lermontov escaped with only an elbow-scratch and a broken sword. The seconds made them change weapons. Ernest fired his pistol but missed; Lermontov aimed at the sky. Honour was more or less satisfied. They shook hands. Lermontov, 'wet as a mouse', rushed straight from the duel to tell Shan Girey all about it.[41] They both thought he had got away with it. But according to Shan Girey some indiscreet and worried remarks of Teresa's, at Court, to 'highly placed persons' betrayed him. An inquiry was launched.

On March 10th, Lermontov was arrested for 'not reporting a duel.' He had fallen into a (one-way) trap, thanks to a Frenchman whom he had dismissed as one of those 'seekers of adventures and sons of bitches' whom he detested – another d'Anthes.[42] Lermontov was taken to the guard house, while the young Attaché stayed free, protected by diplomatic immunity. 'Mongo' Stolypin, Lermontov's second, was also arrested. A Court Martial of Guards officers was convened.

Nicholas himself, the puppet-master in the affair, must have intervened to protect the de Barantes, father and son. Occasionally he took note of a frightened 'public opinion.' With Russia and France on a possible collision course over the 'Eastern question', Lermontov could have appeared as a patriotic young man, who had told an arrogant Frenchman some unpalatable truths. After all, de Barante's own official position in St Petersburg was very exposed. Nicholas had always privately ridiculed Louis Philippe's legitimacy. On the Eastern Question, he had already recalled his own Ambassador, Count Pahlen, from Paris in December 1839. De Barante's private correspondence was purloined and read by Nicholas. It was with great reluctance that he stayed on at St Petersburg, isolated diplomatically – as France was too – by a tripartite axis of Prussia, Austria and Russia.

Nicholas, too, had motives to minimise a Franco-Russian scandal of this character involving an officer of his Life Guards

and the French Ambassador's son. But these were not considerations uppermost in the mind of the amiable and not very
sharp-witted Shan Girey, who told Lermontov, under arrest,
that Ernest was now talking of a second duel, to avenge his
'honour.' The 'insult' had been Lermontov's shot in the air.
Lermontov's hot blood rose. He inveigled Ernest to visit him
secretly. He offered him another duel, as soon as he was free.
Ernest prudently dismissed the offer and, under pressure from
his father, left for France the next day – but not, however,
before he had told his mother about it all. She complained to
Lermontov's regimental colonel that this tiresome Lieutenant
was threatening her son's life with another duel now. The meeting
itself had violated security rules.

Whilst he was confined to the guard-house Lermontov kept
up his morale. He read the *Tales of Hoffman* and translated
Zeidlitz. He dedicated a cheerful ballad to his 'neighbour', the
daughter of a prison officer: he wrote a long dialogue in verse
called 'The Journalist, Reader and Writer', which expressed, at
one level an irritated *ennui* with the state of all three arts, but,
finding satire inadequate, denounced the Journalist for the
corruption of his stale platitudes ('the printer's ink had turned to
dirty water') and concluded that the Writer (i.e. the Poet),
whose 'severe conscience' should guide his pen, would be throw-
ing pearls before swine if the brutish 'ungrateful Crowd' were
allowed to know his bitter prophecies and 'poisoned' secrets.
Lermontov in this, in 'Duma', in 'The First of January', is an
elder brother to Baudelaire, and Gerard de Nerval's contemporary:

> *Je suis le ténébreux, – le veuf – l'inconsolé,*
> *Le prince d'Acquitaine à la Tour abolie.*
> *Ma seule étoile est morte – et mon luth constellé*
> *Porte le soleil noir de la Mélancolie.*

There, too, in the guard house, he was visited by Byelinsky,
who had a piece of unfinished business to be settled to his own
satisfaction, and that was a reconciliation with Russia's greatest
living poet, Pushkin's heir, before he was sent south again. The

meeting was duly recorded for posterity by Byelinsky in a letter
of April 16 to his financial protector Botkin:

> A profound and mighty spirit! How correctly does he look at
> art, what deep and purely spontaneous taste of appreciating
> gracefulness! On, this will be a Russian poet on the scale of
> an Ivan the Great! Marvellous personality! I was absolutely
> delighted when he told me that he rated [Fenimore]Cooper
> above Walter Scott, that the latter lacks poetry and is dry.
> I have thought so for long myself and this was the first man
> I met who thought likewise. He reveres Pushkin and likes
> 'Onegin' best of all. He inveighs against women; of men he
> is likewise contemptuous. He loves several women and usually
> sees only them. A purely Onegin's outlook. Pechorin is
> himself, just as he is.[43]

And he rounded off his panegyric with the description of
Lermontov as the poet of 'merciless truth', asking questions that
'freeze the heart', a writer of 'diabolical talent.'

Adjudged guilty, Lermontov now waited and waited for his
sentence. It was to be degradation to the ranks and loss of his
title and privileges, with, however, a recommendation for
mitigation. Opinions were divided amongst the military establishment. Major-General Plautin of the Life Guards Hussars thought
the sentence should be maintained; Adjutant-General Knorring
of the Guards Cavalry Corps that he should only be transferred
from the Guards to the Army, but with the same rank of Lieutenant (to which he had been promoted in December 1839);
the Grand Duke Michael that, as well, he should serve three
months in a fortress prison. On April 13th, Nicholas cut through
these differences and personally determined the sentences.
Lieutenant Lermontov was to be transferred to the Tenginsky
Infantry Regiment with the same rank. The majority of his
hard-pressed Regiment's battalions were in death-trap fortresses
on the Black Sea Coast, but one battalion was in reserve near Ust
Labinskaya, in comparative safety, training raw recruits.

Once again Lermontov visited the military tailors for the
appropriate and, this time, unglamorous grey of the infantry great

coat. Once again he took leave of a tearful grandmother, half-paralysed with grief. Once again society ladies exchanged views about this stormy petrel, and this time were not so indulgent. Lermontov's own Aunt Vereshchagina roundly blamed Lermontov himself as the trouble-maker who had so muddled up his triumphant return to the capital. 'Nobody is sorry for him; everybody is for his grandmother.'[44] It was his infuriating arrogance and *'imprudences impardonnables'* that so upset his well-wishers.

Lermontov himself, lacking the arts of compromise, went his own way with those who did understand him, and spent his last evening in St Petersburg at the beloved Karamsins, where over the last two years a close friendship had forged itself between him and Sofiya – perhaps on her side love, on his, certainly, trust. Staring out at the scudding clouds over the Summer Garden, he scribbled down a lyric, 'Clouds', comparing his fate of an exile to their freedom:

> You have no torments, no passions beguile you,
> Cold you are always, free you must ever be –
> Having no fatherland, none can exile you.[45]

By mid-May, Lermontov was in Moscow, where he met Gogol, read 'The Novice' to an enchanted audience of literary celebrities, and flirted in his own cat-and-mouse way with the sisters of a former friend and comrade at the Cadet School, Nicholas Martynov.

In June the Tsar, in his letter already quoted to the Empress Alexandra reviewing *A Hero of our Time*, wrote the *envoi* for Lieutenant Lermontov's second official tour of duty in the Caucasus:

> *Bon Voyage à M. Lermontov*. He can go and – if that were possible – brain-wash himself [*se purifier la tête*] in a world where he can put the finishing touches to his character of the Captain always assuming he is capable of painting him in depth.[46]

Lermontov was returning to the Caucasus, but hardly on the terms he had desired.

Lieutenant Lermontov at War

The Tenginsky Regiment, to which Lermontov had been ordered, had been fighting on the Right Flank since the early 1830s. In 1839 their four battalions had been ordered to man the line of garrisons set amidst hostile tribes along the thickly wooded coast of the Black Sea. Fortified by the counsels and Remingtons of gun-running English merchants, and united as never before, the Circassian, Ubykh and Adighe chiefs had fallen like wolves in early 1840 upon the forts of Lazarevskoye and Velimianovskoye, and finally, on March 14, on Fort Mikhailovskoye. The isolated Russians were annihilated. At the last of these, the garrison had decided to fire the power train and blow themselves up rather than surrender. Private Osipov (whose hand lit the fuse) was turned into a military Saint; his name was ordered always to be read first on the roll-call of the Tenginsky Regiment, *pour encourager les autres*: 'he died for the glory of Russian arms at Mikhailovskoye.'[1]

The Tsar received the despatches telling of the collapse of his line of forts in St Petersburg on April 9. A division was immediately ordered from the Crimea – it was hoped – to counter-attack. Four days later, he had Lermontov's case before him. It was not surprising that, in view of the Tenginsky's desperate need to train new recruits and to be provided with fresh officers, the Tsar should have assigned Lermontov for duty with them. One battalion of the regiment was still fighting, though decimated by illness and deaths in battle.

By mid-June Lermontov had arrived in Stavropol – in suffocating heat – to receive his orders from the G.O.C., General Grabbé. So unpromising an assignment as joining the Tenginsky had no attraction for him. Without the opportunity of distinguishing himself there would be little chance of a speedy pardon: medals and awards for gallantry provided the quickest means for peccant officers to return to St Petersburg. Accordingly he applied for a change of duty, on a temporary basis, from the Tenginsky to the punitive expedition shortly to leave Fort Grozny under the command of General Galafayev against Shamyl. General Grabbé, a charming and intelligent man, even writing amateur poetry, gave his willing agreement. Lermontov was posted to Galafayev's staff as a liaison officer. In high spirits he wrote to Varvara's brother before setting off: 'Tomorrow I go into Chechniya to take the Prophet Shamyl – whom I hope I shall not capture. What a rascal!'[2]

Lermontov's reference to Shamyl as a rascal – '*canaille*' in the original of his letter – is the only mention of the Prophet in his writings. This fact, and the somewhat aristocratic contempt of his description, show that Lermontov had not yet had time to take Shamyl very seriously. It betrayed an attitude common to the *jeunesse dorée* of St Petersburg who viewed an 'expedition' such as he was about to undertake as little more than an exciting season's shooting.

General Grabbé, and those who had served in the 1838–9 campaign however, had much to tell the virgin officers joining them in 1840, because that campaign had culminated in the horrible and bloody siege of the rock fortress of Akhoulgo, where Shamyl had made a desperate stand. The hand-to-hand fighting under tall stone towers, shattered by Russian artillery, had been appalling; women and children, fighting with daggers or even stones, had flung themselves at the Russians, and had been bayonetted to death. The alternative, which some had taken, was to throw themselves over the cliffs to certain death in the ravines below. Shamyl, though wounded, and with a pregnant wife to save, had escaped. Grabbé, dismissing him as a spent force, if not already dead, had placed a reward of only three thousand roubles on his head. It was a miscalculation born of culpable ignorance of the psychology of the Daghestan and Chechen tribes. Shamyl had escaped, not only with his arms but with the whole of his amazing reputation as a warrior-prophet intact. Within eight months, his wounds healed, a proud father again, his lieutenants were raiding towns within the line and even abducting Christian girls for his harem. In practical terms he had assembled enough men to take on Galafayev's forces.

The wretched quality of Russian intelligence about Shamyl was an important feature of the war. Neither generals nor officers could speak the obscure Turkish dialects of Shamyl and his lieutenants, nor could they read Arabic, the written language of Daghestan. Lermontov's own efforts to learn 'Tatar' had been given up for lack of time. Other officers did not even attempt it under the nomadic conditions of military life. They were dependent on interpreters, whose loyalties were often suspect, and whose numbers were limited – or, still less frequently, on deserters. To the tribesmen, as Lermontov's poem 'Haroun the Deserter' made clear, the only penalty for deserting was death. There were few who dared risk it.

In the place of more solid information, camp-fire gossip about Shamyl abounded. It was rumoured that the Viceroy of Egypt, Ibrahim Pasha, was sending an army to help Shamyl; credulous tribesmen had heard that the great Queen of England would be doing the same. And to an army full of disgraced exiles, Decembrists and Poles, the story of Shamyl's reply to General von Klugenau was discreetly enjoyable. In 1837 it had been hoped Shamyl would pledge his submission personally to Nicholas whilst the latter was in the Caucasus. Von Klugenau, a grizzled, cigar-smoking General, was sent to negotiate this in a personal meeting which nearly cost him his life. Shamyl ended the 'negotiation' with the following message:

> From the poor writer of this letter, Shamyl, who leaves all things in the hands of God; this is to inform you that I have finally decided not to go to Tiflis for I have often experienced your treachery, and this all men know.[3]

Old hands would speak of Shamyl's amazing prowess as an athlete who could out-swim, out-run, out-fence, out-jump and out-ride any of his own fierce men. His Kabardin horses were magnificent. In his ceremonial green robes over a red silk *beshmet* or tunic, with yellow boots and a huge white turban, he embodied God's justice to terrified villagers; he would arrive flanked by executioners who would cut off first the hands, then the heads of traitors laggard in providing support for his army. Certainly one of the first sights to make young officers shudder were the heads, impaled as visible proof of Shamyl's powers in the *aouls* which they entered, in their turn, to raid for provisions before setting them ablaze. Like General Yermolov, Shamyl believed in terror.

But terror was not his only appeal, and perhaps if the Russians had studied the essential tenets of Shamyl's faith in more depth they would have understood how he could so successfully unite the tribes, proclaim a *Ghazavat* or Holy War, and fuel it for so long. (It was not until 1859 that he finally surrendered, with full honours, to the Russian army.) These tenets were religious fanaticism, love of liberty, and protection of the social and cultural traditions of the tribes. If trapped in a siege, or before a charge of the Russian infantry, such fanaticism showed itself in the collective death chant – noble, threatening, resigned – which the tribesmen intoned:

Weep O ye maidens, on mountain and valley,
Lift the dirge for the souls of the brave!
We have fired our last bullet, have made our last rally,
And Caucasus gives us a grave.

And they would then hurl at the Russians the taunt:

Fame to us, death to you,
Alla ha, Alla hu![4]

Shamyl skilfully adapted the most useful of the *Shariat* or ordinary *Sunni* Moslem social laws to a code acceptable to the mountaineers, thus developing some kind of unity which would override the laws of *Kanli*, or revenge, that until then had always disunited them. Onto this he grafted his own concept of personal holiness, usually achieved through deeds in battle. His troops were graded into fighting orders, the Murids being the rank and file, those making spiritual progress becoming Sheikhs or Khalifs. At their head he set himself up alone, as *Imam*, or Prophet; put before God all the rest were equal. This doctrine of religious equality was convenient too politically; it meant that the poor could attack, without moral or religious scruples, rich Khans, who had sold out to the Russians.

To Lermontov, in 1840, as to his fellow countrymen, the fine points of Muridism, as Shamyl's doctrines were called, remained a closed book, but the campaign on which he was setting out would give him for the first time a real, as opposed to hearsay, experience of the Prophet's ways of waging war.

Lermontov rode into Fort Grozny from Stavropol in early June. He found a welcoming band of Petersburg friends, many from the Circle of Sixteen, now exchanging the stamp of the mazurka on parquet floors for that of dusty boots in the stirrup, and on the muddy floors of bivouacs. Pushkin's jovial younger brother, Lev, was there; the talented painter Prince Grigory Gagarin; Rufin Dorokhov, already known to Pushkin in the Russo-Turkish war of 1828 and later to serve Tolstoy as the model for Dolokhov in *War and Peace*; the Princes Trubetskoy and Dolgoruky, members of the Empress's intimate circle, recently exiled by the Tsar; and 'Mongo' Stolypin, paying somewhat irritably with exile for his loyalty in being Lermontov's second in his duel with de Barante.

On July 6th, in a swirl of dust and screeching gun carriages, General Galafeyev's expedition rode out of the gates of Fort Grozny at dawn. A contemporary, Prince Sayn Wittgenstein, describes one such departure:

> There were Russians in their elegant uniforms, Cossacks of the Line, real Scythian warriors armed to the teeth; Kabardins [the Parisians of the Caucasus], Georgians in their graceful costumes, in wide sleeved capes and pointed sheepskin bonnets; nomadic Kurds, bedecked in turbans and red waistcoats, with long bamboo lances; other tribesmen amongst whom mingled Afghans, Persians and Indians, a rag, tag, and bobtail of unruly and scruffy fellows, living mainly off fermented mare's milk and responsible for the Army's baggage train.[5]

General Galafayev's orders were the traditional ones to 'search and destroy', to capture Shamyl, and to build or re-build various forts. It was hoped – at least in St Petersburg – to create a land blockade similar to the Black Sea line on the Right Flank, which would hem in Shamyl and his men. Lermontov was well aware of the precepts of the 'old tiger' General Yermolov – the terror of the Caucasus in the 1820s – who had said, 'out of pure humanity, I am inexorably severe', and who held that the only way to deal with Asiatics was to carve out Russian dominion at bayonet point 'on the front of the mountains.'[6] He knew the meaning of the order to 'search and destroy' a suspect village, and had written of it when only eighteen – with obvious reference to Yermolov – in his poem 'Ismail Bey':

> Old men and babes he slaughters, pitiless,
> Young girls and mothers smears with the caress
> Of bloody hands; but women of the hills
> Are not like women in their souls and wills;
> After a kiss, a dagger flashes high,
> A Russian reels and falls, and then the cry:
> 'Comrades, revenge!' and in a moment more
> Deserved revenge for death of a murderer
> The simple hut that cheered their humble ease
> Burns high – fire of Cherkessian liberties.[7]

Now he would see such scenes in grim reality, and learn the routine of day march through the primeval beech forests of Itchkeria and Chechniya, and of uneasy bivouac at night. Count Tornau, a veteran of the Caucasus, has left a sober account of the disciplines of this guerilla war:

> The length of the day's march was determined by the distance between the clearings along the river banks, large enough to allow of the camp being pitched a musket shot from the nearest wood. The road lay for the most part through dense forests of lofty trees interrupted here and there by glades, streams and gullies. Fighting went on from beginning to end of each march; there was the chatter of musketry, the hum of bullets; men fell; but no enemy was to be seen. Puffs of smoke in the jungle alone betrayed their lurking places, and our soldiers, having nothing else to guide them, took aim at that.

After a march the troops camped for one or more days according to the number of *aouls* that were to be destroyed. Small columns were sent out on all sides to ravage the enemy's fields and dwellings. The *aouls* blaze, the crops are mown down, the musketry rattles, the guns thunder; again the wounded are brought in and the dead. Our Tartars [native allies] come in with severed heads tied to their saddle bows, but there are no prisoners – the men take no quarter; the women and children are hidden beforehand in places where none care to seek them. Here comes the head of a column returning from a night raid; its rear is not yet in sight; it is fighting in the forest. The nearer it comes to the open space the faster grows the firing; one can hear the yells of the enemy. They surround and press on the rear guard from all sides; they rush in, sword in hand, and wait only the moment when it debouches on the clearing to pour in a hail of bullets. A fresh battalion and several guns have to be hurried forward to disengage it; the running fire of the infantry and canister from the artillery arrest the onslaught and enable the column to emerge from the forest without useless sacrifice.

Men are sent to cut grass, and at once a fresh fight begins. Fuel for cooking purposes, or for the bivouac fires, is only obtained by force of arms. If, on the far side of the rivulet, there is brushwood or any semblance of a hollow, the watering place must be covered by half a battalion and artillery, otherwise the horses will be shot down or driven off. One day is like another; that which happened yesterday will be repeated tomorrow – everywhere are mountains, everywhere forests and the Chechens are fierce and tireless fighters.[8]

After only six days of such skirmishing Galafayev's column reached the river Valerik, and here, in the deep wooded valley through which the river ran, the Russians were engaged in their first pitched battle by the enemy.

Lermontov's long poem, 'The Battle of the Valerik', describing this encounter, begins peacefully enough:

In long deep grasses here we lie,
Dreaming beneath the pleasant shade
Some viny-branched plane tree spreads.
White tents gleam round on every hand,
And Cossacks' lean-ribbed horses stand
In picket lines with drooping heads.
The gun crews sleep by each brass gun,
Fire-wicks emitting scarce a puff,
While ranks of men in pairs, far-off,
Show bayonets bright beneath the sun.

The scene changes to one of disciplined activity:

The infantry move into view;
One gallops, then another. . . . Clink
Of spurs and voices. 'Number two! –
Where is it?' 'Saddle?' 'Chief's Command?'
'Look sharp! Bring up those wagons there!'
'Savelitch! Hi! Bring flints. Prepare
the fire.' Drums sound fall in. The band
Drones, and between the columns spanned
Come clanking guns. A general
Rides by with his attendants all.
Into the spreading meadow land
The shouting Cossacks swarm like bees;
Guidons appear among the trees;
Along the forest's edge beyond.
Then comes a turbaned Meccan riding,
In red *cherkeska* gravely smart,
His prancing light-grey charger guiding
And waves and calls – Where's a brave heart
Who'll to the deadly fight with him?[9]

Lermontov's role in the battle was that of liaison officer, on horseback, between the General and the advance assault troops,*

---

* Consisting of three battalions of Kurinsky *Jaeger* infantry, two Companies of sappers, cossacks, and light artillery, all commanded by Colonel Freitag.

E

a dangerous and difficult role, in which he acquitted himself
with a cool-headed bravery that earned him a commendation
in the expedition's diary. He was soon in the thick of the
fighting:

'On butts!' The rage of slaughter rears
For two hours in the running stream
They fought and fought, with slash and scream,
Damning the course with fallen men.
I stooped to drink, by heat oppressed,
And worn with toil of war – and then
Saw that the murky trampled flood
Was warm and running red with blood.

But even in the midst of battle he is aware of its futility:

Far off, with wild and jagged peaks,
But ever proud and still, on high
The mountains in their snowy clothes
Stretched, and above in loftiest sky
Kazbek's sharp-pointed turret rose.
With secret, bitter sadness then
I thought: 'O miserable men!
What do they want? The earth's great plain
Gives room for all beneath the sky;
Yet ceaselessly and all in vain,
Alone, they war forever – why.'

Lermontov dedicated his poem, once again, to Varvara:

By merest chance I pen this line;
Really I know not how or why.
The right is now no longer mine.
And what have I to say? Do I
Remember you? Just God! For sure,
You knew that long ago, and now
It cannot matter where or how
I am: You have no need to care

In what lost wilderness I fare.
We are soul-strangers now; love wanes,
And scarce a heartfelt tie remains.[10]

However, writing to Varvara's brother, despite a complaint that he had received no letters from home – 'you can't imagine how heavy is the thought that friends forget us' – his tone was livelier as he described the battle and its heavy losses:

Thirty of our officers, and up to three hundred privates were killed, and they left six hundred bodies behind. Imagine, that in the ravine where the fun was, it still smelt of blood an hour afterwards. I've entered into the taste of war, and I'm sure that for a man who is used to the strong sensation of this there are few satisfactions that don't seem cloying.[11]

With his friend Prince Gagarin, he painted a dramatic water-colour of the battle of the Valerik, the inscription reading: '*Dessin par Lermontoff, aquarellé par moi.*' The turbaned follow-ers of the Prophet lie strewn in the path of the inexorably advanc-ing line of Russian infantrymen, their dripping bayonets at the ready. Three Chechens seek to carry out from the field the body of a dead comrade, as ordained by their customs, but it is unlikely that their ferocious flailing with short sword or *kinjal* will save them in fighting at close quarters. The Russian faces are impas-sive, hidden in their beards; those of the Moslems gaunt in hatred, pride and fatigue.

The battle of the Valerik, despite heavy losses on both sides, had ended inconclusively, and by July 15th Galafayev's expedi-tion was licking its wounds back at Fort Grozny; Lermontov had seen action on every day that had followed the battle. After two days' rest, they were off again, on a new quest for Shamyl, this time marching through the arid lunar landscape of Daghestan to the main Russian command post of Temir Khan Shura, in the mountains a hundred kilometres away. More sketches by Prince Gagarin show that Lermontov's companions included Prince Vasiltchikov, son of one of Nicholas' leading ministers, and a remarkable Pole, Prince Xavier Branitsky, who would later become a Jesuit in Paris, and one of Nicholas' fiercest critics from the safety of that capital. In early August, with no exceptional incidents, they returned empty-handed, to Fort Grozny. Lermontov went on leave to Pyatigorsk and Stavropol, where he and Lev Pushkin often found themselves guests at General Grabbé's hospitable table.

In September Galafayev again led his men out, in the course of which Lermontov was commended in despatches for his 'spirited bravery'. During this sortie he came the closest he would ever do to encountering Shamyl, for the Prophet was witness to the burning of the village of Shali by the Russians, standing so close that earth from the Russian cannon balls spattered his clothes. He then withdrew, escorted by his bodyguard, giving the order not to engage the superior Russian force. This self-restraint proved too much for his men, who made a desperate last-minute attempt to butcher the Russian rear-guard – foiled by the courage and quick thinking of Lermontov's comrade, Rufin Dorokhov.

On October 10th, Lermontov had an unexpected further opportunity to show his mettle. Dorokhov had been wounded and Lermontov was entrusted with the command of his troop of irregular soldiers. Numbering about forty men at first, it was later increased to over a hundred. Lermontov described his legacy, in a letter to Alexis Lopukhin, as a 'first-rate command of sharpshooters, volunteers, something like a partisan unit.'[12]

A regular Army colleague commented tartly that Lermontov had gathered about himself 'some sort of gang of dirty cut-throats'[13] that he used their mess-tins, sported a red canvas shirt under his always unbuttoned tunic, never washed, and let his hair grow long. His men, however, fought 'like tigers', for the most part using only cutlasses and swords. Lermontov, too, took to using the *shashka* or short cutlass of the mountaineers. Report after report on his first twenty-two-day expedition through the dangerous forests of Chechniya, and another beginning directly after, speak of Lermontov's extraordinary courage in action, and his success, either in repulsing the hidden enemy or in distracting their attention with his partisans, thus allowing the main force time to ford swift-flowing rivers, or to advance without fear of ambush. 'Even old Cossack *djigits* were amazed at his audacity,' wrote a brother officer. 'His unit was like an errant comet, ever seeking the most dangerous places.' On his white horse, in the forefront of this hand-to-hand fighting, Lermontov's life was constantly at risk, nor was he always sure of the reliability of his own men. Writing to Alexis Lopukhin, he expressed his doubts whether they were wholly to be trusted. At least, so far, there had been no knife in his back.

The contrast between Pushkin, a sedate, top-hatted Apollo visiting the Russo-Turkish front in 1828, and observing the horrors of war with all the aplomb of a *Times* correspondent, and Lermontov, the fiery Dionysus fearlessly ready to receive or dispense death, is striking. (By the same token, poor Byron's efforts in Greece seem worthy of a red-tabbed staff officer in charge of money and stores.)

By late November, after a third expedition, the rewards of gallantry came flowing in. General Galafayev recommended Lermontov's restitution to the Guards, with full seniority. Prince Golitsyn, commanding the Left Flank cavalry, put forward his name for a Golden Sabre, inscribed 'for bravery.' He had already been recommended for the Order of St Stanislas (3rd Class) after the Valerik Campaign. 'This officer,' read the new citation, 'in spite of all dangers carried out his duties with superior courage and cold-bloodedness, and broke into the enemy entrenchments in the first ranks of the bravest. He showed selflessness beyond praise. Taking advantage of our gunfire he suddenly threw himself at a group of the enemy who galloped away in the nearest forest leaving two bodies in our hands.'[14] These recommendations, endorsed by the C-in-C, were forwarded to St Petersburg, where Nicholas would study them in early 1841.

It was time for Lermontov to return to Stavropol, and to pay a courtesy call on his nominal Commanding Officer, (none other than Colonel Danzas, Pushkin's second in his fatal duel) – of the Tenginsky battalion to which he was attached. In Stavropol he made the acquaintance of a burly young career officer named Shultz, who had been badly wounded by the bullets of Shamyl's

men at Akhoulgo in 1839. He had originally applied – like so
many – for service in the Caucasus to earn glory, decorations
and promotion in order to impress prospective parents-in-law in
St Petersburg, and to win the heiress of a grand and somewhat
haughty family. He had found himself instead, lying for a whole
day among the dying and wounded on the battlefield.

'And what was it like, among the dying and the wounded,'
asked Lermontov. 'What did I feel? Well, helplessness; and a
raging thirst under the scorching rays of the sun; but my thoughts
rose – as it were – above the battlefield and turned to the memory
of her for whom I had gone to the Caucasus. Would she remember me? Would she ever realise the wretched fate of her
beloved?'

Lermontov went away silently, but a few days later returned
to Shultz, saying, 'Thank you for giving me a subject. Would you
like to read this?'[15] He handed Shultz the poem, 'The Dream',
later set to music by Balakirev, and translated here by Maurice
Baring:

By hot noon, in a vale of Daghestan,
Lifeless, a bullet in my breast, I lay;
Smoke rose from a deep wound, and my blood ran
Out of me, drop by drop, and ebbed away.

I lay upon the burning sand alone.
Sheer precipices crowded all around.
Their yellow tops were scorching in the sun,
And I scorched too, in death's sleep, on the ground.

I dreamed a dream, and saw the glittering hours
Of evening gaiety in my own place;
And there young women, garlanded with flowers,
Held talk of me in words of happy grace.

But in that happy talk not joining, one
Sat far apart, and sunk in thought she seemed;
And oh! – the cause is known to God alone –
This was the sad dream that her young soul dreamed.

She dreamed she saw a vale of Daghestan. . . .
There on the slope a well-known body lay;
Smoke rose from a black wound, and the blood ran
In cold streams out of it, and ebbed away.[16]

Meanwhile the wheels of military bureaucracy were busily turning in St Petersburg. Lermontov's grandmother had been putting pressure on the War Ministry to allow her young lieutenant from the Tenginsky two months' leave. No one in the capital yet knew of his gallantry on the Left Flank. An adjutant of General Grabbé was set to approve the necessary paper work; it happened that Lermontov came into his office as he was doing so. Had he led a sober and well ordered life? Had he behaved himself correctly? Was he guilty of any misdemeanours? The form was standard.

'Lermontov burst out laughing about such an attestation,' wrote the adjutant, 'and begged me not to change any of the expressions used in it, and to use the very same words as the Minister's.'[17] A satisfactory report was in fact despatched to St Petersburg, permission for leave was granted, and Lermontov was free to set off on January 14th, 1841.

Before Lermontov left for St Petersburg, Grabbé approached him with a somewhat indiscreet request. He asked him to take a letter to Yermolov, his former superior, and respected friend, living in exile and semi-disgrace outside Moscow. Its contents remain unknown, but for Lermontov it was an exceptional opportunity to meet the legendary leader, whose name was still potent in its association for serving officers in the Caucasus. It was he who had tried, for nearly a decade and almost succeeded in subduing the Caucasus in the 1820s. It was he who had built the Georgian Military Highway. To him Decembrists had turned for a lead in Southern Russia in 1826. If his tactics of terror now seemed outdated and inadequate, old campaigners, like Lermontov's Captain Maxym Maxymych, still regarded him with hero-worship. For Lermontov, the meeting must be filled with fascination. Already he was planning a great long novel about the expansion of the Russian state, beginning with the devastations of Pugachev under Catherine the Great, which

would go on to encompass Russia's magnificent hour of trial in
1812 under Alexander when she threw back the French and took
her revenge into the very heart of Paris, and finally the Persian
wars of Yermolov himself, and the conquest of the Caucasus.

A romanticised picture of Yermolov had been painted by
Bestujev in *Ammalat Bek*:

> You should witness his coolness in the hour of battle – you
> should admire him at a conference; at one time overwhelming
> the Tcherkess with the flowing of orientalisms of the Asiatic,
> at another embarrassing their artifices with a single remark.
> In vain do they conceal their thoughts in the most secret
> fields of their hearts; his eye follows them, disentangles and
> unrolls them like worms, and guesses twenty years beforehand
> their deeds and their intentions. Then, again, to see him talking
> frankly and like a friend with his brave soldiers, or passing
> with dignity round the circle of the officials sent from the
> capital into Georgia. It is curious to observe how all those
> whose conscience is not pure, tremble, blush, turn pale, when
> he fixes on them his slow and penetrating glance; you seem
> to see the roubles of past bribes gliding before the eyes of the
> guilty man, and his villainies come rushing on his memory.
> You see the pictures of arrest, trial, judgement, sentence, and
> punishment, his imagination paints, anticipating the future.
> No man knows so well how to distinguish merit by a single
> glance, a single smile – to reward – to reward gallantry with a
> word, coming from, and going to, the heart. God grant us
> many years to serve with such a commander![18]

A Yermolov, rendered warts and all as a Caucasian Cromwell,
would have been perhaps one of Lermontov's most fascinating
portraits. But no evidence exists of his meeting with Yermolov,
though the echo of it, and conclusions inspired by it, can be heard
in his poem 'The Dispute', written some weeks later. It is a poem
of mourning, a dirge for the age-old freedom of the independent
peoples of the Caucasus, now doomed to destruction. 'The
Dispute' is written as a dialogue between the two most fabled
mountains of the Caucasus, Mount Elborus and Mount Kazbek,

each held sacred in myth since antiquity.* The Circassians called them the 'Mountains of Happiness'; the Abkhazians the 'Mountains of the Great Spirit'; the Tartars – romantically – the 'Mountains of the Stars.'

But now Elborus foretells the ending of their proud and inviolable isolation to his brother Kazbek:

> Man will build his smoky cabins
> On thy hillside steep;
> Up the valley's deep recesses
> Ringing axe will creep
> Iron pick will tear a pathway
> To thy stony heart.

Kazbek dismisses this prophecy; the timeless East has its own ways of disarming enemies. But Teheran, Jerusalem and lazy Egypt are all sunk in torpor. Elbrus renews his warning; it is from the North that the attack will come:

> Lo! From Ural to the Danube
> To the mighty stream,
> Tossing, sparkling in the sunlight,
> Moving Regiments gleam;
> Glancing wave the white plumed helmets
> Like the prairie grass,
> While, 'mid clouds of dust careering,
> Flashing Uhlans pass.

He continues, with an obvious reference to Yermolov:

> See! a grey-haired general guides them,
> Threat'ning is his glance.
> Onward move the mighty regiments
> With a torrent's roar;
> Terrible, like gathering storm clouds,
> East, due east, they pour.

Kazbek's reply is the fatalistic response of the East, as he

---

* Lest it should be forgotten, the Dove from Noah's Ark first landed on the top of Mount Elborus.

Drew across his brows, his mistcap
And for aye was still.[19]

And even after conquest, or 'assimilation' into the wondrous
ways of Russia, the processes of peaceful colonisation by efficient
Prussian bureaucrats were not always beneficial. Poor Baron
Rosen, the Governor General in Lermontov's day, removed
so briskly by Nicholas after his visitation, had been defeated by
the 'locals.' His kinsman, the Decembrist Andrei Rosen, had
observed all this in a telling passage of his *Memoirs* that sums up
the tension not yet eradicated between Great Russia and her
minorities:

Why such sudden disgrace after the greatest trust had been
placed in General Rosen? One wonders. However, the system
of centralisation, the desire to impose the same civil administration and the same judicial system on the various different
regions and on subjects of various races, the desire, in short,
to introduce a general division of the land into provinces and
districts, resulted in the sending of a Senator von Hahn to
Tiflis, there to gather all the necessary data on the spot and to
draw up a new plan for the area. As usual, the Senator was
given private secretaries and special functionaries – people
all unfamiliar with the new land – and off they went to write!
What they wrote I do not know; I only know that the country
was divided into provinces and districts, new officials cropped
up everywhere, and judges and district police officers began to
pass sentences on the various mountain tribesmen who understood neither the courtroom procedures nor the language.
The Senator and his officials could have drawn up such a
project in St Petersburg, or in Kostroma, or in their own
homes. Involuntarily, such guests in a country remote from
the centre of government, and distant from the sovereign
power, became the special centre of intrigue.'[20]

Whatever the ultimate fate of the Caucasus, however, there was
no doubt in the meantime that the Caucasian war was being

mismanaged, as Lermontov, from his own experience, must have been well aware. From the marble and malachite palaces of St Petersburg, surrounded by obsequious staff who had not fought in the Caucasus, and conscious of his unlimited power to call up more men and pour in more money, it was perhaps difficult for the Tsar to recognise the error of his strategy, despite the failures of the campaign of 1839 and 1840. For failures they had been. On the Right Flank, along the Black Sea, hardly a fort had withstood the attacks of the tribes, and the naval blockade was ineffective. And on the Left Flank, as Lermontov had seen, Shamyl and his fabled lieutenant Hadji Murad between them by the end of 1840 controlled all the mountains, leaving the Russians with an exposed line of undermanned camps scattered between Fort Grozny and Temir Khan Shura. The expenditure to achieve this was reported as 1.2 million cartridges, 11,000 pieces of shot, and thousands of dead.[21] Between 1839-42, Grabbé lost 64 officers, 1756 men; 372 officers and 6204 men were wounded or missing.

General Veliaminov, who had retired in 1838, and served Yermolov for many years, had given the correct analysis of the strategy needed to take the Caucasus, but it would be twenty years before his prescience would be recognised. 'The Caucasus', he wrote, 'may be likened to a mighty fortress, marvellously strong by nature, artificially protected by military works, and defended by a numerous garrison. Only thoughtless men would attempt to escalade such a stronghold. A wise commander would see the necessity of having recourse to military art; would lay his parallels; advance by sap and mine, and so master the place. The Caucasus, in my opinion, must be treated in the same way, and even if the method of procedure is not drawn up beforehand, so that it may be continually referred to, the very nature of things will compel such action. But in this case success will be far slower, owing to frequent deviations from the right path.'[22]

The bloody ambushes in which Lermontov had so frequently risked his life were perfect examples of the strategy still prescribed by Nicholas in his battle orders: an armed column should deliberately expose itself in the beech forests of Chechniya to draw the enemy out of his cover, and then hope to blow him out of existence with the artillery. Sadly, reality was never so simple. And until the trees, reputedly up to thirty-five feet in girth, and sheltering up to thirty sharpshooters in their luxuriant foliage, could be cleared, the enemy could never be smoked out. So much for the Left Flank.

On the Right Flank, where the Tenginsky had suffered such appalling losses in 1840, official policies were also gravely mistaken. There the Tsar might have tipped the military balance in favour by diplomacy and bribery, a judicious use of free trade concessions on gunpowder and salt, instead of maintaining a blockade, and by a selective wooing of the weaker princes. But his diplomacy was, conspicuous by its absence. He claimed uncompromising sovereignty over all the Circassian and Kabardin Princes, chiefs of Abkhazia and the scores of tribal emirs and beys, a sovereignty supposedly surrendered to him by the Sultan of Turkey in the Treaty of Adrianople in 1829, though in fact only applicable to three ports on the Black Sea. His generals put forward the arguments for submission to the might of Russia in the crudest terms:

You have no chief from the Caspian to Anapa. You have been disobedient, to the Sublime Porte. If you wish for peace you must restore all plunder, return deserters, and admit a chief to be named by Russia. All the English who have come here are impostors. It is better to be under Russian than English rule. What is it that you expect? Do you not know that if the heavens should fall Russia has power enough to support them on her bayonets? The other countries may be good mechanics or artificers but power rests with Russia alone.[23]

Another lively example can be quoted from Bestujev's *Ammalat Bek*, where Yermolov himself speaks to some Tartar prisoners:

Five were led into the presence of the commander-in-chief. A cloud passed over his countenance as he beheld them; his brow contracted, his eyes sparkled. 'Villains!' said he to the *Ouzdens* [Chiefs]; 'you have thrice sworn not to plunder, and thrice have you broken your oath. What is it that you seek? Lands?

Flocks? Means to defend the one or the other? But no! you are willing to accept presents from the Russians as allies, and at the same time to guide the Tcherkess to plunder our villages, and to plunder along with them. Hang them!' said he sternly; 'hang them up by their own thievish *arkans* [girdles]! Let them draw lots: the fourth shall be spared – let him go and tell his countrymen that I am coming to teach them to keep faith, and keep the peace, as I will have it.[24]
The *Ouzdens* were conducted away.

It was hardly the language by which to seduce fierce and independent tribesmen, who had never, in any case, considered the Turkish Sultan as their leader and only accorded him a vague respect on religious grounds. Not surprisingly, they rejected the Russian arguments.

For the Circassians, fighting had changed little since the Middle Ages. The Prussian-trained officers in Russian pay fought against Khans wearing chain-mail armour which could have served in the Crusades and swinging scimitars and iron maces 'to crack helmets.' But English firearms were used in deadly ambushes, for this was essentially a guerilla war, in which the tactical advantage lay with the tribesmen. They knew the country. Their superb horsemanship, and the quality of their horses, fostered along the Terek and Kuban rivers, gave them speed and mobility in surprise attacks, foraging, reconnaissance and escape.

The contrast with Russian regular troops could hardly have been greater. They were skilled above all in drill and square-bashing. 'With us,' wrote a regular officer, 'everything was staked so to speak, on marching and the correct stretching of the toe.'[25] Such techniques were, of course, irrelevant to the conditions of the Caucasus. Nor were their personal weapons much to the purpose, with the exception of their trusted bayonets. The Grand Duke Michael thought little of the smooth-bore breech-loading muskets as a general issue, for 'troops having this weapon would cease to fight hand to hand and there would never be enough cartridges.'[26] Troops were meant to be given enough powder and lead for ten ball cartridges and sixty blanks, but fire power was more often reserved for marksmen only. Whilst the Russians had outmoded flint locks, the coastal tribes bought European weapons and gunpowder, smuggled in by Turkish and British gun-runners who plied their trade along the Black Sea Coast.

The so-called 'forts' were little more than 'disorderly piles of mud', built with earth and brushwood and plagued by tarantulas and scorpions. The soldiers were provided only with salt meat, bread and potatoes, and anything fresh had to be won by fighting. A *shashlik* made from a captured sheep was the greatest luxury a soldier could hope for. Little wonder that 'brigandage reigned in the air', and that any village visited by the army would be plundered before it was set on fire.

On both fronts, malaria, typhus and scurvy – a consequence of the atrocious rations – raged among the troops. With a death rate that averaged 67 per thousand, only 5.8 per thousand were killed in combat. For the wounded medical help was minimal. Brandy, perhaps, would be provided during an amputation, but gangrene was likely to set in during 'convalescence' in some primitive hut. Admission to 'hospital' was a passport to heaven.

In such conditions, discipline was maintained by two complementary means. The first was an appeal to devotion to the Tsar, and the dumb, sentimental, indefinable, completely inexplicable pride of the old soldier. Before fighting the men would form into squares to be blessed by priests, then sprinkled with holy water from the senior officer down to the last private, to the slow rolling of drums. The accompanying chant was traditional and unforgettable: 'We are the sons of the Great North, we are the sons of the White Tsar.'

The other means of discipline was fear. To keep the number of desertions down, to maintain order among brutish *mujiks* serving out their twenty-years term, Decembrists and exiled Poles who had no cause to love the Tsar, there were two punishments, each even worse than the horrors of the British cat – the *knut*, and the running of the gauntlet. A victim to be 'knouted' was bound to a shaped plank implanted on an angle in the ground. The executioner walked slowly up to the man and then brought the lash down with full force on his back. This always drew a groan, as the four-cornered rawhide thong lacerated the flesh and drew blood. After a score of more blows, the executioner poured himself a glass of vodka and then went on with his work. 'All this was done very, very slowly.' When the victim fainted, the doctor revived him with aromatic spirits, and the torment continued. After striking the final blow, the executioner branded the man on the brow and both cheeks with a set of small spikes set to form a letter, which he forced into the flesh of the victim. He then rubbed gunpowder into the bleeding flesh, so that the mark would be permanent. An eye witness[27] described the 'running of the gauntlet.' Two battalions, totalling fifteen hundred men, formed two concentric circles, facing each other. Every man held his musket in his left hand, a rod in his right. Fifteen men, with bared back, were led between the circles by sergeants. Each sergeant held the butt of a bayonet musket pointing at the breast of the victim, whose hands were bound to the musket. As the sufferer passed the soldiers, each man struck him with his rod. As the beating progressed, the voices of the victims were audible: 'Brother, be merciful! Brothers, be merciful!' If the prisoners fell and could not continue, they were laid upon sleds which soldiers pulled, and the flogging continued, often until they died. Officers such as Lermontov were expected to watch the soldiers closely, to make sure they did not strike lightly out of pity.

By 1830 Nicholas sought to prohibit the *knut* (except for Cossacks) and a limit was set to the punishment of running the gauntlet (to six times through one thousand men). Desertion called for once through five hundred men for the first flight, up to six times through five hundred for the second. And yet there were deserters.

Leadership, at the highest levels, was divided and uncertain. Nicholas himself called the Caucasus a 'Generals' Republic.' Ever since the days of Yermolov there had been rivalry among local commands, split between Stavropol, north of the mountains, Tiflis, well to the south of them (where the Commander-in-Chief lived), Temir Khan Shura and Fort Grozny, the tactical headquarters in Daghestan and on the Terek. Each had its own generals, and senior officers, worried as to their influence on the Tsar.

Nor had Nicholas, despite his visit in 1837, yet grasped the changing nature of the war. His generals – Yermolov in the van – had turned it into a social war of destruction of whole communities, tribes and age-old ways of life. With survival at stake, Shamyl's proclamation of a *Ghazavat* or a holy war had found increasing acceptance, hardening the tribesmen's opposition into fanaticism.

The style of Nicholas' methods, especially applied to a military campaign, did not encourage his subordinates to vary their orders, brought at the gallop all the way from St Petersburg to them by relays of couriers. Of the many sharply etched pen portraits of Nicholas, that of Andrei Rosen will serve as well as any to explain some of Nicholas' self-made difficulties by failing to practice the art of delegation:

The Emperor Nicholas I was generously endowed by nature both in physical appearance and in intellectual abilities. No one will question his decisiveness or bravery. By temperament, he was highly energetic, but had great strength of self-control also, with which he would often overcome an innately hot temper. He sought the love of no man; he was content to inspire fear, and the man whom he had terrified he always treated kindly, or with condescension. But self-sufficiency and self-confidence, tolerable qualities, and sometimes even useful ones, in a private individual, become a shortcoming in a monarch, and especially in an autocrat. Nicholas I listened to no one, tolerated no advice and, indeed, would not be advised. He had submissive, zealous servants, and they flattered him and even praised his errors at the outsets of the Hungarian and Crimean Wars; how, then, was he to restrain himself from self-sufficiency?

Among us, everything flows from the will of one man, the autocratic Sovereign. And this Sovereign, be he a Trajan or a Caligula, will care faithfully for his subjects – if not out of love for the Fatherland or mankind, at least for present glory and for glory in posterity. Why, then, do his helpful ukases not achieve their ends? Because there are those persons who find injustices and oppression to their advantage. Neither the cudgel of Peter, nor the kindness of Catherine, nor Alexander's wishes nor Nicholas' threats have yet removed abuses.

All Nicholas' educated contemporaries unanimously called him a tyrant. He ruined his own glory, it seems, crushed by the weight of his unlimited power.[28]

In St Petersburg, therefore, illusions continued to dictate the attitudes of court and official circles. Service in the Caucasus, according to Government opinion, was not in a war. The government were merely conducting a series of 'civilising' campaigns to bring Christianity and the benefits of imperial rule to bloodthirsty ruffians who disguised themselves as Moslem patriots. Russia was 'disengaged from any desire for conquest.' Ostensibly since 1801 she sought to protect the Georgians from possible invasion by Persia, and to stop the mass traffic in Circassian girls to the harems of Constantinople. Privately, far-sighted armchair imperialists would admit that they were planning Russia's ultimate expansion, and the containment of the British, for the Caucasus could be seen as the gateway to India.

The attitudes of young aristocrats – whether exiled, transferred or pressurised into a tour of duty – fitted in well with those of the Government. The Caucasus was a kind of jousting place, which would give them a brief chance to earn or justify reputations for gallantry before returning to the *salons* of St Petersburg. The officers in the Independent Caucasian Corps – a force numbering over 70,000 active soldiers – were thus split, socially and spiritually, into two opposing groups. On the one hand, were the long-serving professionals, who had served out most, if not all, their military lives there, and developed a seasoned, if not battle-weary knowledge of the ever-present problem of death from disease, ambush or sheer ineptitude; and on the other, those who came to joust briefly in some kind of an Eastern Eglinton Tournament.

Captain Maxym Maxymych, the kindly, grizzled veteran put the point bluntly to his friend, the narrator, in *A Hero of our Time*: 'How can we uneducated old men keep up with you? You young society people are proud: for a time you're in the midst of Circassian bullets, then you go off here and there, and afterwards when you meet, you're even ashamed to stretch out a hand to the likes of me.'[29]

Lermontov's friend and fellow writer, Count Sollogup, describes the veteran's resentment of the visitors: 'The army officer hates all those who come from St Petersburg. . . . He does not dance much because he is disappointed. Every minute he exclaims: "Our kind! The army kind! We are plain soldiers. We are not guardsmen. How could we be? We would never make it. Narrow waists, high neckerchiefs, stamping the floor when dancing the mazurka, writing love verses – all these have long since passed us by." '[30]

In an essay entitled *The Caucasian*, obviously unprintable in his day, and only published in 1929, Lermontov described the typical long-serving Caucasian officer. Written in early 1841, fresh from his return from the Caucasus, it was the epitaph of Maxym Maxymych, whom only three years ago he had portrayed as the embodiment of all that was best in humanity, his qualities developed under the stress and strain of war. But it was an epitaph now shot through with irony, indeed mockery, at the Captain's wasted gallantry. The poor fellow would have started off his service under the old Tiger, Yermolov, would have become half Russian, half Asiatic. In fact, like his English counterparts, paying the 'great game' of imperialism in India or Afghanistan, he had 'gone native.' He would adopt Circassian dress, a sheepskin hat, have a smattering of Tartar, dream of a General's epaulettes, knightly exploits and a captured Circassian mistress. His true fate, wrote Lermontov, would turn out very differently. At worst his bones would bleach on a stony hillside. At best he might be lightly wounded in the legs and be invalided out on a pension, or survive to become a veteran, marry and develop a red nose drinking his way to retirement in the mortally dreary conditions of garrison life somewhere in Central Russia. In 1840, writing of *A Hero of Our Time* in a letter to the Empress, the Tsar had expressed the hope that Lermontov's second exile would enable him to 'finish the character of the Captain.' It had indeed done so, in a chilly broadside against the false romanticism of war, whose horrors had turned the amiable portrait of the captain to a caricature, in which his very virtues of loyalty and obedience have become the vices of dumb acquiescence in a senseless holocaust.[31]

Lermontov had shared the romanticism of his aristocratic contemporaries towards the war, and now had shed it. His mood was one of sombre resignation to its waste, and sadness at its sacrifices. A moving poem, described by Maurice Baring as one of the 'most poignant poetical feeling, and consummate poetic art', gives the final testament of an officer dying in Daghestan, with a melancholy that was his own:

> I want to be alone with you,
> A moment quite alone.
> The minutes left to me are few,
> They say I'll soon be gone.
> And you'll be going home on leave,
> Then say . . . but why? I do believe
> There's not a soul who'll greatly care
> To hear about me over there.
> And yet if some one asks you there,
> Let us suppose they do –
> Tell them a bullet hit me here,
> The chest – and it went through.
> And say I died and for the Tsar,
> And say what fools the doctors are; –
> And that I shook you by the hand,
> And spoke about my native land.[32]

Such was Lermontov's lament for an unknown soldier. On a more intimate note, a Last Post was sounded for Prince Alexander Odoyevsky, one of the Decembrists he had met in 1837 during his Caucasian tour, that self-same Odoyevsky who in 1825 had cried so touchingly and naively at the meeting of the conspirators, 'We shall die, oh! how gloriously we shall die!' This death sentence did not come until 1839, and then of malaria fever in some tent by one of the Black Sea forts. But Lermontov loved him with his 'boyish laugh' and had admitted him into his company of the elect:

I knew him, yes in Eastern mountains journeying,
We travelled once, and there our joint exile
In friendship shared. . . .

and ended his epitaph as if for a Homeric hero:

And here amid those sombre mountains, groved
About your unknown grave – how greatly, see
With all that in your happy life you loved
Has fate united you – how gloriously!
Blue is the quiet steppe, and with a crown
Of silver spires Kavkas encircles it,
Frowning upon the sea, in silence sealed,
Like some great giant leaning on his shield,
Hearing the wandering waves soft legends sing,
Hearing the Black Sea's ceaseless thundering.[33]

Last Leave

Lermontov arrived in St Petersburg on February 5th, 1841. His mood seemed one of bravado. Only a few days after his return he amused himself by going to a fashionable Shrove Tuesday ball at the Vorontsov Dashkovs' – a solecism of the first order, since as an officer on probation he had no right to attend a ball where the Imperial Family would be present. His friend Count Sollogup greeted him with some alarm, and took credit for giving him the following advice:

> I was somewhat surprised to find him so carelessly merry . . . his whole future was shaken by this exile, but he was twirling around in a waltz as if nothing had happened. Vexed, I went up to him:
> 'What are you doing here?' I shouted at him – 'Get out of here, Lermontov, they may arrest you at any moment! See how sternly the Grand Duke Michael Pavlovitch is looking at you!
> 'They won't arrest him at my place!' Count Ivan [Vorontsov Dashkov] made this passing remark as he walked by us, screwing up his eyes through his lorgnette.
> I was watching Lermontov the whole evening. Some kind of feverish merriment took possession of him, but at times a strange look crossed his features; after supper he came up to me. . . . 'When I come back I shall probably find you a married man; you will settle down, come to your senses, and so will I, and you and I together will start publishing a thick journal.'[1]

It is not surprising that he now had hopes for a serious literary career. During his absence Andrey Krayevsky had skillfully manœuvred the Censors into allowing the publication of his poems in the July, September, October and January issues of

Notes of the Fatherland. Byelinsky had devoted long and important articles to him; so had Bulgarin in the *Northern Bee.* Most
important of all, negotiations begun by Krayevsky in June for a
collected edition of Lermontov's poems had ended in August with
the whole Committee of Censors approving its publication.
From October 1840 onwards, it had been on sale, at a subscription
price of one silver rouble. The public could now see for themselves whether Lermontov was entitled to fresh laurels as Pushkin's successor. Most literate Russians since then have known the
best of this collection by heart: 'Borodino', 'The Gifts of the
Terek', 'Mtsyri', 'Prayer', 'When o'er the yellowing corn a
fleeting shadow rushes' and many others. 'The Novice' and the
'Tale of the Merchant Kalashnikov' were included. His friends
were delighted at his achievement. Sofiya Karamsina declared
herself 'in ecstasy.' Meanwhile reviews of *A Hero of our Time*
continued to appear. His poem 'The Last Testament' was published in the *Notes of the Fatherland* in February, with an editorial
welcome by Krayevsky. In the same issue, Byelinsky reviewed
his poetry in general using the adjective 'Pushkinian' – for him,
the supreme accolade:

> We shall call him neither a Byron nor a Goethe nor a Pushkin,*
> but we do not consider it excessive praise to say that such
> poems as 'The Water Nymph' [*Russalka*], the 'Three Palm
> Trees', and 'The Gifts of the Terek' could be found only in
> poets such as Byron, Goethe and Pushkin.[2]

To English readers, knowing no Russian, such claims may
sound excessive, and indeed a poor translation – for example –
of 'The Gifts of the Terek' could confirm them in their views.
The first translation of 'The Gifts' was made by the Imperial
family's English tutor – a certain Thomas Shaw – who also
taught at the Lyceum of Tsarskoye Selo and at the University of
St Petersburg, and who popularised Pushkin, Bestujev, Lermontov, and other Russian writers in *Blackwood's Edinburgh
Magazine.* It was there in 1843 that 'The Gifts' appeared in his

---

* For a comparison of Lermontov and Byron, see Appendix 1.

translation, and to give some inkling to the English reader that
Byelinsky's accolade about the original in Russian is justified
the translation with its period charm is given here in full:

Terek bellows, wildly sweeping
Past the cliffs, so swift and strong;
Like a tempest is his weeping,
Flies his spray like tears along.
O'er the steppe now slowly veering –
Calm but faithless looketh he –
With a voice of love endearing
Murmurs to the Caspian Sea:
Give me way, old sea! I greet thee;
Give me refuge in thy breast;
Far and fast I've rush'd to meet thee –
It is time for me to rest.
Cradled in Kazbek, and cherish'd
From the bosom of the cloud,
Strong am I, and all have perish'd,
Who would stop my current proud.
For thy son's delight, O Ocean!
I've crush'd the crags of Dariál,
Onward my resistless motion,
Like a flock, hath swept them all.'

Still on his smooth shore reclining,
Lay the Caspian as in sleep;
While the Terek, softly shining,
To the old sea murmur'd deep: –

Lo! a gift upon my water –
Lo! no common offering –
Floating from the field of slaughter,
A *Kabardinetz** I bring
All in shining mail he's shrouded –
Plates of steel his arms enfold;

*   A mountaineer of the tribe of Kabarda.

Blood the Koran verse hath clouded,
That thereon is writ in gold:
His pale brow is sternly bended –
Gory stains his wreathed lip dye –
Valiant blood, and far-descended –
'Tis the hue of victory!
Wild his eyes, yet naught he noteth;
With an ancient hate they glare:
Backward on the billow floateth,
All disorderly, his hair.'

Still the Caspian, calm reclining,
Seems to slumber on his shore;
And impetuous Terek, shining,
Murmurs in his ear once more: –

'Father, hark! a priceless treasure –
Other gifts are poor to this –
I have hid, to do thee pleasure –
I have hid in my abyss!
Lo! a corse my wave doth pillow –
A *Kazachka** young and fair.
Darkly pale upon the billow
Gleams her breast and golden hair;
Very sad her pale brow gleameth,
And her eyes are closed in sleep;
From her bosom ever seemeth
A thin purple stream to creep.
By my water, calm and lonely,
For the maid that comes not back,
Of the whole *Stanitza,*** only
Mourns a *Grebenskoi Kazak.*

* A Kazak girl.
** Village of Cossacks.

'Swift on his black steed he hieth;
To the mountains he is sped.
'Neath Cchechen's *kinjal* now lieth,
Low in dust, that youthful head.'

Silent then was that wild river;
And afar, as white as snow,
A fair head was seen to quiver
In the ripple, to and fro.

In his might the ancient ocean,
Like a tempest, 'gan arise;
And the light of soft emotion
Glimmer'd in his dark blue eyes;

And he play'd, with rapture flushing,
And in his embraces bright,
Clasp'd the stream, to meet him rushing
With a murmur of delight.[3]

In February a second edition of *A Hero of our Time* appeared. After announcing its publication in an enthusiastic editorial note, Krayevsky continued, 'By the way, Lermontov himself is now in Petersburg, and has brought back from the Caucasus several delightful new poems which are to be printed in the *Notes*. The anxieties of military life did not permit him to surrender himself serenely and completely to the art which has named him as one of its highest priests; precious gifts are being prepared for Russian literature' – doubtless his trilogy.[4]

As a further expression of his admiration, Krayevsky commissioned a portrait of Lermontov by the fashionable painter Kirill Gorbunov. It is the portrait that has probably graced more editions of the poet's works than any other. Dressed in the dark grey of the Tenginsky regiment, with red facings and gold buttons, he wears a handkerchief knotted carelessly round his neck and holds a short Caucasian sword. His moustache is longer and turned up at the ends in military fashion, and his hair

parting seems to have changed sides since earlier paintings. But
the greatest contrast with previous likenesses lies in the expression. The lips now have a grim and downturned set to them,
there is not a semblance of a smile. The eyes, large and brown,
stare back at the painter with their fabled intensity. The total
effect of maturity and melancholy is given the final touch by the
grey white pallor of the skin, so much at variance with the rosy
coloured cheeks that match the red and gold of his Life Guard's
uniform in Zabolotsky's picture of 1837.

A new and important friendship during his brief return to St
Petersburg was that with Countess Evdokiya Rostopchina,
daughter-in-law of the famous Governor of Moscow in 1812,
who had set his own mansion on fire and proclaimed the destruction of Moscow. A gifted and amiable young woman, her salon
was a centre for the leading literary figures of the day. According to her the three months spent by Lermontov in the capital
were

... the happiest and most resplendent of his life. Very well
received in society, beloved and spoiled by the circle of his
nearest and dearest, he wrote some charming verses in the
morning and came to us in the evening to read them. A
cheerful disposition came to life in him again in his friendly
atmosphere, he would devise some joke or prank and we
spent whole hours in merry laughter, thanks to his inex-
haustible jollity. Once he announced that he was going to
read us a new novel entitled *Shtoss** and calculated that it would
take him at least four hours to read it. He demanded that we
should foregather early in the evening and that the doors
should be locked to keep out strangers. All his wishes were
complied with and the select, numbering about thirty, fore-
gathered; at long last, Lermontov entered with a huge notebook under his arm; the lamp was brought, the doors were
locked and then the reading began. A quarter of an hour later
it was finished. The incorrigible joker tempted us with the
first chapter of some terrible story which was begun by him

---

*   *Shtoss* means faro.

only the day before; there were about twenty handwritten pages and the rest of the notebook was just blank. The novel stopped there and was never finished.[5]

Both *Shtoss* and a ballad in verse, 'The Tale for Children' (attributed to 1839), contained elements of the fantastic, of the Gothic, and of a St Petersburg more familiar to Gogol and Dostoyevsky than to Pushkin. In both of them Lermontov mocked his earlier Demoniac self. There was a figure of evil in *Shtoss*, but he was a grey-haired, tight-lipped old man in slippers and dressing-gown who arrived mysteriously every night at the flat of Lugin, the anti-hero. The latter – consumed by spleen – was ready to gamble away his possessions and finally his soul at faro. The story, short enough, and unfinished, could hardly be lengthened, but is powerful in its evocation of a gloomy, dank Petersburg where the isolated individual was at the mercy of his diseased imagination and the supernatural, there being nothing else to occupy him. In 'The Tale for Children' (which Byelinsky thought amongst the finest verse Lermontov ever wrote) Lermontov dismissed the Demon of whom he had previously sung (with his 'mad, passionate ravings') in favour of some 'sly devil', who had come to prey on a seventeen-year-old princess, wistfully lonely in her granite palace on the Neva. Another victim, another Tamara: but this time her tormentor was made to resemble some corrupt dandy of the 1840s. Strong contrasts succeed. The blue stars smile down on the proud city; but within the dirty walls of these palaces and slums there are 'terrible secrets', and everywhere 'deceit, madness or suffering.'

But the pleasures of gaiety and literary success were to be short lived. The true feelings of those in authority towards him were shown when on March 5th the recommendations of General Grabbé and of the G.O.C. for the whole of the Caucasus for him to receive the order of Saint Vladimir or that of Saint Stanislas were formally turned down. From elation his spirits fell into depression. He saw that his bravado had been foolish. 'I've no chance of staying here because I get into such scrapes,' he wrote to a friend. 'They've crossed me off the Honours List

for the Valerik so I don't even have the consolation of wearing a
red ribbon when I put on a civilian frock coat. . . . On March 9th
I leave, to earn my retirement in the Caucasus.'[6]

To his intense pleasure, at the end of an icy March his grandmother managed the long journey from Tarkhany to St Petersburg. Perhaps thanks to her influence with the ever-helpful
General Filosofov, his leave was, in fact, extended. It was not
until April 11th that the interlude came to an end, with an order
from General Kleinmichel – his interrogator in 1837 and one of
Nicholas' desk officers on the General Staff, to leave St Petersburg
within forty-eight hours. Lermontov left the best of his unpublished poems in a large exercise book with Krayevsky, and
spent his last evening at the beloved Karamsins. There, over-
coming his gloom, he broke a long-standing reluctance to address
Pushkin's widow Natalie, now back in Society. Lamely ascribing
his past failures to shyness, he charmed her and begged for
her forgiveness. Later, when she heard of his death, so her
daughter recounts, her heart was deeply touched.

Evdokiya Rostopchina bears witness to Lermontov's forebodings; he openly predicted that he would not return. They
exchanged poems, his beginning with the line:

I know that we were born together under the same star

and hers:

There is a long dreary difficult way
Without a woman's face or mind to comfort the poet's soul.[7]

Passing through Moscow too, there were five days of farewells,
chance meetings recorded by Bodenstedt and Samarin, and
moments of gloom and wild gaiety. He gave Samarin a copy of
'The Dispute' and in a tearful moment read him his 'Battle of the
Valerik' in a shaking voice. The trouble with Russia, he told
Samarin, was not that 'some people were suffering but than an
immense number were suffering without realising it.' In this
mood he scribbled his unpublishable farewell to the Russia of
Nicholas:

Farewell, unwashed Russia
Land of slaves, land of lords,
And you blue uniforms,
And you submissive hordes.
Perhaps beyond Caucasian peaks,
I'll find a peace from tears,
From Tsars' all seeing eyes,
From their all hearing ears.[8]

One is reminded of de Custine's gibe at the tribe of Russian courtiers that they 'are like trained bears who made you long for the wild ones.'[9]

Even after Lermontov's departure his tearful grandmother made desperate attempts to get the orders rescinded. She implored Madame Karamsina to ask Jukovsky's intercession, through the Empress, for a pardon; the occasion was to be the wedding of the Heir to the Throne to Princess Marie of Hesse-Darmstadt when a number of other disgraced 'lions' from the Guards were, in fact, given a second chance. But for Lermontov there was no respite. By mid-April, he was on his way south again, in the company of his cousin, 'Mongo.' 'Wish me well and a light wound,' he wrote to Sofiya Karamsina. 'That is the best that you can hope for me.'[10]

The Cup of Life

We drink the cup of life while yet
A veil our eyes is keeping;
And the cup's golden brim is wet
With tears of our own weeping.

But when the veil falls from our eyes,
As Death appears before us,
Then with the veil the mystery flies
That held enchantment o'er us.

Oh then we see the golden cup
Was empty in its gleaming,
That only dreaming filled it up,
Nor even ours the dreaming![1]

(transl. by C. M. Bowra)

Nicholas' orders for Lermontov in April 1840 had been specific. He learnt now from the list of recommendations for gallantry arising out of the Right Flank campaign how Lermontov had thwarted his will. He minuted on June 30th, 1841 his displeasure.

His Majesty the Emperor, upon noticing in the recommendation for awards No 543 of March 5th submitted by the Corps Commander, that Lieutenant Lermontov, transferred on April 15th, 1840 from the Hussar Regiment of the Life Guards to the Tenginsky Regiment for a misdemeanour, was not with his regiment but had been used in an expedition to Chechniya with a special Cossack detachment under his command, desires to inform the Corps Commander confirmation of the order that Lieutenant Lermontov be present, in person in

[his] formation, and that Commanding Officers under no pretext dare withdraw him from drill duties [*frontovoi slujby*] in his Regiment.[2]

Nicholas, in fact, was using the word '*frontovoi*' in the nineteenth-century meaning of drill formation and not 'front' line. If this interpretation is accepted of the Imperial Minute, a completely different construction may be put upon Nicholas' motives than the traditional one that he had signed Lermontov's death warrant. He knew that the four battalions of the Tenginsky on active service had been ordered to the Fort of Navaginskoye on the Black Sea. From there, they were to adventure themselves deep into the Ubykh territory, from whence, it was hoped they would return, having slaughtered their opponents, in the late autumn. It was an expedition designed to wipe out the humiliations of the 1840 campaign, and, for those involved in it, the next best thing to a sentence of death. As Lermontov's posting was not to the active battalions but to one of the two reserve battalions, where he was to act as training officer to new recruits, Nicholas, it seems clear, was destining Lermontov to a role humiliating perhaps for so fiery a cavalry man, but one which would save his life. The death toll among leading Russian writers of his reign – Griboyev murdered in Teheran, Pushkin killed in a duel – had been too high; it seemed quite unnecessary to earn the cumulative op-probrium of letting Lermontov, too, meet his death. It is worth quoting again his letter to the Empress the year before, which had made his intentions clear as to his thoughts; Lermontov should finish the character of the gallant Captain from *A Hero of our Time*, a task impossible under campaign conditions, but perfectly feasible in the dull routine of a Cossack village somewhere along the Line – as indeed Tolstoy was to discover in his turn a few years later.

Lermontov, however, had as little intention of accepting a tame assignment of troop training behind the Line in 1841 as in 1840. No sooner had he arrived in Stavropol than he applied once more to General Grabbé for a further posting, on a temporary basis, to the Left Flank. The Imperial Minute had not yet arrived. After some days in the bustling atmosphere of G.H.Q., his spirits had returned. His grandmother received a letter asking her to persuade his cousin Akim Shan Girey to drop a plan to visit America and instead to join him. 'It's gayer here. I do hope, grandmother, all the same that I will be pardoned, and can retire.'[3] She was expected to keep up the pressure by staying in St Petersburg.

General Grabbé played the game. On May 9th Lermontov got his change of posting. Orders were given that he and 'Mongo' should ride to Temir Khan Shura in the heart of Daghestan, where Grabbé was marshalling a force of no less than 9000 men to rebuild old forts, build new ones and create a land blockade which would seal off Shamyl's forces.

The two set off together with a Tartar escort. On the way there, for reasons which remain uncertain – perhaps genuine ill health, perhaps a mood of defiance, perhaps the determination to push his luck still farther – Lermontov abruptly changed his plans. They had stopped at a primitive post house, somewhere in the foothills between Pyatigorsk and Vladikavkaz. An eyewitness, a supplier of remounts to the Borisoglebsky Lancers, who had fallen in with them, gives a racy account of Lermontov's sudden decision to plead illness, disobey orders and install themselves at Pyatigorsk. The scene took place in the tea room:

I had just started drinking tea when Lermontov and Stolypin came into the room. The superintendent warned the travellers of the dangers of night travel. Lermontov replied that he was an old Caucasian, had taken part in expeditions and would not be put off, even after the superintendent's story that a passing non-commissioned officer had been murdered the day before yesterday by the Circassians, only seven *versts* away. . . . But the rain was pouring hard outside, Kakhetinsky wine appeared on the table, and he and his companions stayed the night after all.'

The next day Lermontov began arguing with Stolypin:

'Listen, Stolypin, it's really nice in Pyatigorsk now, the Verzilins [he also mentioned several other names] are there. Let's go to Pyatigorsk.'

The village of Sioni, near Kobi, and Mount Kazbek, Caucasus, by Lermontov

'*Souvenir of the Caucasus*', by Lermontov

*Drawing by Lermontov of the hut and rowing boat which feature
in the chapter, 'Taman', in* A hero of our Time

Caucasian view with buffaloes and mounted Circassians, by Lermontov

'Bataille de Valerik, 11 Juillet, 1840'. 'Lermontov delineavit, Gagarin pinxit'

(Above) '*At the Valerik, 12 July, 1840: The burial of the dead*', by Lermontov and Ga
(Right top) *Major N. Martynov (Lermontov's opponent), by Thomas Wright*
(Right middle) *Prince A. I. Vasiltchikov, by Prince G. G. Gagarin*
(Right below) *Lermontov in army forage cap by Baron D. P. Pahlen*

Lermontov on his deathbed in Pyatigorsk, July, 1841, by P. K. Shvede

Stolypin replied that it was impossible:

'Why?' asked Lermontov quickly. 'Old Ilyashenkov is the Commandant there and there is no need to appear before him, nothing hinders us. Make up your mind, Stolypin, let us go to Pyatigorsk.' He left the room.

Stolypin was in a serious dilemma:

'Well,' asked the horse *coper*, 'have you made up your mind, Captain?'

'For goodness sake!' said Stolypin, 'how can we go to Pyatigorsk when I have been charged to take him to the Regiment? There,' he continued, pointing to the table, 'is our order for post horses and there are our instructions – look for yourself.'

Just then Lermontov came back in again, and forced the issue in a manner worthy of his own short story, *The Fatalist*:

'Stolypin, let us go to Pyatigorsk,' he cried, and taking from his pocket a purse full of money, he drew a coin from it.

'Now listen, I am going to toss this half rouble. If it falls heads – we go to the Regiment; if it falls tails – we go to Pyatigorsk. Agree?'

Stolypin silently nodded his head. The half rouble was tossed and came down tails at their feet. Lermontov jumped up and shouted happily:

'To Pyatigorsk, to Pyatigorsk! Call the men, the horses have already been harnessed!'

The men, two thick-set Tartars, having found out what was going on, prostrated themselves before their masters and thanked them with unfeigned delight.

It was still pouring with rain as the little party set off on the three-hour ride to Pyatigorsk. The horse *coper*, who was travelling there as well, invited the two young officers to share his carriage, and listened, half appalled, to Lermontov's views on the state of Russia and his criticisms of a 'certain exalted person' – in other words the Tsar.

They arrived in Pyatigorsk drenched to the skin and booked in together at the hostelry on the boulevard which was managed by the Armenian landlord, Naitaki.

Twenty minutes later, the fascinated horse *coper* recalled,

F

Lermontov and Stolypin appeared, having changed into fresh linen, white as driven snow, and dressing gowns, Lermontov wearing dark green silk, with a thick cord belt ending in golden acorns. He seemed in a high good humour. Rubbing his hands with pleasure he told Stolypin:

'Well, then, even Monkey* is here. Monkey is here. I told Naitaki that they should send for him.'[4]

'Monkey' was Major Nicholas Martynov, an old friend from Moscow and the Officer Cadet School, one of whose sisters had been one of Lermontov's half-serious loves in the spring of 1840.

The next day they reported to the Commandant in Pyatigorsk, having obtained Medical Certificates confirming their illnesses and his permission to remain in Pyatigorsk. Lermontov's woes included 'scrofula', 'unusual loss of weight', and 'swelling of the gums.' He was obviously shaken by the Moscow-Stavropol journey.

There then ensued an exchange of reports and medical certificates between Pyatigorsk, Colonel Traskin (officially Chief-of-Staff at G.H.Q., Stavropol), and the two officers. G.H.Q. thought their 'illnesses' should be 'cured' at Georgievsk Hospital or in the front line. The exchange was inconclusive, and Lermontov stayed on, backed by the support of the Medical Officer in Pyatigorsk, Barclay de Tolly, with Traskin finally approving Lermontov's holiday.

The reaction of the Commandant to Lermontov's arrival reads like a scene out of Gogol at his funniest. Colonel Ilyashen-kov, a man of the old school, was none too clever, and timid to boot. When the town-adjutant reported that Lermontov and Stolypin had arrived in Pyatigorsk, he clutched his head in his hands, and, jumping up from his office armchair, said excitedly:

'So this hare-brained fellow has decided to grace us again by his presence! What is this for?'

'He has come to the water spa,' replied the town-adjutant.

'To play tricks and cause trouble!' said the old man, flying into a rage, 'and we shall be held responsible afterwards! . . .

* '*Martyshka*': Russian original.

And we have not even got any room at the hospital. Can't we get rid of them by sending them to Yegoryevsk? What? . . . I do not even know, really, what we should do with them?'

'We shall have to keep a stricter eye on them,' his adjutant replied respectfully, 'but we cannot refuse to receive them as they have permission of the Chief-of-Staff, and medical certificates about the necessity of taking the mineral water cure.'

'Well then, call them in,' gave up the commandant. Stolypin and Lermontov were shown into the office.

'Ah, good morning, gentlemen,' the representative of the Powers-that-be greeted them, knitting his brows, and taking a pace forward, 'Why are you here? How long do you intend to grace us with your presence?'

'We are being driven by illness, colonel, sir,' Lermontov began to reply, but Ilyashenkov, wishing to exercise his authority, interrupted him.

'Permit me!' he cried, addressing himself to Stolypin,

'You are the senior, therefore reply.'

Stolypin explained their reasons and handed over the medical certificate requiring them to undergo medical treatment in Pyatigorsk. Lermontov followed his example.

The commandant read the statements and handed them over to the town-adjutant. He ordered that these should be presented to the General-Staff, and, shaking the young men by the hand, said to them:

'I have no vacant beds at the hospital, but what am I to do with you? You might as well stay here! Only on one condition, gentlemen, not to play any tricks and not to cause trouble, otherwise I shall send you back to your regiments, you might as well know that!'

'Sick persons have no inclination to play tricks, colonel, sir,' replied Stolypin bowing his head respectfully.

'We shall not cause any trouble, but permit us to amuse ourselves a little, colonel, sir,' said Lermontov, bowing respectfully in his turn, 'otherwise we shall surely die of boredom and then you will have to bury us yourself.'

'Fie, fie!' spat Ilyashenkov, 'what are you talking about?

I cannot stand burying people. But if one of you happened to get married here, then I would come to your wedding with pleasure.'

'Get married! ... Fie, fie!,' exclaimed Lermontov with feigned horror, imitating the commandant. 'What is this you are saying, colonel, sir? I would much rather die!'

'This is it, this is it! I just knew it,' said Ilyashenkov, waving his arms. 'You are incorrigible, you will bring bad luck onto yourselves. Well now, off you go, and God be with you, and get fixed up! ... And afterwards, whatever God grants, so it shall be.' And he took his leave. The meeting was over.

A conversation started in the office regarding lodgings. Chilyaev, offering a wing of his house, added that the living accommodation in the old house was already occupied by Prince A. I. Vasiltchikov.

'Let us go and have a look!' said Lermontov.

'We might as well,' replied Stolypin, 'but not just now; we should call at the hotel and get changed; it will soon be noon – what is the pleasure in going about town in full uniform?'[5]

With their status as invalids thus formally recognised at the price of taking a twice-daily bath, Lermontov and Stolypin soon settled down in a rented cottage to the comfortable and sociable routine of fashionable spa-dwellers. Lermontov immediately acquired a grey steeplechaser, 'Circassian', and a second horse in reserve, and enjoyed himself in dawn gallops across the steppes and foothills in Circassian dress, or showing off to the ladies, 'almost teaching his horse Georgian dances.' He became a familiar sight, too, pacing up and down the acacia and lime boulevards, stocky in his grey lieutenant's tunic, a cherry stick in hand. Two serfs appeared from his estates, one, the *valet de chambre*, had been his male nurse, the other a groom. A Georgian of astonishing good looks was engaged as a second valet, and so was a cook. His grandmother was asked to send him Jukovsky's latest edition of collected poetry, and a complete set of Shakespeare in English. An Empire writing desk was placed at the window of his study, where he could reach out and pick cherries from a wild cherry tree as he worked. With such an establishment, a piano, a cook and plenty of champagne, the charming and good-looking Stolypin and the famous, if not notorious, Lermontov were ready to take Pyatigorsk society by storm.

The summer season in Pyatigorsk began in May. The weather was just right. Rich visitors arrived to take the waters. Bands playing music on the boulevards could be called in at whim to contrive a 'ball' at Naitaki's hotel, the ladies even dressed in their ordinary day clothes. If the dance were more formal, the hotel turned itself into a 'Club for the Nobility.' Apart from dancing, the favourite occupation was playing cards, Pyatigorsk's traditional activity, which went on without interruption from morning till night, and from night till morning. The hale and hearty included those who did not know what to do with their time, and who considered a day lost if they did not play cards. The scene had not changed since Lermontov's stay in 1837.

Enchanting is our Caucasian Monaco,

he wrote,

It is crowded with dancers, gamblers and brawlers;
Gambling, wine and fighting make us feverish,
We are inflamed by women by day and by bed bugs at night.[6]

Pyatigorsk society was soon divided into those amused by Lermontov's caricatures, and impromptu verses at their expense, and fascinated by his flashes of poetry, gaiety and wit, and those who reflected the Establishment view that a disgraced Guards officer and duellist, out of favour with the Sovereign and the authorities, such as himself, would do best to lie low.

In the first camp were bound to be placed the unmarried girls, only too glad to be amused and perhaps wooed by exiles from St Petersburg. Amongst those who shone most brightly were the three Verzilin sisters whose presence in Pyatigorsk had influenced Lermontov's decision not to go to the Front. There was Emilia, '*la Rose du Caucase*', 'silly and good natured', who would later marry Lermontov's cousin, Akim Shan Girey, Agrafena, and

Nadejda, the youngest barely sixteen, whose 'gentle neck' and 'careless curls' he celebrated in a charming poem. Their house, which adjoined the Lermontov-Stolypin cottage, and where their mother kept an open house for their friends, was known as the 'temple of the graces.' Another beauty often to be seen there was Ekaterina Buikhovetz, '*la belle noire*', a distant cousin of Lermontov's, whose dark good looks had something in them of his lost Varvara.

Less distinguished, but a well-known magnet for the local bachelors, were the two pretty daughters of a German hotel-keeper, Herr Roshke; his hotel at Karass, a few miles outside the town, was a familiar meeting-place for mounted picnics.

Amongst the men, Lermontov's chief companions and supporters were old campaigning friends or contemporaries from St Petersburg. They included Prince Sergey Trubetskoy, wounded at the battle of the Valerik and now convalescing without permission in Pyatigorsk; Rufin Dorokhov, the local d'Artagnan, whose band of irregulars Lermontov had taken over the previous summer; Mikhail Glebov, another wounded veteran of the Valerik, like Lermontov before his disgrace a member of the Life Guards; Lev Pushkin, the gambling brother of the poet; and Gagarin, his painting friend, called almost daily in June. '*Martyshka*' or 'Monkey' Martynov, whose presence in Pyatigorsk Lermontov had greeted with such pleasure, was another member of this set. A retired major, son of a rich Moscow property developer, disappointed in his military career despite his gallantry at the siege of Akhoulgo, he nursed under a thick skin a vulnerable, if not vain, character* which made him an easy target for Lermontov's jokes, which at first he patiently endured. They had, after all, known each other since Moscow childhood and Cadet School. Lermontov was a close friend of his two sisters, despite their mother's disapproval. Martynov made things worse for himself by 'going native' in the style which Lermontov had parodied in his essay *The Caucasian*. His good looks had not been

---

* Akim Shan Girey called him a 'ninny and *poseur*.' He thought he could write poetry. For unknown reasons in 1841 Nicholas refused to approve a recommendation for gallantry in favour of Martynov.

improved by his shaving his head like a Tartar, and he dressed only in Kaftans, black and white surcoats and sheepskin hats, with the largest dagger a silversmith could make stuck into his silver belt. He changed his regalia daily and considered himself the Beau Brummel of the spa. Lermontov guyed him unmercifully, addressing him as '*le chevalier des monts sauvages*' and '*Monsieur Sauvage Homme*', and filling his album with wickedly funny caricatures. An old friendship was now at risk. He lived with Glebov in a cottage behind Lermontov's own quarters.

Lermontov's habit of teasing was not confined to Martynov alone. Even the ladies of Pyatigorsk were not immune. He would make up verses on the spur of the moment with varying refrains: 'cuckoo, cuckoo', if the victim were pock-marked, 'heron, heron', if she were tall, or 'canary, canary' for the pretty ones. One of the 'cuckoo' ladies, it is pleasant to record, shouted back to Lermontov, 'you *shelapoot Kirghis*' ('you Kirghis ragamuffin'), and the incorrigible joker for once apologised.[7]

As another of Lermontov's circle pointed out,

> there were two men in Lermontov; one good-natured to the small circle of his intimate friends, and to the few for whom he held a special respect; the other arrogant and irritable towards all the rest of his acquaintance. To the first group belonged in the last years of his life, Stolypin, Glebov, Prince Alexander Dolgoruky, the Decembrist Nazimov, and a few others. To the second group belonged in his estimate the whole mass of humanity, and he thought it the best of his pleasures to make fun of their small and large peculiarities, with jests and sarcastic remarks. He was mischievous in the whole meaning of that childish word, and his day was divided into two parts, between serious study and reading, and such pranks as could only come into the head of a fifteen year old schoolboy.[8]

But Lermontov had never concealed his views on 'friendships' with ordinary mortals. As he wrote in 'Sashka':

What's a good chap in the end?
A weary burdensome, and faded friend

What's clever's more to taste and tolerable,
Than a thousand friends, however good of will.
Therefore, he gained (counting just those one sees)
In a month a hundred charming enemies.[9]

At the beginning of July, Colonel Prince Vladimir Golitsyn, commander of the cavalry on the Right Flank in 1840, who had recommended Lermontov for a golden sabre, was on leave in Pyatigorsk. Lermontov took orders during a campaign, but he had no intention of doing so on social questions. The Prince suggested giving a ball in the Government botanical gardens. Lermontov objected that this might not be convenient since the gardens were far outside the town and it would be difficult to escort the ladies, fatigued after dancing, back home so late. It was not as if they were in St Petersburg. There were only three or four public *droshkies* for hire, and few private carriages. They could hardly be dragged home on carts. 'Why not?' said the Prince. 'That would teach the local savages a lesson!'[10]

Lermontov said nothing, but disliked this snobbish reference to the people amongst whom he was living. He turned to his other friends, who were present. 'Gentlemen,' he said, 'is it really necessary that the Prince should be at the head of all our picnics? If he doesn't wish to be with us – well, we can manage without him.'

So on July 8th Lermontov and his friends decided to throw an alternative ball, by public subscription, in front of the Grotto of Diana, a folly designed by the Bernadazzis under the leafy limes by the Nikolayevsky Baths. Persian carpets were laid out, Naitaki's best wines flowed, regimental linen was commandeered for the tables, and two thousand lanterns were fixed, under Lermontov's feverish supervision, to the roof of the Grotto. Prince Golitsyn was neither invited nor even told of the plan.

His cousin Ekaterina Buikhovetz has left an evocative Watteau-like picture of the ball:

Oh, how merrily we passed the time. That day the young men arranged a picnic for us in the Grotto, the whole of which was decorated with shawls; flowers in green bowls wound round the columns and the chandeliers too were made entirely of flowers.

We danced in a small square near the grotto; the benches were draped with charming carpets; the illuminations were marvellous; the evening was enchanting, the sky was so clear; the trees looked lovely in the lights; the alley was also lit up, and at the end of it there was a most elegant dressing room; the music was provided by two bands. Sweets, fruit and ice cream were being offered all the time; we danced until we could drop with fatigue; the young people were so nice in welcoming their guests; we had supper; after supper we danced again; even Lermontov who was not fond of dancing, even he was so merry. We walked back from there. The young men all accompanied us with lanterns; one of them started to fool around a little. Lermontov, as my cousin, immediately offered me his arm, we started walking faster and he accompanied me up to the house.

We were so friendly, he and I. He is my third cousin and always called me '*ma charmante cousine*' and I called him 'cousin', and I loved him as my own brother. Whenever any young people came here they immediately asked me to intro-duce them to him.[11]

Despite the distraction of *fêtes champêtres*, flirtations, cards, headlong gallops and a course of medical baths, Lermontov's chief preoccupation continued to be poetry. In April, upon leaving St Petersburg, his friend and admirer Prince Vladimir Odeyevsky had entrusted to him an old and treasured album, a sort of 'occasional book', dedicating it to Lermontov in the hope that he himself would fill its four hundred odd blank pages with his poems. The album has been found, half-filled, the first poem ('The Dispute') in a jolting handwriting, suggesting perhaps that it had been written on his journey to Pyatigorsk. The themes that Lermontov felt most passionately once more run through this last collection, including his search for some religious truth that would transcend the hypocrisies of conventional religion. The Christ-like protagonist of his poem 'The Prophet' is a figure 'despised and rejected of men':

Since the Eternal Judge to me
The Prophet's power of vision lent,
In human eyes I read and see
Pages of vice and folly blent.

To preach of love when I began,
Teaching of truth and purity,
My neighbours all, like devils, ran
And took up stones to throw at me.

Upon my head I ashes cast
And from the towns, a beggar, fled;
And now I dwell in deserts vast,
Just like the birds, by God's hand fed.

Keeping the laws of Providence,
The brute creation serveth me;
The stars hear me with confidence,
With bright rays playing joyously.

When through the city's noisy way
I hurry onwards, in distraction,
The old men to the children say,
With smiles of selfish satisfaction –

'Behold, from him a warning take!
He was too proud with us to dwell;
The fool! That God through his lips spoke –
This was the tale he strove to tell.

Look, children! on him cast your eyes!
How sad he is! how thin and pallid!
How all the wretched man despite!
How naked, and how poor and squalid!'[12]

If 'The Prophet' is to be read with any confessional meaning
at all, it is that Lermontov did still believe in a God: that God was
his own and not one of State-supported orthodoxies; and God's

laws were to be found in Nature, not in 'the city's noisy way.'
He described his feelings in the same album in another poem
of stately resignation almost incredible in a young man not yet
twenty-seven: that reaffirmed his sense of communion with his
God:

Lone, I wander where the pathway glistens
In the mist with twinkling points of spar;
Night is still, to God the desert listens,
And in heaven star communes with star.

Solemn wonder holds the heights of heaven,
Earth in cold blue radiance sleeps, and yet
Why am I with pain and anguish riven?
Why this exception? this regret?

Nothing now in life tempts my desiring,
Nothing in the past claims my regret;
Peace and freedom are all my requiring, –
Ah, could I sleep soundly and forget!

No, not in the grave's cold sleep to moulder –
I would lie in everlasting rest,
So but in me living forces smoulder,
So but tranquil breathing stir my breast,

So but, night and daytime, those that love me
Lull my ear with songs to drowse and drowse,
And an oak-tree, ever green, above me
Stoop, and make a dusk of murmuring boughs.[13]

Another poem, poignant in its mood of longing and regret, was
addressed to Varvara:

No, not for you, for you, does my love flame;
'Tis not for me, your beauty brightly shining.
In you my love is for old anguish pining,
For youth once mine before disaster came.

And when at times I look into your eyes
And dwell on them with long and lingering glances,
I converse in mysterious utterances –
'Tis not in words to you that my heart lies.

I speak to a companion of young days;
In yours, I seek another's face once cherished,
In living lips, lips that have long since perished,
In eyes, a flame that was long since ablaze.[14]

This, or 'The Prophet', was perhaps the last poem that Lermontov would ever write. Hundreds of blank pages remained in Prince Odoyevsky's album.

The day that would sound his death-knell began lightheartedly. On July 13th the three Verzilin sisters invited their friends to the 'temple of the graces' for another party. Lermontov had planned to go that day to the medicinal baths at Jeleznovodsk, but he postponed his treatment till the next day in order not to miss it.

He arrived at the house that evening to receive a scolding from Emilia, who was, she declared, fed up with Lermontov's incessant teasing. Lermontov begged for mercy. '*Mademoiselle Emilie*,' he pleaded, '*je vous en prie, un tour de valse seulement pour la dernière fois de ma vie*.'* and 'for the last time' she agreed. Lermontov seized the moment to promise that never again would he irritate her.

Emilia takes up the tale. 'We sat down to chat peacefully,' she wrote:

Lev Pushkin joined us . . . and the two of them started vying with each other and sharpening their tongues. . . . They did not say anything particularly malicious, but a lot of it was funny. Then they saw Martynov, who was talking very amicably to my younger sister Nadejda, standing by the piano which Prince Trubetskoy was playing; as usual he was in Circassian dress and wearing an enormous dagger.

Lermontov could not contain himself and began being witty

* 'I beg of you, for the last time of my life, a waltz.'

at Martynov's expense, calling him that ferocious 'highlander with the big dagger' [*montagnard au grand poignard*]. It so happened that when Trubetskoy struck the final chords the word 'dagger' got carried loudly around the room. Lermontov added cheerfully in French: 'Mademoiselle Emilie, beware, here comes that ferocious highlander.'

Martynov paled and bit his lips; his eyes sparkled with anger. He came over to us and in a voice he could hardly restrain, said to Lermontov:

'How many times have I asked you to abandon your jokes, at least when ladies are present?'

He turned and walked away so quickly that Lermontov had not time to gather his thoughts, but upon my quoting the proverb 'my tongue is my enemy', he answered calmly:

'It doesn't matter, tomorrow we will be good friends.'

The dancing continued, and I thought that the whole quarrel was thus over. The next day Lermontov and Stolypin were due to go to Jeleznovodsk. I was told afterwards that as they were leaving us, Martynov repeated his phrase in the entrance hall, in reply to which Lermotov asked:

'Come on, are you going to get really angry and challenge me to a duel for this?'

Martynov obstinately answered, 'Yes, I am calling you out'[15] and the day of the meeting was fixed there and then.

In another version of the quarrel (from the memoirs of the Clerk* to the Commandant who was in Pyatigorsk at the time though not at the party,) the damning possibility arises that Lermontov sketched Martynov waltzing with the slender young Nadya, the former's face distinctly simian, the latter's elegant and pretty as in life. When the music stopped, Lermontov showed it to Nadya, with the cruel question: 'To be frank, Nadejda Petrovna, how could these two names be united?' Despite her tender years, Nadya counter-attacked: 'You are the devil himself, and mad! Leave me please,' and then rushed from the room in tears. Martynov had observed all this but could not see the caricature. He moved over and asked to see it, but Lermontov managed to

* A 'Major' Karpov.

shut his notebook just in time. As they left the party, the formal challenge then took place in the street.[16]

To undertake a duel, in Lermontov's already compromised position with the authorities, was rash in the extreme. Should the affair leak out, he would certainly be downgraded to the ranks, losing his status as a nobleman and property, and suffer the risk of corporal punishment. The seconds had to be appointed, bearing in mind the danger of severe punishment from the Tsar for them too if their part should be discovered. It was decided that Mikhail Glebov, recently wounded, with a gallant fighting record, and Prince Alexander Vasiltchikov, son of the President of the Council of Ministers, would be the safest candidates for the role, Glebov acting for Martynov and Vasiltchikov for Lermontov. Extra 'unofficial' seconds would be Stolypin and Prince Trubetskoy, neither of whom could afford a false move in the light of recent brushes with authority. Rufin Dorokhov, with all his experience of matters of honour, would naturally be on hand as well. But all the seconds believed that this, like previous storms in glasses of vodka, would be settled cheerfully on the morrow with Martynov. They would all celebrate a reconciliation that evening at Prince Golitsyn's party.

The morrow came, but Martynov, whether, as Soviet biographers have suggested, encouraged secretly by messages from 'highly placed persons' or – more likely – from vanity and mulishness, refused to accept any compromise. Lermontov's mood about the duel at first remained sanguine; he still thought it might all blow over with some good-natured apology accepted by Martynov, whom after all he had known for so long. He even bought tickets for five days at the medicinal baths at Jeleznovodsk, where he had gone on the day after the party.

The duel had been fixed for July 15th. On the morning of that day, his cousin Ekaterina, chaperoned by her aunt in a carriage, and young Constantine Benckendorff (a nephew of the Chief of the Gendarmes), Lev Pushkin and another friend on horseback, went to meet Lermontov for a picnic at Karras. Once again, Herr Roshke, the genial hotel-keeper, greeted them; once again his pretty daughters offered freshly-baked rolls and honey to the guests; once again there seemed to reign the frivolous mood of a promenade in carriages or on horseback such as Constantin Guys might have painted. But later, as Lermontov and Ekaterina strolled together through the heather and juniper and vines of the Scottish colony, his air of gaiety fell away. She leaves a touching record of their final walk together:

> I took his arm and we strolled like that all the time. I wore a *bandeau*. I really don't know how it happened but my plait got loose and the *bandeau* fell off, which he took and hid in a pocket. In front of everyone else he was merry and joking, but when there were just the two of us he was terribly sad, and talked to me in such a way which I can quite understand now, but then it never entered my head there could be a duel. I knew the reason for his earlier sadnesses [i.e. Varvara Lopukhina] and thought that it was still the same, tried to persuade him, consoled him as best I could. With his eyes full of tears he thanked me for having come, wished me to come back to his lodgings to have something to eat – but I did not agree, we went back and he came with us too. We dined in the roadhouse. On leaving us at five o'clock, he kissed my hand several times and said, '*Cousine*, my darling, there will not be happier day than this in my life.'[17]

He had not breathed a word about the impending duel.

There is a curious account of a last-minute attempt at reconciliation attempted by Martynov. He may have hoped the friendly atmosphere, food and especially wine of the Roshkes would put Lermontov in a mellow mood. Martynov and Dorokhov entered the dining-room to see Lermontov flirting with Frau Elisabeth. Martynov bowed 'very politely to him' and turned to kiss the hand of the pretty innkeeper. Lermontov at that moment 'smiled ironically' but continued his conversation even more attentively with her, ignoring him. Martynov, clearly upset at this, stood aside, walked up and down, and then interrupted the *tête à tête*: 'You seem to have forgotten your obligation to give satisfaction? and instead you disappeared, and now are playing at being Lovelace?' Lermontov, equally true to form, slightly turned his head and quietly replied: 'I was prevented. . . . I am always ready; why not now? As you wish.' This version (of Karpov's) does not take into account the premeditated arrival of the other seconds, with duelling pistols, nor Ekaterina Buikhovetz' presence, who surely would have mentioned it in her letter to her sister.[18]

In the late afternoon, Lermontov rode off with Glebov, nominally Martynov's second, and 'Mongo', to the site of the duel near Pyatigorsk's cemetery. All the way there, Glebov recalled, he was in a cheerful mood; there was no talk of dying, no instructions as to what to do should he be killed. He rode, said Glebov, as though he were going to a feast. The one regret that he expressed was that he could not get released from the army, and that, being a serving soldier, it was doubtful whether he would be able to accomplish all the work he hoped to do.

'I have already worked out the plot of two novels,' he told Glebov, 'one from the time of the fight to the death between two great nations, beginning in St Petersburg, continuing in the heart of Russia and near Paris, and ending in Vienna. The other – from life in the Caucasus, Tiflis during the time of Yermolov, his dictatorship and the bloody pacifications of the Caucasus, the partisan war and the catastrophe during which Griboyedov perished in Tehran. But now I have to kick my heels until I can start laying the foundations of these stories. In about a fortnight I shall have to leave to join the Regiment, and who knows how soon we'll return from the expedition?'[19]

If Lermontov had inner misgivings, he did not show them. In *A Hero of Our Time* Pechorin had described his sensations on the way to the duel with Grushnitsky:

I remember that on this occasion, more than ever before, I was in love with nature. How curiously I inspected every dewdrop that trembled on a broad vine leaf and reflected a million iridescent rays.

And to Doctor Verner he makes his final confession of his feelings:

When I think of near and possible death I am thinking of
myself ... of women who, while embracing another, will
laugh at me so as not to make him jealous of a dead man. ...
what do I care for them all? Out of life's storm I carried only
a few ideas and not one feeling. For a long time now I have
been living not with the heart but with the head. I weigh and
analyse my own passions and actions with stern curiosity
but without participation. Within me are two persons: one
of them lives in the full sense of the word, the other cogitates
and judges him.* The worst will, perhaps, take leave of you
within an hour, while the other ... what of the other?[20]

Indeed, the 'other' had to face Fate, that grim, ineluctable
reaper of the bodies and souls of Lermontov's heroes, Ismail Bey,
Arbenin, the Novice, Pechorin, and now of their author. What
had usually counted had been to fight to the last breath: Lermontov, after all, never feared death, only oblivion, a humiliation he
was to be spared. But the hourglass was almost empty; how
would Lermontov, so like 'The Fatalist' at this moment, play
his card?

The contestants turned off the road not far from the cemetery
on the slopes of Mount Mashuk and stopped at the first meadow
that appeared convenient. Suddenly the summer's sun disappeared behind a dust storm. The sun then briefly reappeared.
Martynov and the others, probably Trubetskoy, Stolypin,
Vasiltchikov and Dorokhov took up discreet positions in the
long grass just in case any gendarmes appeared. There was no
doctor standing by – all the doctors in Pyatigorsk having refused
to be involved in the affair – nor any carriage to remove bodies.
Even though behind-the-scene efforts by the seconds to effect a
formal reconciliation had failed, none of them could take the
thing too seriously. Lermontov had already told them that he
would not shoot at Martynov.

Glebov and Vasiltchikov measured off thirty paces, placing

* Alfred de Musset once said to his brother Paul: 'I must try everything.
Within me are two men, one who acts, and another who looks on.' (Paul
de Musset: *Biographie d'Alfred de Musset*, 1877, p. 86.)

swords to be the 'barrier', with hats at ten paces from it as markers, and having led the two adversaries to the furthest distance apart instructed them to walk ten paces towards each other,* on the command 'March'. The pistols were loaded by Glebov. Vasiltchikov handed one to Martynov, Glebov the other to Lermontov. Each duellist, whether moving or stationary, would have the right to three shots. The two seconds gave the command to come forward. According to the seconds, Lermontov remained where he was: then, having cocked his gun, he raised the pistol with the muzzle pointing upwards, at the same time covering himself with his arms and elbow, following the drill of practised duellists. Either duellist could fire without waiting for the other's shot, but it was clear Lermontov had declined to fire.

'At that moment, and for the last time,' wrote Vasiltchikov, thirty years later in *Russky Arkhiv*, 'I glanced at him and I shall never forget the calm, almost cheerful expression which flitted across the poet's face as he faced the pistol muzzle already pointed at him.'[21]

But Vasiltchikov later told his son, Boris (who committed it in writing to as yet unpublished memoirs) that in his article he had suppressed one vital detail, to 'spare' Lermontov's memory. It was that as Lermontov came up to the barrier, not only was the muzzle of his pistol pointing skywards, but he said to his second (i.e. Alexander Vasiltchkov) in a loud voice, 'so that Martynov could not but hear it: "I shall not fire on that fool!" [in the Russian: *Ya v etovo duraka strelyat ne budu*]'.[22] Martynov, who so far had stood aiming his pistol at Lermontov was now goaded beyond control, the inferiority complex of a weak man crystallising into hatred. Stolypin heightened the tension by crying out impatiently to Martynov: 'Fire, or I will separate you.'

Martynov 'came to the barrier with quick strides and fired.'[23] Lermontov fell on the spot, as if mown down by a scythe, making

---

* There are other conflicting stories as to distance at which shots might be exchanged at closest range, varying from five paces only (Polevodin), six paces, (Lyubomirsky), ten paces (Viskovaty) and twelve paces (Shan Girey).

no further movement of any kind, not even clasping the wounded spot, as the wounded usually do.

The seconds rushed up. Stolypin said to Martynov, 'Clear off, you have done your worst.'*[24] There was a gaping wound in Lermontov's right side and blood was oozing out of the left. The bullet had penetrated his heart and lungs. Though all signs of life had apparently disappeared, it was nevertheless decided to call a doctor. Vasiltchikov galloped off to Pyatigorsk. 'I called on one or two of the medical profession,' he wrote, 'but got the same answer, namely, that because of the bad weather (it was raining cats and dogs), they would not go to the site of the duel, but would come to the lodgings in the town when the wounded man was brought there. When I returned, Lermontov was lying on the same spot, dead.' It was about seven o'clock.[25]

Later, wrote Emilia Verzilin, Glebov told her, 'what eerie hours he spent, having remained alone in the forest, sitting on the grass in the pouring rain. The head of the dead poet was resting on his knees – it was dark, the tethered horses neighed, reared, pawed the ground with their hooves, the thunder and lightning was incessant, it was frightening beyond words. Glebov wanted to lower the head carefully onto his great coat, but this movement caused Lermontov to yawn convulsively. Glebov froze motionless and remained so until a police cart arrived in which poor Lermontov was to be carried to his lodgings.'[26] Due to the unexpectedly fatal outcome of the duel, to the inexperience of the official seconds, to the almost solid cascades of rain blurring all vision following the dust storm, and turning doctors and *droshky* drivers into heartless stay-at-homes, there was a wait of two hours, charged with pitiful horror. Vasiltchikov and Glebov were left to perform the minimal acts of decency for their dead comrade; they finally placed the corpse on the cart for the macabre journey to his house at about ten o'clock.

Glebov and Vasiltchkov as seconds were incarcerated to the guard room of Pyatigorsk. Martynov, as a civilian, was already in the local prison. A female sympathiser, visiting him there,

* '*Allez vous en, votre affaire est faite*': French original.

later commiserated with him on spending 'three terrible nights in the company of two arrested criminals, one of whom was reading a book of psalms the whole time, while the other was swearing most horribly.'

Lermontov's body was laid out on his own bed, and the curious were refused admittance. During that nightmare night Lermontov's servant had to stay up, holding a copper bowl under the body to catch the blood and to keep the flies away. He was crying. Alexander Arnoldi, an old friend, came in next morning. 'Lermontov was in a white shirt, strewn with flowers. The room was empty and in a corner hung his raspberry-coloured taffeta shirt, with the bloody mark on the left side.' The painter Shvede came to paint him in oils, hair closely cut, eyes half closed, a 'wicked smile' still lingering on his lips.[27]

Society in Pyatigorsk rose to the tragedy. For two days the orchestras did not play on the boulevards. 'Everyone talked in whispers.' The ladies all called at Lermontov's lodgings and the little room where his body lay was filled with flowers.

The duel had another consequence. Pyatigorsk had never before seen a blue-coated gendarme. Suddenly the little town was full of them, 'like ravens sensing carrion.'[28] Colonel Traskin, Grabbé's Chief of Staff in Stavropol, had arrived in Pyatigorsk three days before from Kislovodsk (where the General's wife had been convalescing) and naturally – as senior officer present – took charge. He knew perfectly well that Grabbé viewed Lermontov sympathetically as a poet as well as a soldier, and had put him forward for battle honours the year before, which had been refused by the Tsar; he could judge the exact nuances of disciplinary measures to be inflicted on seconds, princes or commoners in fatal duels; he knew, too, the subtleties of favouritism and patronage in St Petersburg's War Ministry, where Chernyshov, the Minister, would do his best to interpret the Tsar's brief Minutes, or, in their absence, his August Will. Traskin, furthermore, had many military friends amongst the 'Yermolov' set. He took charge, probably willing to salvage Lermontov's reputation – within the measure possible – which would mean not disclosing anything detrimental to him such as his last words, and spiriting away awkward witnesses who were not officially 'caught', as had been the two seconds, Glebov and Vasiltchikov. A highly interesting personal letter from him to Grabbé has been found written on July 17, two days after Lermontov's death, covering the official report of Commandant Ilyashenkov to Grabbé. After some gossip about Madame Grabbé's state of health, Traskin continues:

You will learn from the attached Report of the Pyatigorsk Commandant [*Ilyashenkov* – author] about the unfortunate and disagreeable business that happened here the day before yesterday. Lermontov had been killed in a duel with Martynov, formerly in the Cossack Grebensky Regiment. The witnesses were Glebov of the Horse Guards, and Prince Vasiltchikov, one of Georgia's new legislators. We only learnt the reasons for this quarrel after the duel; a few hours before they were seen together, and nobody thought they would fight. This was not the first time Lermontov had poked fun at Martynov, and put about caricatures of the latter in the manner of Monsieur Mayeux, and of Martynov's ridiculous clothes dressed up as a Circassian with a long dagger, and he called him '*M. Poignard du Mont Sauvage.*' At an evening party of the Werzilines, he mocked Martynov in front of the ladies. On leaving, Martynov told him he would make him hold his tongue; Lermontov replied that he was not frightened of his threats and would offer him satisfaction if Martynov felt himself offended. Thereupon Martynov called him out ['*cartel de la part de Martynov*'] and the witnesses they chose could not smooth matters over, despite all the efforts which they made; they were going to fight without witnesses. Their animosity makes one think they were settling other differences. They fought at a barrier of fifteen paces which the seconds lengthened to twenty paces. Lermontov had said he would not fire, and that he would await Martynov's shot. They arrived at the barrier at the same time. Martynov fired first, and Lermontov fell. The bullet crossed the body from right side to left, and pierced the heart. He lived for only five minutes, and could not utter a single word.

Pyatigorsk is half full of officers coming from their units

without any permission, oral or written, coming here to distract themselves and not for the cure; amongst others, M. Dorokhov who is certainly not ill. Commanding Colonels of Regiments allowed almost anyone to come here, even officer cadets ['*Junkers*']. It is vital to stop this. Old Ilyashenkov is a worthy and honourable man, but cannot cope with such hot headed youth, and they are twisting him round their fingers. I have sorted it all out, and sent back a number who were hanging around without leave, amongst others Prince Trubetskoy, but I cannot deal with the whole situation, as a number of people are not under my orders. . . .

A. Traskin.[29]

Traskin's own sympathies in the case may be gauged by the strange little story that Martynov, in jail, asked to pay his last respects to Lermontov's corpse in his house. Opposite the request in writing, Traskin minuted '!!!Refused. Traskin.'[30] And it was to Traskin that Grabbé sent his own heartfelt regrets about Lermontov. Finally, from Martynov's words in Traskin's letter, it was Martynov who had insulted Lermontov by saying, 'he would make him hold his tongue' – sufficient reason for Lermontov to take offence and ask for satisfaction; and this version is exactly opposed to the official seconds' evidence later concocted under Traskin's supervision. There must have been good reason for this contradiction.

Ilyashenkov's official account of the duel (see Appendix III) indeed left important points unexplained, or was silent about them. Curiously, a young officer called Lissanievitch had been encouraged earlier (by unknown troublemakers) to challenge Lermontov to a duel, but had indignantly refused. His evidence was not called. Curiously, a senior police officer, Colonel Kuvshinnikov, had been present in Pyatigorsk, throughout Lermontov's stay, as Benckendorff's personal representative. Curiously, the first evidence of all in a duelling case, the fatal Kuchenreuter pistol belonging to 'Mongo' had, at least temporarily, disappeared.[31] Any evidence of Lermontov's stated intention not to fire – thus making of the duel effectively a murder – was not heard. When the Tsar heard of the duel in the report of July 16th, he issued an order (August 4th) that the investigation was to be immediately transferred from the Civilian Court to a Military Court, to prevent scandal, and – so Soviet commentators allege – to ease Martynov's plight. Traskin, to mastermind the 'cover up' and, as already suggested, to save reputations, supervised the seconds' statements, and, as Martynov was none too clever, the seconds were encouraged to collate in writing their submissions, to agree a common story. As a gesture of benevolence, neither Glebov nor Vasiltchikov were to remain under arrest. Stolypin and Trubetskoy remained silent, and they were not arrested as official seconds. (Stolypin's participation was not even known publicly until 1885. The Tsar let him depart for Paris in 1843, perhaps as a reward for his silence.)

The silence of all the witnesses corroborates the unpublished version Prince Vasiltchikov gave to his son Boris of Lermontov's last words. If, indeed, at such a moment fraught with danger, Lermontov had thought it appropriate, witty, or necessary to pile Pelion upon Ossa by insulting Martynov a second time, and saying that he was too great a boor to merit his serious attention in a duel, it would be natural that all concerned should unite to suppress such an example of, at the best, bad manners, and, at worst, arrogant behaviour of their now dead comrade-in-arms.

He, rebel, craves a storm, as though
In storm were peace

the last two lines from 'The Sail' seem apt in the context of Lermontov's last words.

There is some corroborating evidence, too, from a second-hand source, P. T. Polevodin, who wrote within a week of the duel from Pyatigorsk to a friend that he had heard from the seconds that 'Lermontov had first coolly approached the barrier, crossing his arms, *lowered* his pistol, and with a look had called on Martynov to fire. Martynov, at heart a scoundrel and coward, knew that Lermontov always kept his word, and delighted that Lermontov would not be firing, took aim at him. At that moment, Lermontov fixed Martynov with a look of such contempt that even the seconds could not bear it and looked down at the ground.' After a moment's further hesitation during which he lowered his pistol, Martynov finally nerved himself to pull the trigger.[32]

Other accounts by friends of Lermontov in Pyatigorsk that week, speaking to the seconds, substantiate various details of the unpublished Vasiltchikov version. A. I. Arnoldi, one of the pall-bearers, was sure from what he heard that all the seconds thought there would be a reconciliation, and that Lermontov had fixed Martynov with an almost unendurable look of contempt. He even suggests that Martynov – insulted by Lermontov again in front of so many of his friends – felt obliged as only a man of weak character would, to 'prove himself.'[33] N. F. Turovsky reports Lermontov's last words as 'I shall not raise my hand against you; if you want to, fire.'[34] Two others, whose evidence is of lesser importance as they were not in Pyatigorsk at all, also mention phrases such as 'Is it possible I should aim at him?' (E. P. Rostopchina) and 'I shall fire, but not at you' (A. Bulgakov). In his own evidence for the Military Court Martial, Martynov said he had waited a certain time for Lermontov's shot before firing his own.

All in all, the probability is that neither protagonist had intended to fire; hence the carelessless, so criminal otherwise, of the seconds in not providing doctors, nor carriages; hence Lermontov's relaxed conversation with Glebov on the way to the duel. Psychologically, too, Martynov's conduct fits a last-second provocation by Lermontov leading in a panic and fury to his murderous act. Lermontov, too, was perfectly capable of a biting, wounding remark to a man he had so continuously mocked. And the silence later observed by all the seconds and Colonel Traskin (who must have been told) about Lermontov's conduct would be the decent thing.

Martynov at first feared that he would be sent to Siberia, but the Tsar was determined his punishment should be mild. After a three-month 'stint' in a guard house, he was sentenced to excommunication, and sent to repent at leisure – in fact for four years – in the Monastery of Kiev. The sentence came direct from the War Minister, Chernyshov, and caused – privately – some disgust amongst the Generals and officers in the Caucasus,

who knew how strictly Nicholas usually interpreted the duelling
laws. The various violations of the duelling code – the absence
of a doctor above all – went unreproved as far as the seconds
were concerned. General Grabbé was one who did not fail to
mince his words; and the Commander-in-Chief in the Caucasus,
Golovin, washed his hands of the farce of the court martial,
knowing 'they' in St Petersburg would intervene.

Yermolov's reaction was outspoken:

> I would not have let off this Martynov. Had I been in the
> Caucasus, I would have got rid of him. There are certain
> engagements to which it is possible to send a man, and taking
> out a watch, to count after how much time that man will no
> longer be amongst the living. I would not let him get away
> with it. One can allow anyone else to be killed, even if he
> bears a name of great distinction, there will be plenty of such
> tomorrows, but one must wait so long for such as Lermon-
> tov![35]

There was an autopsy on July 17th.

Lermontov's funeral took place on July 18th. A Decembrist
friend, Nicholas Lorer, himself a pall-bearer, described it:

> Representatives of all the regiments in which Lermontov had
> served willy nilly during his short life were discovered, who
> wished to pay their last respects to the poet and comrade.
> Colonel Bezobrazov was the representative from the Nije-
> gorodtsy regiment of dragoons, myself from the Tenginsky
> Infantry, Tiran from the Life Guards Hussars and A. Arnoldi
> from the Grodnensky Hussars. On our shoulders we brought
> the coffin out of the house and carried it to the secluded grave
> in the cemetery on the slopes of the Mashuk. In conformity
> with the law* the priest was on the point of refusing to accom-

---

* Death by duelling was considered a suicide, excluding therefore a Church
Service. Father Paul, the local priest, under pressure from Traskin, accompanied the body but did not hold any service in church. A band had to be
sent away.

pany the mortal remains of the poet, but money produced its usual effect and the funeral was conducted with the rites and ceremonial due to a Christian soldier. Sadly we lowered the coffin into the grave, with tears in our eyes, threw a handful of earth and it was over.[36]

Ekaterina, who had failed to retrieve her blood-soaked golden *bandeau*, kept by Lermontov in his pocket, accompanied the Verzilin girls to the funeral. 'He was as handsome dead as alive.' The lady who had called him a 'Kirghiz ragamuffin' was there in tears; so were most of the other bystanders of the fair sex. There was no music. 'It was so quiet that only the rustle of dry grass under the feet could be heard.'[37]

The Tsar agreed to the tearful request of Lermontov's grandmother that his body should be moved from Pyatigorsk to the family vault in Tarkhany in 1842. She died, heart-broken, three years later. Shortly after Lermontov's death, Varvara's sister wrote of her to a friend that she was ill:

Her nerves are so shattered that she had to spend two weeks in bed. Her husband proposed that she should go to Moscow, she refused; or abroad, she refused and said she did not really want to be healed. Perhaps I am mistaken, but I link this to the death of Michel.[38]

Martynov, released from his monastery in 1846, wooed the rich daughter of a general in Kiev, married her, fathered eleven children and settled down to a long life of boredom as a moderately unpopular clubman. He died in 1875. 'Mongo' Stolypin, who might have described the duel for posterity, stayed silent till the end despite even Tolstoy's efforts to get him to divulge the truth during the Moldavian campaign in 1854. He was the first translator of *A Hero of our Time* into French, in 1844. He died in Florence in 1858.

As for the Tsar, his first comment on Lermontov's death had echoed uncannily the reaction of Lermontov's grandmother on the suicide of her husband. On leaving mass to have tea with his family, he had turned to his courtiers and said loudly: 'Information has been received that Lermontov has been killed in a duel – a dog's death for a dog.' His sister, the Grand Duchess of Weimar, had been so horrified by this that she forced him to return, and he came back to say: 'Gentlemen, the man who could have taken Pushkin's place for us has been killed.'[39]

The wily Shamyl was captured at last by the Russians in 1859, and was kept by the Tsar in a gilded captivity till his death in 1871. On one occasion in Kaluga the Prophet agreed to receive some Russian veterans of the war, speaking to them through an interpreter. One of them told the caged tiger that he came from Tchembar, 'close to Lermontov's grave.'

'Lermontov?', said Shamyl. 'I have heard of him; he wrote of my Caucasus.'[40]

> Hushed forever is the sound of his wild song,
> Never shall the echo of his sweet notes be heard again,
> Dark and narrow is the poet's grave,
> And on his lips is laid the seal of death.
> *Lermontov*

Byron and Lermontov

Lermontov was born in 1814; Byron died in 1824; and within four years of his death Lermontov was already writing poems under his influence. There seemed no generation gap. Lermontov as a child had an English tutor, a Mr Winston, provided for him by his rich grandmother. He had already learnt 'The Prisoner of Chillon' (in Jukovsky's translation) aged thirteen. By 1829–30, aged sixteen, or thereabouts, at the Noble Pension in Moscow, he had already begun to translate Byron, both literally and in 'free' verse. One of Lermontov's first loves, a beauty (Katherine Sushkova) nicknamed by him 'Miss Black Eyes', reminisced that in 1830 Lermontov was 'inseparable' from a large volume of Lord Byron that he always carried around with him. He translated 'Darkness', 'Napoleon's Farewell', some stanzas from 'Beppo' and 'The Giaour.' There were also translations from Tom Moore and Ossian, and he knew Moore's biography of Byron. He set 'Farewell' to verse, Canto XVI of *Don Juan*, and 'Lines written in an album in Malta.' In 1831 he composed a free imitation of 'Stanzas to a lady on leaving England', and an 'Epistle to a Friend.' By 1832 he translated 'On this day I complete my 36th year'; and verses from 'Mazeppa.' In 1836 it was the turn of the 'Jewish Melody', 'My soul is dark', 'Lines written in an album', and the 'Dying Gladiator.'

As a matter of family pride he could quote Canto the Eighth, verse IX of *Don Juan* that referred to his great grandfather, at the Siege of Ismailia under Suvorov, 'The columns ... though led by Arseniew, that great son of slaughter/As brave as ever faced both bomb and ball.'

And there were any number of apposite epitaphs and epigraphs at the head of Lermontov's own poems, especially in the Eastern Tales and ballads. For example, his 'Ismail Bey', the story of a Circassian officer who deserts his Russian Regiment and returns to the mountains to lead his tribesmen against the Russians, is prefaced – in one Canto describing Ismail's love for a Circassian girl – by a quotation from Byron's 'Giaour':

So moved on earth Circassia's daughter,
The loveliest bird of Franguestan.

'Parisina' and 'The Giaour' are extensively quoted elsewhere.

Russian readers knew Byron mainly through French translations, or through translations by second-rate Russian poets such as Kozlov. But, as elsewhere in Europe, everything that he did or wrote was of the greatest interest to them. Russia's own poets, including Pushkin, were also fascinated by Byron. Indeed, Pushkin had a brief affair with a gypsy fortune-teller's daughter in 1821 in Moldavia, Calypso Polichroni, who was thought – to Pushkin's delight – to have also been Byron's mistress.

The Government, too, and its chosen instrument to deal with literature, the Censors, watched Byron's writings and acts with anxiety: godless free-thinking, sexual licence, and calls to revolution were not to be encouraged under Autocracy. It was no coincidence that the Decembrist revolutionary poets such as Ryleyev, Bestujev 'Marlinsky,' and Kuchelbecker had all been inspired in varying degrees by Byron. His sacrifice for Greece called for no less an idealism. On top of the grim legacy of 1825 in Russia came the failure of the 1830 Revolution in France, and of the Polish Revolt.

If ever there had been a hope for a free growth of literature in Russia, these three events put paid to it. Literature became the only battlefield for the opposition, but she had to speak forth in public in sly, double meaning. And in private, young students such as Lermontov wrote fiery 'liberal' denunciations which, if found, would certainly earn them exile to Siberia or to the Caucasus. Poets turned to the greyer themes of doubt, resignation, scepticism, or despair born allegedly out of frustrated loves. Byron's appeals for freedom sounded sweetly in Russia after 1828, herself now muzzled so effectively, by Nicholas' *'Corps de Gendarmes'* working hand in glove with the Censors and the 'official' press. Lermontov (and others of his generation such as

Herzen and Byelinsky), thus turned away from an inadequate and frustrating world controlled by Censors, to console themselves with their own thoughts, passions and ideals; and in Lermontov's case, Nature as well, especially in such a magnificent and beautiful setting as the Caucasus.

Lermontov wrote in 1830:

I am young, but echoes set my heart on fire
And I wish to emulate Byron
Our souls are one, our sufferings alike
I, too, seek oblivion and freedom
Were but our destinies the same.

And again

No, I am not Byron but another as yet unknown
Chosen as he to be exiled, pursued by the World,
But with a Russian soul.

As one might expect of one poet greatly attracted by another, Lermontov's 'borrowings' are many, and the subject of countless textual criticisms and comparisons. Yet such scholarship about possible plagiarism misses the point; he 'borrowed' because emotionally he felt this need, and there are examples of Byronic ideas and attitudes even in Lermontov's most mature prose writings, as well as the obvious cases in poetry between 1830 and 1835–36. Lermontov too wrote a 'Corsair.' In his 'Two Brothers' and 'Caucasian Prisoner', and 'Ismail Bey', there is the familiar Byronic cast of desperate heroes and heroines, eventually meeting death or some ineluctable fate against exotic backgrounds, in Lermontov's case painted from careful observation of wild mountains in their ever-changing glory. 'Lara', 'The Giaour', 'Cain', 'Childe Harold' are not so much models as pace-setters against which the young poet measured himself.

It could even be argued that some themes of Byron's are developed by Lermontov, in this sombre context of censorship and threatened or actual repression, beyond the range of the older poet, with an intensity born of two political exiles, and parti-

cipation in a very cruel, full-scale war being waged in the Caucasus
against the tribes.

Lermontov naturally expounded the Byronic theme of the
futility of human sufferings, the aimlessness of life. In two
versions of a poem 'Night' he developed the ideas in Byron's
'Darkness':

> The bright sun was extinguished, and the stars
> Did wander darkling in the eternal space
> Rayless, and pathless, and the icy earth
> Swung blind and blackening in the moonless air
> Morn came and went – and came, and brought no day.

Stars, cliffs, trees, waves in Lermontov have hearts and souls,
and speak as noble and stoic humans, albeit usually resigned.
For Byron, Nature provided perhaps a more limited expression of
beauty, to Lermontov, religious by nature, Nature had to provide
an alternative God for the one who had deserted human beings,
and displayed an apparent indifference to their suffering, amidst
much beauty.

Lermontov was also fascinated by the myth – as was Byron
in 'Cain', Tom Moore, Alfred de Vigny in '*Eloa, La Soeur des
Anges*', and others, of the theme of the fallen Angel, of Lucifer.
Lermontov's 'Demon' differs markedly from the sceptical,
elegant Lucifer created by Byron. The latter is not dismayed by
his damned state; hardly gives a thought to redemption of his
own lost soul; does not fall in love with Eve or her daughters;
and generally is a heartless agent of temptation. Lermontov's
Demon, on the other hand, is bored with his own trail of destruction and seeks redemption and reconciliation with God – to be
denied to him by the pitiless Deity and his humourless Guardian
Angels.

The whole problem of freewill, good and evil, and predestination is raised, seriously, and for the first time in Russian literature,
in the poem. There is also an intensity of sensuality in the love
scenes between Tamara, the Georgian Princess seduced by the
Demon, that excite the reader more effectively than any of
Lucifer's blandishments in 'Cain.' Lastly, the poem has a passage

where the words become music to a degree and pitch never present in 'Cain.' Lermontov's use of Caucasian landscape and Georgian scenery, surveyed by the Demon as he circles the earth, are based on his own detailed knowledge, and thus carry the stamp of accuracy and realism, in a way no conventional 'eastern' imagery of English poets could convey.

Russian romanticism had a very special character, and the need to protest, and the art of saying it, had moved by the 1830s into the medium, as Byelinsky emphasised, of 'prose, prose, prose.' The pupil here out-distanced his master.

In prose, Lermontov in *A Hero of our Time* created two characters who were partly Byronic, partly not. The 'Hero', Pechorin, physically very like Lermontov, has been described in 'Childe Harold in a Russian Cloak.' Certainly his aristocratic dandyism (attributed to the English as the 'evil of the age'), his haughty indifference, and his cynical experiments with the hearts of women are Byronic. The desire for revenge and the idea that personality alone can triumph over the vulgar crowd dominate Pechorin. These, too, were Byronic attitudes. The 'Hero' is a confessional novel; Lermontov revealed much about himself in it. Pechorin's 'I love to doubt everything' is Byronic in character. But his unhappiness and attempt to escape from his fate through the proud exercise of his will at whatever cost set him aside from Byronic heroes who in the end are more story-tellers than human beings in all their complex sufferings and joys. And in Grushnitsky, the fatuous, irritating officer killed in a duel by Pechorin, Lermontov created a kind of parody of the Byronic dandy, taking words for reality, and declamations for passion.

Lermontov, with his scowling face, droopy cavalry moustache, bow-leggedness and chronic arthritis, could not rival Byron's flamboyant good looks, nor his legion successes with women. In the kingdom of the heart, Byron found more experiences and satisfactions to gratify his super-ego than poor Lermontov who only loved once, lost his true love to an obese, elderly rich husband chosen by her parents, and nursed a bitter grievance and frustration forever thereafter. As a result, it could be argued that his feelings and perceptions about love became more intense than those Byron experienced. As Soloviev said of Lermontov, 'the most characteristic feature of his genius is the terrific intensity of thought concentrated on himself, his ego, a terrific power of personal feeling.'

But there were curious coincidences, too, in the lives of the two poets. Lermontov knew neither his father nor mother except in the most formal way, and Byron grew up a lonely child. Both remained childlike in their vanity. Both were impetuous in action; the only conclusion from an idea was fatalistically to try it out. Both would retreat into the private melancholy of their 'tender souls' when the mood overtook them, but would tell the world about it in their poetry. Both were, sometimes, as Lermontov was once described, 'diabolically naughty.' Both loved drink and gaiety, both had deep depressions. Both allowed themselves *'le plaisir aristocratique de déplaire.'* Both adored women. Both lived nomadically – Lermontov through force of circumstance, Byron hounded by his own legend. Both showed great moral courage against society, against self-appointed censors – and in Lermontov's case, against the official Censors. Both had to fulfil their need to write, whatever the personal consequences.

G

Appendix 2

Poems

A Book of Russian Verse, ed. C. M. Bowra (Macmillan, 1943)
Written in 1830. Not published in Lermontov's lifetime.

Hope

I have a bird of paradise;
Upon a springing cypress-tree
She sits for hours while daylight flies,
And not a song by day sings she.
Her back is of celestial blue,
Her head is purple; flaming dye
Upon her wings, of golden hue
Like dawn's reflection in the sky.
Only when earth is slumbering,
Hidden, as night mists silent roll,
Upon her bough she starts to sing
So sweetly, sweetly to the soul,
That forced by it, your load of pain
Forgetting, you must sing away,
And in your heart each tender strain
Is a dear friend who comes to stay.
Often in tempests I have heard
That song which means so much to me,
And always for my peaceful bird
I listen, listen hopefully.

(C. M. BOWRA)

The Waggon of Life – Transl. Sir Cecil Kisch (Cresset Press).
Written in 1831, not published in Lermontov's life-time.

The Wish

Would I were a bird like the raven that flew
    By me now o'er the steppe far above!
Would I could but soar up aloft in the blue,
    So that freedom alone I might love!

I westward – I westward would haste to keep tryst,
    Where the fields of my forefathers bloom,
Where castle long empty, mid hills clad in mist,
    Guards their ashes forgot in the tomb!

On time-honoured wall hang their shield, with the coat
    Of their sires, and the sword red with rust,
And over the sword and the shield I would float,
    With my wings I would scatter their dust!

The strings of my own Scottish harp I would sound,
    And each vault with its chords I would fill;
By each they are heard and from each they rebound,
    Till their echoes at last become still.

In dreams is no profit, in wishes no worth
    When stern destiny makes her decree.
'Twixt me and the hills of the land of my birth
    There are spread the wide waves of the sea.

This scion, the last of those warriors rare –
    Amid alien snows withers he.
My birth befell here, but my soul belongs there.
    Would that I a steppe-raven might be!

A Book of Russian Verse, ed. C. M. Bowra (Macmillan, 1943). Written in 1831, signed and first published in the *Odessa Almanack for 1840*, passed by the Censor V. Pakhman.

The Angel

An Angel was flying through night's deep blue,
    And softly he sang as he flew.
Noon, stars and clouds in a wondering throng
    Listened rapt by that heavenly song.

He sang of the blest, who live without stain
    In God's garden, a shining train.
He hymned the Lord's might, and his voice rang clear,
    For he sang without guile or fear.

He bore in his arms a young soul to its birth
    On the dark and sinful earth,
And the Angel's song remained in the soul
    Without words yet unblemished and whole.

Long after on earth when the soul would tire,
    It felt a strange, aching desire
For the music of heaven which it sought for in vain,
    In earth's songs of sorrow and pain.

(V. DE S. PINTO)

A Book of Russian Verse, ed. C. M. BOWRA (Macmillan, 1943). Written 1832, signed and first published in the *Notes of the Fatherland*, 1841 Vol. xviii, No. 10, p. 161. Passed by the Censors A. Nikitenko and S. Kutorg.

A Sail

A solitary sail that rises
White in the blue mist on the foam –
What is it in far lands it prizes?
What does it leave behind at home?

Whistles the wind, the waves are playing,
The labouring masthead groans and creaks.
Ah, not from pleasure is it straying,
It is not pleasure that it seeks.

Beneath, the azure current floweth;
Above, the golden sunlight glows.
Rebellious, the storms it wooeth,
As if the storms could give repose.

(C. M. BOWRA)

Poems from the Russian chosen and transl. by Francis Cornford and Esther Salaman (Faber, 1943).

Signed, and first published in *The Contemporary* 1837, Vol. vi, No. 2, pp. 207–211. Passed by the Censors A. Krylov and S. Kutorg.

Borodino

'Come tell me, was it all for nought
That Moscow burned, although we fought
   And would not yield?
Come, Uncle, tell the tale again
Of how we fought with might and main,
And men remember, not in vain,
   Our Borodino's field.'

'Yes, in our time the men were men,
And from the heat of battle then
   How few returned,
How few returned their fields to till!
Heroes – not lads like you – they still
Fought on, but could not stay God's will,
   That Moscow burned.

'We beat retreat by day and night,
We fumed and waited for the fight;
   The old men jeered:
"We'd better winter in the bogs,
And build up huts and bring in logs,
But never turn to face the Frogs,
   And singe their beard."

'But then a noble stretch of ground
To build a great redoubt we found,
   And there entrench.
All night we listened. Nought astir!
But when the dawn touched fir by fir
And lit the guns – why then, good sir,
   We saw the French.

'I had my powder tightly rammed.
I'll serve you now and you be damned,
   My fine Mounseer!
No hope for you to lurk and crawl;
We'll stand against you like a wall;
And if needs must, we'll give our all
   For Moscow, here.

'For three whole days without a change
We only shot at distant range;
   No use at all!
You heard men saying left and right,
It's time to buckle to and fight –
Until across the fields the night
   Began to fall.

'I lay to sleep beside my gun,
But heard the cheer, till night was done,
   The Frenchmen made.
Our men were quiet. One would sit
And mend his coat where it was slit,
Or bite his long moustache and spit
   And clean his blade.

'The very hour night was fled
Our guns began to move ahead:
   My God, the rattle!
Our officers were gallant then;
They served their Tsar and loved their men,
They lie asleep in field or fen,
   Who led the battle.

'The Colonel set our hearts astir;
"Moscow's behind. My lad, for her,
   As all have heard,
Our fathers fought with might and main.
Let's swear to die for her again.'

And there on Borodino's plain
　　We kept our word.

'That was a day. Towards our redoubt
We saw the Frenchmen gallop out
　　Through smoky air,
Dragoons as bright as on parade,
And blue hussars with golden braid,
And Uhlans – what a show they made!
　　They all were there.

'That was a day will never die:
The flags like spirits streaming by –
　　A fire ahead –
The clash of steel – the cannon's blast –
Our arms too weak to slay at last:
But few the bullets were that passed
　　Our wall of dead.

'That day the foeman learned aright
The way we Russian soldiers fight –
　　Fierce hand to hand,
Horses and men together laid,
And still the thundering cannonade;
Our breasts were trembling, as it made
　　Tremble the land.

Lermontov, Transl. by C. E. l'Ami and A. Welikotny (University of Manitoba Press, 1967).
Written in January 1837. Not published in Lermontov's lifetime.

The Poet's Death

Revenge, sire, revenge!
Here I shall fall at your feet!
Be just and punish the murderer,
So that his execution in remotest ages
Thy just tribunal shall announce to posterity,
And villains shall know the example of it.

The poet died, to honour fated;
Fell, by foul rumour's tongues betrayed;
Lead in his breast, revenge unsated,
Down to the earth he bowed his head.
Certain it was his soul could never
Endure the shame of men's disdain;
He braved the world's harsh frown – as ever
Alone! – and struggled – and was slain!
Slain! . . . And why now these wailings loose,
This needless blare of eulogy,
This wretched lisping of excuse?
It was Fate's sentence – let it be!
Did not you all in those first years
His free great gift reject and shame?
Did not you all with jibes and sneers
Fan that scarce-hidden fire to flame?
What, then? Rejoice! He could not bear
Those his last tortures! His light was shaded
Like a quenched torch; his genius rare
Like a triumphal garland faded.
Coldly the murderer took his stand,
Coldly . . . No mercy could there be!
The empty heart beat evenly,

The pistol shook not in his hand.
Why should it shake? From far away,
Like all these swarming fugitives
Come here to cadge for rank and pay,
Tossed by Fate's whim into our lives,
He laughed, and brazenly despised
This barbarous country's law and story,
Could spare no mercy for our glory –
Dolt, in that black hour could not know
Against what thing his hand was raised! . . .

And he is dead, and taken by the grave,
Like that unknown beloved minstrel brave,
Prey of blind jealousy, whose story he
In mighty verse such deathless glory gave,
Slain, as he was, alas! so pitilessly!
Why from luxurious peace, from honest friendship severing,
Did he approach this world, envious and vile and smothering
For flaming hearts, for passionate souls a hell?
Why did he walk with them, with false and worthless
    slanderers,
Why take for truth the words of fawning, lying panderers –
He who from earliest youth had known men's hearts so well?
They tore away his garland, and instead
Gave him a crown of thorns, with the laurel twined;
But harshly on the ever-glorious head
The hidden needles cut with anger blind . . .
So did their mocking ignorance' crafty tongue
Poison his life's last moments cold and brief,
And by vain thirst for vengeance fiercely wrung,
With hope deceived and secret burning grief,
He died . . . The great music's unforgotten strain
Ceased . . . and shall not resound on earth again.
Grievous and narrow is the earthy shield
He rests in, and his prophet's lips are sealed.

And you, proud sons of famous fathers – you,
Known to the world for vileness unsurpassed,

Who spurn with coward heels the remnant few
Of tribes afflicted by ill-fortune's blast!
You, greedy crew that round the sceptre crawl,
Butchers of freedom, genius, and renown!
Hid by the bulwark of the law, and all –
Law, truth, and honour – in your steps cast down!
Vile panderers of lewdness, there is law –
Stern law of God that waits to claim its own:
It will not heed the jingling gold you paw,
Your thoughts and deeds to it are all foreknown,
Then will your slanderous gossip make small pay,
In vain your vipers' tongues with poison dart,
And all your black blood will not wash away
The godly lifeblood of the poet's heart!

Lermontov Transl. by L. E. L'Ami and Welikotny. (University of Manitoba Press, 1967).
Signed and first published in *The Notes of the Fatherland*, 1839, Vol. 5, No. 8, pp. 168–170. Passed by the Censors A. Nikitenko and V. Langer.

The Three Palm Trees, an Eastern Legend

In the sandy desert of Araby,
Three palms grew proud and tall,
And under them, out of the earth set free,
A cool spring murmured small;
Guarded beneath the leafy strands
From burning rays and flying sands.

And silent seasons came and went,
And yet no traveller wayfaring,
Rested beneath the palms' green tent,
Or cooled his breast beside the spring;
And withering under the sun's hot beam
Were the beautiful leaves and the sounding stream.

And the three palms murmured against their God:
– Why were we born, to wither here?
Useless we bloomed on the desert sod,
Shaken by storms and sun-rays sere.
To no kind eye have we given joy.
Shall naught, O Heaven, our years employ? –

Even as they ceased, far in the blue,
Dense clouds of golden sands made play,
And bells' discordant jinglings flew
From packs with coloured carpets gay,
Where, tossed like shallops on the main,
Long rows of camels ploughed the plain.

And up between the hard humps swaying,
Dark hands moved softly out and in,

On patterned travelling tent-flaps straying,
While dark eyes glistened from within;
And crouched above his saddle high,
A slender Arab spurred nearby.

Rearing and prancing, the steed out-broke
Like a panther leaping, arrow-stung;
And the beautiful folds of his long white cloak
Flapped, on the horseman's shoulder hung,
As he crossed with a whistle the sand-drift sheer,
And galloping, threw and caught his spear.

Noisily up to the palms they rode,
And there in the shade their gay camp spread;
Pitchers gurgled as water flowed
And, proudly nodding each two-crowned head,
The palms made welcome their sudden guests,
While the spring flowed free to all behests.

But as twilight over the desert spread,
An axe rang loud on pliant roots,
And the nurslings of silent years fell dead . . .
Small children tore their brown bark suits,
And their bodies to little logs were sawn,
And burned in the Bedouins' fire till dawn.

When the morning mists had fled to the west,
The caravan moved on its hourly way;
And there on the ground, a sad bequest,
A heap of cold grey ashes lay;
And what remained the hot sun battered,
And the wind on the open desert scattered.

Now all round was desert made,
And no leaves whispered by the spring;
In vain to the Prophet it prayed for shade –
Only the hot sand came to sting;
And the desert hermit, the crested kite,
Over it, clutched his prey in flight.

A Book of Russian Verse, ed. C. M. Bowra (Macmillan, 1943).
Signed and first published in the *Notes of the Fatherland* 1839,
Vol. vi, No. 11, p. 272. Passed by the Censors A. Nikitenko and
P. Korsakov.

Prayer

When life's oppressive hour is mine
And in my heart griefs crowd,
A prayer of wondrous power is mine
That I repeat aloud.

Blest is the strength that flows to me
In concords of sweet sound;
Past reckoning it blows to me
Divine enchantment round.

Doubt, like a burden, leaping then
Far from the spirit flies;
From words of faith and weeping then
How light, how light we rise!

(C. M. BOWRA)

Poems from the Russians. Chosen and transl. by Francis Cornford
and Esther Salaman (Faber, 1943).
Signed and first published in the *Notes of the Fatherland*, 1840,
Vol. viii, No. 2, pp. 144–154. Passed by the Censors P. Korsakov
and A. Freigang.

Cossack Lullaby

Now fall asleep, my lovely babe,
   Baioushki, baiou;
The moon into your cradle looks
   The clear night through.

A story I will tell you now,
   A song I'll sing for you;
So shut your eyes and fall asleep,
   Baioushki, baiou.

The foaming Terek rushes on
   His stony shores between,
And there the wicked Chechen creeps
   And whets his dagger keen.

But Father is a warrior bold,
   A fighter hard and true;
So sleep, my baby, calmly sleep,
   Baioushki, baiou.

Then when the time is come you'll know
   The way a man should fight,
And leap into the saddle straight
   And sling your gun aright.

And I will work your saddle-cloth
   With scarlet silk and blue;
So sleep, my dearest, fall asleep,
   Baioushki, baiou.

And you will have a Cossack's heart
  And be a champion high,
When I come out to see you go,
  And you shall wave good-bye.

How many bitter quiet tears
  I'll weep that night for you!
Sleep sweetly, quietly, my love,
  Baioushki, baiou.

For you I shall begin to long
  And comfortless to wait;
Be kneeling early at my prayers,
  And telling fortunes late.

And I shall think how, far away,
  You must be pining too;
Oh, sleep, while not a care is yours,
  Baioushki, baiou.

A Book of Russian Verse ed. C. M. Bowra (Macmillan, 1943). *Verses* by M. Yu. Lermontov, 1840. First published at I. Glazunov. 1000 copies printed, pp. 161–62. Passed by the Censor A. Nikitenko.

When o'er the yellowing corn a fleeting shadow rushes,
And fragrant forest glades re-echo in the breeze,
And in the garden depths the ripe plum hides its blushes
Within the luscious shade of brightly verdant trees;

When bathed in scented dew, the silver lily,
At golden morn or evening shot with red,
From out behind a leafy bush peeps shyly,
And nods with friendly mien its dainty head;

When down the shady glen the bubbling streamlet dances,
And lulling thought to sleep with its incessant song,
Lisps me the secrets, with a thousand glances,
Of that still corner where it speeds along;

Then does my troubled soul find solace for a while,
Then vanish for a time the furrows from my brow,
And happiness is mine a moment here below,
    And in the skies I see God smile.

(W. A. MORRISON)

A Book of Russian Verse ed. C. M. Bowra (Macmillan, 1943). *Verses* by M. Yu. Lermontov, 1840, first published at I. Glazunov. 1000 copies printed, pp. 167–168. Passed by the Censor A. Nikitenko.

We parted, but my heart still wears
    Thine image, gracious yet,
Pale token of those better years
    I never can forget.

What though new passions rule my will?
    Deserted and untrod
The temple is a temple still,
    The idol still a god.

(MAUD F. JERROLD)

Poems from the Russian. Chosen and transl. by Frances Cornford and Esther Salaman (Faber, 1943).
Signed, and first published in the *Notes of the Fatherland* 1841, No. 4, Vol. xv, p. 283. Passed by the Censors A. Nikitenko and S. Kutorg.

My Country

I love my country with a singular love
That reason cannot move:
'Tis not her glory
Bought with our Russian blood, nor her proud story
Of strength impregnable, nor heritage
Of legends handed down from age to age,
That stirs my dreams. But I must testify:
These things I love, and cannot tell you why.

Rivers in flood like seas,
Deep in her woods the swaying of the trees,
In the cold fields her silence – I love these.

Those endless days
Jolting my cart along her dusty ways,
Till, sighing for a place to spend the night,
And peering through the darkness left and right,
Far off one sees
The trembling lights of her sad villages.

I love the wispy smoke
From the singed stubble-fields on soft winds borne;
The covered wagons of the wandering folk
In the wide steppes asleep when day is done;
And on the hill among the yellow corn
The two white birches shining in the sun.

With comfort few can share,
I love to see a barn filled full of hay,

Or the poor huts straw-covered by the way,
With rough-carved shutters round their windows bare –
And many a feast-day evening I am found,
Eager to watch upon the dewy ground,
Till dawn is near,
The tramp and whistle of the dance, and hear
The drunken babble round.

Modern Russian Poetry: an anthology – chosen and transl. by
Babette Deutsch and A. Yarmolinsky (John Lane, The Bodley
Head, 1923).
Signed and first published in the *Notes of the Fatherland*, Vol.
xvii, No. 8, p. 268, 1841; Passed by the Censors A. Nikitenko and
S. Kutorg.

Captive Knight

Silent I sit by the prison's high window,
Where through the bars the blue heavens are breaking.
Flecks in the azure, the free birds are playing;
Watching them fly there, my shamed heart is aching.

But on my sinful lips never a prayer,
Never a song in the praise of my charmer;
All I recall are far fights and old battles,
My heavy sword and my old iron armor.

Now in stone armor I hopelessly languish,
And a stone helmet my hot head encases,
This shield is proof against arrows and sword-play,
And without whip, without spur, my horse races.

Time is my horse, the swift-galloping charger,
And for a visor this bleak prison grating,
Walls of my prison are heavy stone armor;
Shielded by cast-iron doors, I am waiting.

Hurry, oh fast-flying Time, fly more quickly!
In my new armor I faint, I am choking.
I shall alight, with Death holding my stirrup,
Then my cold face from his visor uncloaking.

Anthology of Russian Literature by Leo Weiner, Pt. II 19th Century (Putnam's, 1953).
Signed and first published in *Moskvityanin*, 1841. Passed by the Censor N. Krylov.

The Dispute

Once, before a tribal meeting
   Of the mountain throng,
Kazbék-hill with Shat-the-mountain
   Wrangled loud and long.
'Have a care, Kazbék, my brother,'
   Shat, the grey-haired, spoke;
'Not for naught hath human cunning
   Bent thee to the yoke.

Man will build his smoky cabins
   On thy hillside steep;
Up thy valley's deep recesses
   Ringing axe will creep;
Iron pick will tear a pathway
   To thy stony heart,
Delving yellow gold and copper
   For the human mart.
Caravans, e'en now, are wending
   O'er thy stately heights,
Where the mists and kingly eagles
   Wheeled alone their flights.
Men are crafty; what though trying
   Proved the first ascent! –
Many-peopled, mark, and mighty
   Is the Orient.'

'Nay, I do not dread the Orient,'
   Kazbék, answering, jeers;
'There mankind has spent in slumber
   Just nine hundred years.

Look, where 'neath the shade of plane-trees
    Sleepy, Georgians gape,
Spilling o'er their broidered clothing
    Foam of luscious grape!
See, 'mid wreaths of pipe-smoke, lying
    On his flowered divan,
By the sparkling pearly fountain
    Dozeth Teheran!
Lo! around Jerusalem's city,
    Burned by God's command
Motionless, in voiceless stillness,
    Deathlike, lies the land.

'Farther off, to shade a stranger,
    Yellow Nilus laves,
Glowing in the glare of noonday,
    Steps of royal graves.
Bedouins forget their sorties
    For brocaded tents,
While they count the stars and sing of
    Ancestral events.
All that there the vision greeteth
    Sleeps in prized repose;
No! the East will ne'er subdue me!
    Feeble are such foes!'
'Do not boast thyself so early,'
    Answered ancient Shat;
'In the North, look! 'mid the vapours,
    Something rises! What?'

Secretly the mighty Kazbék
    At this warning shook,
And, in trouble, towards the nor'ward
    Cast a hurried look.
As he looks in perturbation,
    Filled with anxious care,
He beholds a strange commotion,
    Hears a tumult there.

Lo! from Ural to the Danube,
    To the mighty stream,
Tossing, sparkling in the sunlight,
    Moving regiments gleam;
Glancing wave the white-plumed helmets
    Like the prairie grass,
While, 'mid clouds of dust careering,
    Flashing Uhlans pass.
Crowded close in serried phalanx
    War battalions come;
In the van they bear the standards,
    Thunders loud the drum;
Streaming forth like molten copper
    Batteries, rumbling, bound;
Smoking just before the battle
    Torches flare around;
Skilled in toils of stormy warfare,
    Heading the advance,
See! a grey-haired general guides them,
    Threat'ning in his glance.
Onwards move the mighty regiments
    With a torrent's roar;
Terrible, like gathering storm-clouds,
    East, due east, they pour.

Then, oppressed with dire forebodings,
    Filled with gloomy dreams,
Strove Kazbék to count the foemen,
    Failed to count their streams.
Glancing on his tribal mountains,
    Sadly gloomed the hill;
Drew across his brows the mistcap,
    And for aye was still.

        – From J. Pollen's *Rhymes from the Russian.*

Lermontov, transl. by L. E. L'Ami and A. Welikotny (University of Manitoba Press, 1967).
Written in 1841. Not published in Lermontov's lifetime.

A Princess of the Sea

A prince, at the shore to bathe his steed,
Hears from the water: 'Prince, give heed!'
And his good horse snorts and pricks his ears,
Splashes and sprawls, as away he veers;
And the voice cries: 'I am the Sea-King's daughter!
Stay tonight with me under the water!'
A hand came up from the ocean grot
To clutch at his silken bridle-knot;
And a young head rose from the waters fair,
Seaweed twisted in raven hair,
Blue eyes flaming with love in the swirls,
Ocean spray on her neck like pearls.
And the prince laughed: 'Good! Now hold, my lass!'
And he twined his hand in the raven tress,
And held. His battle-arm was strong.
She pled and wept for long and long,
But the prince swam firmly to the strand,
Leapt out, and called to his waiting band:
'Hi-hi! Come all together, braves!
Look how this fish of mine behaves! . . .
But why do you all stand gaping there?
Have you never seen a maid so fair?'
Then the prince looked down, and stopped . . . a sigh,
And the merry triumph fled his eye.
He saw: On the golden sand asleep,
A green-tailed wonder out of the deep:
A maid with snaky scales for gown,
Trembling, writhing, sinking down;
Cold drops upon her forehead's rise,
A mortal shadow in her eyes;

Pale hands that in the sand-spit broach,
Pale lips that murmur wild reproach . . .
The prince rides pensive by the water:
He will not forget the Sea-King's daughter!

A Book of Russian Verse, ed. C. M. BOWRA (Macmillan, 1943).
Written in 1841. Not published in Lermontov's lifetime.

The Crag

In the night a golden cloudlet straying
    Slumbered on a crag's breast, huge and burly;
    Rose the damsel in the morning early,
Gaily fled through heaven's azure, playing.

But upon the wrinkled rock remaining
    Faintly still a trace of brightness wandered:
    Lone the giant stood, and deeply pondered
Softly, for air's emptiness complaining.

(V. DE S. PINTO)

Appendix 3

The Official Report on the Death of Lieutenant Lermontov

'On the 16th day of the month of July in the year 1841 the coroner, town-major lieutenant-colonel Untilov, assessor of Pyatigorsk rural police court Cherepanov, police inspector Marushevsky and acting attorney Olshansky 2nd, having invited cornet Glebov and titular councillor prince Vasiltchikov, who were the seconds, to accompany them, went to inspect the site where the duel took place on the 15th at 7 p.m. This site is situated at a distance of about four verts from the town of Pyatigorsk, on the left hand side of the Mashuk mountain near its foot. A road runs there, leading to a German Colony founded by Tzar Nicholas. On the right hand side of the road there is a hollow which extends from the top of Mashuk to its very foot, and on the left hand of the road a small mountain stands in front, which is separated from Mashuk. The above-mentioned road passes between them to the colony. The first shrubs commence from this road, which meandering to Mashuk mountain, surround a small meadow. It was here that the duellists chose the spot for shooting it out. Having tied their horses to the shrubbery, where grass which has been trodden down and wheel tracks of a racing *droshky* are visible, they, so Glebov and prince Vasiltchikov informed us – the persons charged with the inquest, measured off along the road a barrier of 15 paces and placed a hat at each end of it, then starting from these hats they again measured off 10 paces along the road in both directions, at the ends of both of which they again put hats, thus making it four hats altogether. The duellists to start with stood at the extreme points, i.e. each 10 paces from the barrier; Martynov from North to South, and Lermontov from South to North. On the signal given by the seconds, they came to the barrier. Major Martynov, firing the fatal pistol, killed lieutenant Lermontov, who did not manage to fire his pistol. On the spot where Lermontov fell and lay dead the blood which he lost can be seen. His body, in accordance with the arrangements made by the seconds, was brought the same evening at 10 o'clock to his (Lermontov's) lodgings.'

References

Preface

1 *Pushkin on Literature*, translated and edited by Tatiana Wolff (Methuen, London, 1971) p. 60.

2 *Michael Lermontov, Biography and Translation*, by C. E. L'Ami and Alexander Welikotny (University of Manitoba Press, 1967) p. 65.

3 *Oxford Book of Russian Verse* (Clarendon Press, 2nd Edition, 1948) p. xxvi.

4 *Russian Poets and Poems etc.* by Mme. N. Jarintzov, Vol. 1 (Blackwell, 1917) pp xiv–xv.

5 Prince George Vasiltchikov's letter to Author of July 21, 1976: Alexander V. [Lermontov's second] was an uncle of my paternal grandfather [the latter's father was A.'s half-brother]. A. V. had a son, Boris (whom I still remember well, as he died only in the mid-thirties in Paris). This Boris served most of his life in senior posts of the provincial administration, ending up as Stolypin's first Minister of Agriculture. He left a fascinating thick volume of handwritten memoirs, the manuscript of which I was able to locate during the war in Paris and which I later typed out. It is now in my possession. According to Stanford and Columbia universities (to whom it has been shown), it is one of the most interesting records of the last quarter of the nineteenth century in Russia known to scholars.

Chapter 1 – Childhood in the Wild East

1 Born 2/3rd October 1814 (old style) in Moscow. The Julian Calendar used in Russia in the nineteenth century was twelve days behind the Gregorian Calendar. All key dates follow those given in V. Manuilov's *Chronology of the Life and Works of M. Yu. Lermontov* ('Nauka', Moscow and Leningrad, 1954).

2 *Chronology of the Life and Works of M. Yu. Lermontov*, op. cit., pp. 17–18.

3 *M. Yu. Lermontov in the Memoirs of his Contemporaries* (*Artistic Literature* 1972) ed. by V. V. Grigorenko and others, quoting M. N. Longinov, p. 150.
4 Op. cit., p. 56, quoting P. K. Shugaev.
5 Alexandre Dumas: *Adventures in the Caucasus,* transl. and ed. by A. E. Murch, from *En Caucase,* (Peter Owen, London, 1962).
6 *Russian Journal of Lady Londonderry 1836–7* ed. by W. Seaman and J. Sewell (John Murray, 1973) pp. 137–8.
7 *Blackwood's Edinburgh Magazine,* pp. 471–2, 1843, from *Ammalat Bek* by N. Bestujev – 'Marlinsky.' Transl. by Thomas Shaw.
8 *Travels in Russia; the Krimea, the Caucasus and Georgia* by Robert Lyall, M.D. (reprint two vols. in one, Arno Press, New York, 1970) pp. 401–2. First published 1825 for T. Cadell, The Strand & W. Blackwood.
9 Op. cit., p. 457.
10 *Blackwood's Edinburgh Magazine,* op. cit., p. 477.
11 Lyall, op. cit., pp. 434–5.
12 *Michael Lermontov,* biography and translation by C. E. L'Ami and Alexander Welikotny (University of Manitoba Press, 1967) p. 288.
13 *Don Juan,* Canto the Eighth, Verse LX. Byron even mentioned Lermontov's maternal great-great-uncle:
 Thicker than leaves the lives began to fall
 Though led by Arseniev, that great son of slaughter.
14 B. 1772, d. 1861. Chief of Staff in 1812 to the Russian Grand Army. Served under Suvorov. Appointed as G.O.C. in the Caucasus from 1815 to 1827.
15 *Travels in Circassia, Krim Tartary, etc.* (1836) by Edmund Spencer. Second edition in two vols (Henry Colburn, London, 1838) pp. 218–219.
16 *Voyage au Mont Caucase et en Georgie, par M. Jules Klaproth,* Vol. 1 (Paris, 1823) p. 251.
17. 'Ismail Bey', Part II, Canto IX. Transl. from *A Book of Russian Verse* (Macmillan, 1943) transl. by J. S. Phillimore.
18 Lyall, op. cit., p. 426.
19 Translated privately for the Author by Philip Longworth.

Chapter 2 – The Education of Cornet Lermontov

1 *The Rebel on the Bridge* by Glyn Barratt (Paul Elek, 1975) p. 66.
2 Barratt, op. cit., p. 67.

3 *M. Yu. Lermontov in the Memoirs of his Contemporaries*, op. cit., p. 178, quoting V. P. Burnashov.

4 Translated by the Author. Original text in *Complete Edition of the Works of M. Yu. Lermontov* ed. by Professor D. I. Abramovitch (St Petersburg, 1910) Vol. I, p. 144. All subsequent references to original Russian texts of Lermontov's writings will be to this edition unless otherwise stated.

5 *M. Yu. Lermontov in the Memoirs of his Contemporaries*, op. cit., p. 36, quoting A. P. Shan-Girey.

6 *Complete Edition of the Works of M. Yu. Lermontov*, op. cit., Vol. 4, p. 307. Letter of August 1832 to Sofiya Alexandrovna Bakhmetieva (transl. by the Author).

7 L'Ami and Welikotny, op. cit., p. 239 (from 'Ismail Bey').

8 *Complete Edition of the Works of M. Yu. Lermontov*, op. cit., Vol. I, p. 105 and p. 96.

9 L'Ami and Welikotny, op. cit., p. 239 (from 'Ismail Bey').

10 Op. cit. p. 269 (part III of 'Ismail Bey').

11 *M. Yu. Lermontov in the Memoirs of his Contemporaries*, op. cit., p. 36, quoting A. P. Shan-Girey.

12 *Complete Edition of the Works of M. Yu. Lermontov*, op. cit., Vol. 4, p. 316 and p. 318. Letters of 1832 and 19 June 1833 to M. A. Lopukhina.

13 L'Ami and Welikotny, op. cit., pp. 373–374.

14 David MacDonald: unpublished translation of *Masquerade* for stage performance at Citizens Theatre, Glasgow 1976.

15 *Complete Edition*, op. cit., p. 319. Letter of August 4th to M. A. Lopukhina.

16 Op. cit., p. 311 and p. 322. Letters of 28 August 1832 and 23 December 1834 to M. A. Lopukhina.

17 L'Ami and Welikotny, op. cit., pp. 337–338, Canto CXLVII.

18 *The Russian Conquest of the Caucasus* by J. F. Baddeley (Longmans, 1908) p. 96.

19 Quoted and translated by Sir Isaiah Berlin in his 1970 Romanes Lecture. Letter of Byelinsky to Gogol of July 15, 1847.

20 Review of *Masquerade* in *Financial Times*, October 4, 1976, by Michael Coveney:

 Mikhail Lermontov (1814–1841) is renowned as the poet who shot to notoriety for writing a long poem about the death of Pushkin. That was in 1837, and soldier Lermontov, while delighting the intelligentsia with his enthusiastic, and brilliant championing of virtues of liberty and free thought (virtues the

old Decembrist Pushkin had celebrated to the embarrassment of
Nicholas I), was rewarded by peremptory dismissal to the
Western line in the Caucasus. In his last five years of life he was
banished twice and wrote his extraordinary novel, the cynically
entitled *Hero of our Time*. That book is well-known in English.
But *Masquerade*, his chief play on many of the same themes, is
not. It had never been translated into English – until Robert
David MacDonald did so for the Glasgow Citizens and gave
jaunty notice of his intentions by replacing 'qu' with a 'k'.

Although I am assured that most of the original play is
faithfully followed, the action is placed in a *fin de siècle* design,
brilliantly realised by Philip Prowse in order to make more
immediate to contemporary British audiences the quality of life
in those Petersburg salons of the 1830s. Foppish gamblers and
lovelorn aristocracy in elegant evening dress gossip round the
card tables. Huge mirrors duplicate images of well-dressed
decadence; ladies draped in huge furs, their necks elongated
inside large, jewelled collars, adorn a scene of club-land exclu-
sivity. The central character, Eugene Arbenin, has rejected this
shallow scene and laconically committed himself to marriage.
But his flair, not to mention his money, is missed at the gambling
tables and there are plans in motion to recapture him.

He sees his own past reflected in the antics of a pathetic Prince
who, at the beautifully staged masked ball, declares undying
commitment to a haughty Baroness. As the plot slowly unwinds,
it becomes clear that the Baroness is, in real life, pining for the
Prince; he, however, does not return the affection. Arbenin is ten
years older than the callow Prince and uses his apparent folly to
fuel a savagely articulated contempt for a society that encourages
people like him, who, says the Baroness, are 'glittering but worthless'. As might be expected at this theatre, the ambiguous
attitude of Lermontov to the crimes of vanity and egoism receive
a lavish treatment that both demonstrates and criticises the
current morality. Mr MacDonald's translation, too, is full of
such racy neo-Wildean epigrams as 'You must expect the cream
of society to be both rich and thick.'

Arbenin is deceived as to his wife's fidelity by identifying a
bracelet he gave her in the possession of the Prince; he, in fact,
has received it from the Baroness. Arbenin resolves to kill his wife
and does so by poisoning her ice-cream at a grand ball. In a long
and astonishingly gruesome scene, he watches her die very slowly

while ruminating on the awfulness of Life. 'I'm dying,' squeaks Nina with sudden realisation; 'Not yet,' says Arbenin, 'there's still half an hour to go.' As she wilts, protesting her innocence, he turns on her with vitriolic accusations of being a liar. The melodrama is under-pinned with surging quotations from Rakhmaninov's First and Second Symphonies.

The stage is divided into two levels. The lower depths are occupied by the salon society while, above, in grandly cobwebbed secrecy, a mysterious stranger oversees the action, descending intermittently to spy on the protagonists and assume the role of reluctant valet or waiter. Who is this man? It transpires that he is an old and dissatisfied friend of Arbenin and, having heard of his marriage and himself deprived of youth, health and money, has returned to plague the malcontent and, in some mysterious way, effect his downfall. The former guardian angel has turned avenger. The power of the final scenes is immeasurably enhanced by the visual emphasis given to what is, presumably, a small Dickensian character on the periphery.

One of the gamblers, an oily busy-body played with devastating precision and smarminess by Jonathan Hyde, comments drily 'Someone has clearly had a hand in all this; I should like to shake him by it.' Arbenin enters, Lear-like, with his wife's corpse. The downfall of Byronic Man is complete. The music swells, the curtain falls. The production, by Mr MacDonald, is beautifully controlled, exquisite to look at, full of pungent detail: Mr Hyde lights a cigarette from the funeral candles that have been solemnly lit in the dead woman's memory; when the disgraced Prince (he has been heavily defeated at the tables and has fled to the Caucasus) returns to Arbenin's house with the stranger, they enter the lower level through a mirror that has been, until that point, stationary – as it swings open the theatre and its dumbstruck audience are seen in swift and brilliant reflection.

Mark Lewis as Arbenin conveys with charm and accuracy the essential unpleasantness of Lermontov's hero – his brusque treatment of old friends recalls the odd behaviour of Pechorin in *Hero of our Time*. And there is impressive work, too, from Paola Dionisotti as the Baroness, abandoning her position in Petersburg with broken heart and emancipated philosophy ('George Sand was right – almost.') and Julia Blalock as the wronged Nina.

The most vivid evidence illustrating the relationship of writers, the Censors, the Third Department, and the Tsar, comes in *The Diary of a Russian Censor, Aleksandr Nikitenko,* ed. and transl. by Helen Jacobson (University of Massachusetts Press, Amherst, 1975) pp. 87–89.

December 12, 1842 An unexpected and absurd episode occurred which deserves a detailed account. Yesterday morning, around noon, I returned from my lecture at Catherine Institute and worked in my study, not suspecting that anything was amiss. Suddenly a gendarme officer appeared and graciously asked me to pay a visit to Leonty Vasilievich Dubbelt. 'Probably something to do with censorship,' I thought, and immediately headed for the Third Section of His Majesty's Own Chancery.

On the way, I mentally sorted through all my censorship dealings and searched in vain for a solitary blunder. In the course of ten days I had managed to acquire a certain acumen, but I was now hopelessly lost in guesswork.

The officer who had come to fetch me inquired about Kutorga's apartment, for he, too, was ordered to appear before Dubbelt. This meant that trouble was brewing for us over *Notes of the Fatherland.*

I arrived in the chancery before Kutorga; he arrived half an hour later. We were taken to Dubbelt.

'Oh, my dear gentlemen,' he said, taking our hands. 'How distressing it is for me to see you concerning such an unpleasant case. You'll never guess why the emperor is displeased with you.'

With these words, he opened the No. 8 issue of *Son of the Fatherland* and pointed to two passages marked off with a pencil. Here they are, from Efebovsky's story, *The Governess.* He describes a ball at the home of a government official in Peski: 'May I ask you, what's so bad about the figure, for example, of this courier with his splendid, brand-new aiguilettes? Since he considers himself a military man and, even better, a cavalryman, *Gospodin*'s courier is fully entitled to consider himself attractive when he rattles his spurs and twirls his mustaches, which are smeared with a wax whose rosy smell pleasantly envelopes both himself and his dancing partner ...' The other objectionable passage: 'an ensign from a construction unit of the Engineer Corps, wearing enormous epaulettes, a high collar, and a still higher tie ...'

'And that's it?' I asked Dubbelt.

'Yes,' he replied. 'Count Kleinmichel complained to the Emperor that his officers were insulted by this.'

I was so noticeably relieved, that Vladislavlev remarked:

'It appears that you are very pleased.'

'Yes, I am,' I said. 'I was very upset until I learned what we were being accused of. Because of the complexity and difficulty of censorship, we could easily have overlooked something and given cause for punitive measures. But now I see that this case is like a lump of snow falling down on you from some roof as you chance to be walking along the sidewalk. There are no precautions one can take against such punitive measures because they are beyond the sphere of human logic.'

Dubbelt escorted us to Benkendorf.

Benkendorf, a venerable old man, whom I met for the first time, received us with a serious and grieved expression.

'Gentlemen,' he said in a gentle, soft voice, 'I deeply regret that I must give you some unpleasant news. The Emperor is very upset by the passages in the journal which have already been shown to you. He considers it improper to attack members of his Court or officers. I presented the most favorable evidence about you and spoke about your fine reputation among the public. In short, I did everything I could in your favor. Despite my efforts, he ordered your arrest for one day.'

After expressing regret at having incurred the Emperor's wrath, I said, 'Your Excellency, speak to His Majesty for us. Explain to His Majesty the difficult position we censors find ourselves in. We never know what is expected of us and what position to take; we frequently suffer only because some outsider takes it into his head to meddle in our affairs. Thus, we are never safe; there will be no end to punitive measures, and we shall find ourselves unable to fulfill our responsibilities.'

Benkendorf took our hands and assured us that he would report all this to the emperor. We left. Vladislavlev prepared a paper for the commandant and gave it to us. It was almost 4 p.m. We were permitted to go home to eat, provided we would report to the commandant by ten. At eight I went to get Kutorga, who was terribly upset. He didn't know how to break the news of his arrest to his sick wife. Finally, we left to report to the commandant at the Winter Palace. He wasn't in, and we gave our dispatch to the aide-de-camp. He led us to a tiny room where a clerk was working on some papers, placed a sentry at the door, and then went to the commandant for orders. He returned in half an hour and announced that I would be confined in either the Petrovsky or Senate guardhouse, and Kutorga in the Sennaya guardhouse.

I was led away first. I found myself in an enormous basement room with vaulting in the company of the sentry officer. The town adjutant was always very courteous to us. Then, he and Kutorga left and I remained alone with the officer. He was a young man from the Obraztsov Regiment, apparently a very decent fellow. He took a kindly interest in me, saw to it that I received a bed and gave me his overcoat to cover myself for the night. In short he surrounded me with attention and concern.

The next day the same aide-de-camp came to tell me that I was free. We went together to the Sennaya to release Kutorga. After parting with the town adjutant and thanking him for his kindness, we went to see Prince Volkonsky, our superintendent.

He not only received us kindly, but even warmly. I spoke plainly about everything that had been seething inside me. Censors are treated like little boys or smooth-faced ensigns; we are placed under arrest for trifles not worthy of attention. At the same time we are saddled with the responsibility of protecting minds and morals from anything that might lead them astray, of safeguarding the public spirit, the laws, and finally, the very government itself. What kind of logical activity can be expected of us when everything is decided by blind whim and arbitrary desire.

After leaving the prince, we went to see the minister. The same regrets and kind words.

'Who can you complain about or blame in this case?' said the minister. 'This case was unusual. I couldn't do a thing; it was already over with before I learned about it. I would have gone to the Emperor immediately, but couldn't because we have the measles at our house. All I could possibly do was write a letter and ask Benkendorf to present it to the emperor.'

The prince read us this letter. It was written intelligently and forcefully. While describing us, that is, Kutorga and myself, as the finest of censors and professors, the minister stated that he was now in a great predicament with regard to the censorship. Reliable people didn't want to take on this wretched responsibility, and if Kutorga and I were still at our posts, it was only because the minister had pleaded with us to stay. He is afraid that censorship duties will soon become abhorrent to everyone.

They say the Emperor read this letter without saying a word.

21 *My Past and Thoughts: The Memoirs of Alexander Herzen*, transl. by Constance Garnett, revised by Humphrey Higgens (Chatto and Windus, London, 1968) pp. 418–419.

22 Op. cit., p. 419.

23 Op. cit., p. 1761.

24 Op. cit., p. 1761.

25 L'Ami and Welikotny, op. cit., p. 290.

26 Op. cit., p. 291.

27 Op.cit., pp. 320–324.

28 Op. cit., p. 310.

29 Op. cit., p. 335.

30 V. G. Byelinsky, quoted in *A Guide to Russian Literature 1820–1917* by Moissay J. Olgin (Harcourt Brace, New York, 1920) pp. 29–30.

31 *M. Yu. Lermontov in the Memoirs of his Contemporaries*, op. cit., p. 182, quoting V. P. Burnashov.

32 Op. cit., pp. 184–185. Translation of poem by Maurice Baring, *Russian Literature* (Williams & Norgate, 1914), p. 110.

33 *M. Yu. Lermontov in the Memoirs of his Contemporaries*, op. cit., p. 184.

34 *The Tales of a Literary Man* by I. Andronikov ('Literature for Children', Moscow, 1968) p. 253. Letter of February 10, 1837 to Andrei Karamsin.

35 *Duel and Death of Pushkin* by P. E. Shchegolev, p. 293.

36 *M. Yu. Lermontov in the Memoirs of his Contemporaries*, op. cit., p. 186.

37 *My Past and Thoughts*, op. cit., p. 441.

38 *The Third Department* by P. S. Squire (Cambridge University Press) p. 122.

39 *Chronology of the Life and Works of M. Yu. Lermontov*, op. cit., p. 72.

40 *My Past and Thoughts'*, op. cit., p. 44.

41 Marquis de Custine: *Lettres de la Russie* 11th letter.

42 *Chronology of the Life and Works of M. Yu. Lermontov*, op. cit., p. 73.

43 *M. Yu. Lermontov in the Memoirs of his Contemporaries*, p. 391, quoting S. Rayevsky's official apologia.

44 Op. cit., pp. 19–20, quoting V. Stasov.

Chapter 3 – The Grand Tour

1 *Chronology of the Life and Works of M. Yu. Lermontov*, op. cit.,
   p. 78.

2 Op. cit., pp. 82–83.

3 Barratt, op. cit., pp. 177–178.

4 *M. Yu. Lermontov in the Memoirs of his Contemporaries*, op. cit.
   pp. 343–345, quoting N. F. Turovsky.

5 '*A Hero of Our Time*', translated by Philip Longworth (New
   English Library, Mentor Edition), pp. 109–110.

6 *Travels in the Steppes of the Caspian Sea, The Crimea, Caucasus* by
   Xavier Hommaire de Hell (Chapman and Hall, 1847) p. 286. (This
   descriptive passage was written, in fact, by Mme de Hell.)

7 *A Hero of Our Time*, op. cit., pp. 85–86.

8 *Chronology of the Life and Works of M. Yu. Lermontov*, op. cit.,
   p. 80.

9 *M. Yu. Lermontov in the Memoirs of his Contemporaries*, op. cit.,
   pp. 201–202, quoting N. M. Satin.

10 Barratt, op. cit., p. 127.

11 *A Hero of Our Time*, op. cit., p. 94.

12 *M. Yu. Lermontov in the Memoirs of his Contemporaries*, op. cit.,
   p. 516, quoting M. A. Nazimov.

13 Op. cit., pp. 298–299, quoting Yu. Samarin.

14 Alexandre Dumas found his mistress' grave thirty years later and
   had inscribed the following verses:

> *Elle atteignait vingt ans; elle aimait, était belle,*
> *Un soir elle tomba, Rose effeuillee aux vents,*
> *O terre de la mort, ne pèse pas sur elle*
> *Elle a si peu sur celle de vivants.*

   quoted by L. Blanch: *The Sabres of Paradise*.

15 *A Hero of Our Time*, op. cit., p. 88.

16 *Chronology of the Life and Works of M. Yu. Lermontov*, op. cit.,
   pp. 88–89. Letter to S. Rayevsky, Nov–Dec. 1837.

17 Op. cit., pp. 88–89 transl. by Philip Longworth.

18 Barratt, op. cit., p. 173.

19 *Blackwood's Edinburgh Magazine*, 1843. T. Shaw's translation of
   'Ammalat Bek'.

20 *A Hero of Our Time* transl. by V. & D. Nabokov (Doubleday
   Anchor, 1958) p. 30.

21 Transl. by the Author.

22 *Chronology of the Life and Works of M. Yu. Lermontov*, op. cit.,
   pp. 88–89.

23 *Travels in the Transcaucasian Provinces of Russia, 1837*, by Captain R. Wilbraham, 7th Royal Fusiliers (John Murray, London) p. 1839. Op. cit. pp. 198–199.

24 L'Ami and Welikotny, op. cit., p. 204.

25 Wilbraham, op. cit., p. 205.

26 *Chronology of the Life and Works of M. Yu. Lermontov*, op. cit., p. 83.

27 Op. cit., p. 89. Letter of Nov/Dec 1837 to S. Rayevsky.

28 L'Ami and Welikotny, op. cit., p. 202.

29 Op. cit., pp. 202–203.

30 Klaproth, op. cit., pp. 10–11.

31 Barratt, op. cit., p. 175.

32 *Russian Poets and Poems* by Mme. N. Jarintzov (Blackwell, Oxford, 1917) Vol. I, p. 180.

33 Private letter of 29/1/1974 to the Author from Mr D. Barrett of the Department of Oriental Books, Bodleian Library, Oxford:

> In Lermontov's time, the dominant dialect in the Caucasian region would have been Azeri Turkish ... and all the Turkish speaking peoples outside Turkey would have been called Tatars. It differs very little from the Turkish of Turkey, even less so when written in the Arabic script. 'Azerbaidjani' is only another way of referring to 'Azeri Turkish'.

34 Wilbraham, op. cit., p. 120.

35 Op. cit., p. 129.

36 Lyall, op. cit., pp. 522–523.

37 Transl. by the Author. Original quoted I. Andronikov, *Lermontov in Georgia* in 1837 (Zarya Vostoka, Tiflis, 1957) pp. 110–111.

38 L'Ami and Welikotny, op. cit., p. 224.

39 I. Andronikov, op. cit., p. 42.

40 Baring, op. cit., p. 115.

41 Janko Lavrin: *Lermontov* (Bowes and Bowes, London, 1959) p. 62.

42 Vladimir Nabokov, in *Speak Memory* (Penguin Books, 1969), has an unusual account of his own indoctrination into the marvels of the Novice (pp. 127–129):

> Never shall I forget that first reading. Lenski (Nabokov's tutor) had selected a narrative poem by Lermontov dealing with the adventure of a young monk who left his Caucasian retreat to roam among the mountains. As usual with Lermontov, the poem combined pedestrian statements with marvellous melting fata morgana effects. It was of goodly length, and its seven hundred and fifty rather monotonous lines were generously spread by

Lenski over a mere four slides (a fifth I had clumsily broken just before the performance).

Fire-hazard considerations had led one to select for the show an obsolete nursery. ... Despite the ejection of an ancient wardrobe and a couple of trunks, this depressing back room, with the magic lantern installed at one end and transverse rows of chairs, hassocks, and settees arranged for a score of spectators (including Lenski's fiancee, and three or four governesses, not counting our own Mademoiselle and Miss Greenwood), looked jammed and felt stuffy. On my left, one of my most fidgety girl cousins, a nebulous little blonde of eleven or so with long, Alice-in-Wonderland hair and a shell-pink complexion, sat so close to me that I felt the slender bone of her hip move against mine every time she shifted in her seat, fingering her locket, or passing the back of her hand between her perfumed hair and the nape of her neck, or knocking her knees together under the rustly silk of her yellow slip, which shone through the lace of her frock. ...

The lights went out. Lenski launched upon the opening lines:

> The time – not many years ago;
> The place – a point where meet and flow
> In sisterly embrace the fair
> Aragva and Kurah; right there
> A monastery stood.

The monastery, with its two rivers, dutifully appeared and stayed on, in a lurid trance (if only one swift could have swept over it!), for about two hundred lines, when it was replaced by a Georgian maiden of sorts carrying a pitcher. When the operator withdrew a slide, the picture was whisked off the screen with a peculiar flick, magnification affecting not only the scene displayed, but also the speed of its removal. Otherwise, there was little magic. We were shown conventional peaks instead of Lermontov's romantic mountains, which

> Rose in the glory of the dawn
> Like smoking altars,

and while the young monk was telling a fellow recluse of his struggle with a leopard –

O, I was awesome to behold.
Myself a leopard, wild and bold
His flaming rage, his yells were mine.

– a subdued caterwauling sounded behind me.
43 *A Hero of Our Time*, op. cit., p. 55.
44 *Chronology of the Life and Works of M. Yu. Lermontov*, op. cit., p. 89.

Chapter 4 – The Rise and Fall of a Society Lion

1 S. N. Shchukin: *Iz Vospominani ob A. P. Tchekove, Tchekov in the Memoirs of his Contemporaries* (Moscow, Leningrad, 1954) p. 542.
2 *A Hero of Our Time*, op. cit., p. 10.
3 Op. cit., p. 60.
4 Op. cit., pp. 61–62.
5 Op. cit., pp. 62–63.
6 Op. Cit., p. 127.
7 Op. cit., p. 46.
8 *M. Yu. Lermontov in the Memoirs of his Contemporaries*, op. cit., p. 50, quoting A. P. Shan-Girey.
9 *A Hero of Our Time*, op. cit., p. 166.
10 Original in French. Translated by the Author. Quoted by Emma Gershtein: *The Fate of Lermontov* (Moscow, 1964) pp. 467–468.
11 *A Hero of Our Time*, op. cit., p. 69.
12 Op. cit., p. 143.
13 Op. cit., p. 10.
14 Op. cit., p. 68.
15 L'Ami and Welikotny, op. cit., p. 70.
16 *Catalogue for Victoria and Albert Exhibition on Lord Byron* by Anthony Burton and John Murdoch, 1974.
17 'Lara' by Lord Byron, C. I. St xviii.
18 *M. Yu. Lermontov in the Memoirs of his Contemporaries*, op. cit., p. 45.
19 *Anthology of Russian Literature* by Leo Wiener, Part II (Putnam's, The Knickerbocker Press, 1903) p. 166.
20 'The Demon', transl. by Alexander Condie Stephen (Trubner and Co. London, 1875) p. 65.
21 'The Demon' transl. by Robert Burness (Douglas and Foulis, Edinburgh, 1918) pp. 48–49.

22 'The Demon' transl. by A. C. Stephen, op. cit., p. 81.
23 *The Poetical Works of Lord Byron* (John Murray, 1863) pp. 331–332.
24 *M. Yu. Lermontov in the Memoirs of his Contemporaries*, op. cit., p. 242, quoting Byelinsky's letter to V. P. Botkin of 18 April 1840. See John Bayley: *Tolstoy and the Novel*, p. 42: 43.

Both 'The Demon' and to a lesser extent, Pechorin, are excellent examples of what John Bayley has called the 'Timon effect' where Shakespeare's Timon 'puts himself outside humanity', but still 'knows' the 'image of the good':

Put armour on thine ears and on thine eyes
Whose proof nor yells of mothers, maids, nor babes,
Nor sight of priests in holy vestments bleeding,
Shall pierce a jot.

'The ferocity shows its opposite with agonising certainty. Satan in *Paradise Lost* moves us for the same reason: not because he is a hero and a rebel, but because he alone in the poem is invested with the idiom to convey dramatically what goodness is, because he is aware of the rent in his nature which separates him from "pleasures not for him ordained", so that he must cry out "Evil, be thou my good." Hamlet's tirades against his mother and Ophelia have the same perversity, and Byron – a great Timon lover – occasionally achieves the effect. His bitter poem on hearing that his wife was ill conveys in spite of himself a yearning for reconciliation, affection and "the common good of life", as great as that of the underfloor man when the despised Lise came to see him. Lermontov, whose understanding of Byron was more deeply intuitive than that of any other Russian author, Pushkin included, dramatises through Pechorin – the *Hero of Our Time* – a comparable impression.

'Their satanic division of rent in their nature – the *nadryv* as Dostoevsky calls it – this is what separates his characters so completely from those of Tolstoy. When crisis or alienation comes to one of Tolstoy's characters it comes from outside, like a thief reconnoitring and breaking into an orderly house. Whereas Dostoevsky's can live with – and even live *by* – the cracks and contradictions in themselves, to be penetrated by the outside world is for Tolstoy's people the supreme anguish, a catastrophe not to be healed or overcome. In terms of the construction of a

novel, the dramatic principle of the *nadryv* is replaced in Tolstoy
by the static principle of *samodovolnost* – self-sufficiency, or self-
esteem. When that is gone, the Tolstoyan character is lost indeed.'

25 *M. Yu. Lermontov in the Memoirs of his Contemporaries*, op. cit.,
   pp. 228–229.
26 *Chronology of the Life and Works of M. Yu. Lermontov*, op. cit.,
   p. 96.
27 Op. cit., p. 98.
28 *M. Yu. Lermontov in the Memoirs of his Contemporaries*, op. cit.,
   p. 229, quoting I. S. Turgeniev.
29 V. Byelinsky, *Articles and Reviews* ('School Library', Moscow
   Workers' Press, 1971) p. 174, originally published in the *Annals of
   the Fatherland*, 1841, Vol. XIV, Book II.
30 *A Book of Russian Verse* ed. by Maurice Bowra (Macmillan, 1943)
   transl. by C. M. Bowra, pp. 45–46.
31 *Chronology of the Life and Works of M. Yu. Lermontov*, op. cit.,
   p. 98.
32 *A Book of Russian Verse*, op. cit., transl. by Maud Jerrold, p. 41.
33 '*Complete Edition of the works of M. Yu. Lermontov*', op. cit.,
   Vol. 2, p. 294.
34 A. Herzen: '*My Past and Thoughts*', translated by C. Garnett,
   revised by H. Higgens, p. 1670.
35 *The Marquis de Custine and his Russia in 1839*, George F. Kennan,
   (Hutchinson, London, 1972), p. 40.
36 *Articles & Reviews*, op. cit., p. 153.
37 *Studies in Russian Literature*, Charles E. Turner (Sampson Low,
   1882) p. 342.
38 *M. Yu. Lermontov in the Memoirs of his Contemporaries*, op. cit.,
   pp. 166–167, quoting D. A. Stolypin and A. V. Vasiliev.
39 *The Penguin Book of Russian Verse*, introduced and edited by
   Prince D. Obolensky, p. 159 (plain prose translation).
40 Emma Gershtein, *The Fate of Lermontov*, op. cit., p. 11.
41 *M. Yu. Lermontov in the Memoirs of his Contemporaries*, op. cit.,
   p. 47, quoting A. P. Shan-Girey.
42 *The Fate of Lermontov*, op. cit., p. 15, quoting P. A. Viskovatov,
   who in turn heard this remark attributed to Lermontov by the
   officer of the guard.
43 *Chronology of the Life and Works of M. Yu Lermontov*, op. cit.,
   pp. 127–128.
44 Op. cit., p. 129. Letter of E. A. Vereshchagina to her daughter.
45 L'Ami and Welikotny, op. cit., p. 155.

46 *The Fate of Lermontov*, op. cit., p. 468, transl. by the Author from French.

Chapter 5 – Lieutenant Lermontov at War
1 *The Russian Conquest of the Caucasus*, op. cit., p. 347.
2 *Collected Edition of the Works of M. Yu. Lermontov*, op. cit., p. 338. Letter of 17 June 1840, from Stavropol to A. A. Lopukhin.
3 J. F. Baddeley, op. cit., pp. 310–311.
4 *Blackwood's Edinburgh Magazine*, 1843, *Ammalat Bek* by Bestujev 'Marlinsky' transl. by T. Shaw, p. 477.
5 *Souvenirs et Correspondances de Prince Emile de Sayn Wittgenstein Berleburg*, ed. Calmann-Levy (Paris, 1888) Vol. I, p. 36, transl. by the Author.
6 *The Russian Conquest of the Caucasus*, op. cit., p. 97.
7 L'Ami and Welikotny, op. cit., p. 270, quoting from 'Ismail Bey'.
8 *The Russian Conquest of the Caucasus*, op. cit., pp. 267–270, quoting Tornau.
9 L'Ami and Welikotny, op. cit., pp. 185–186.
10 Op. cit., pp. 187–189.
11 *Collected Edition of the Works of M. Yu. Lermontov*, op. cit., Vol. IV, pp. 339–340. Letter to A. A. Lopukhin of 12 September 1840 from Pyatigorsk.
12 Op. cit., p. 340. Letter of November (undated) to A. A. Lopukhin, from Fort Grozny.
13 *Chronology of the Life and Works of M. Yu. Lermontov*, op. cit., p. 140, quoting K. X. Mamatzev's account, as told to V. Potto, in the newspaper *Kavkaz* of 1897.
14 *Chronology of the Life and Works of M. Yu. Lermontov*, op. cit. p. 140, quoting Mamatzev.
15 *M. Yu. Lermontov in the Memoirs of his Contemporaries*, op. cit., pp. 306–307.
16 *A Book of Russian Verse*, op. cit., pp. 49–50.
17 *M. Yu. Lermontov in the Memoirs of his Contemporaries*, op. cit., pp. 261–262. quoting Ya. I. Kostenetsky.
18 *Blackwood's Edinburgh Magazine*, *1843 Ammalat Bek* op. cit., pp. 478–479.
19 *Russian Songs and Lyrics* by John Pollen (East and West, 1916) pp. 49–52.
20 Barratt, op. cit., p. 185.

21 '*Les Peuples du Caucase et leur guerre d'Independance contre la Russie.*' par F. Bodenstedt. (E. Dentu, Paris, 1859) p. 591.
22 *The Russian Conquest of the Caucasus*, op. cit., p. 112.
23 *Journal of a Residence in Circassia, 1837/9* by James Stanislaus Bell (London, 1840) Appendix (p. 425) quoting 'Letter brought back from the Russian General in answer to a verbal communication of the Circassian Heralds.'
24 *Blackwood's Edinburgh Magazine*, 1843, op. cit., p. 480.
25 *The Russian Army under Nicholas I, 1825–1855* by John Shelton Curtiss (Duke University Press, Durham, N.C., 1965) p. 121.
26 Op. cit., p. 120.
27 Op. cit. p. 284, quoting Seriakov's eyewitness account in *Russkaya Starina*, 1875, Vol. CIV, pp. 161–171.
28 Barratt, op. cit., p. 235.
29 *A Hero of Our Time*, transl. by Philip Longworth, op. cit., p. 66.
30 *M. Yu. Lermontov in the Memoirs of his Contemporaries*, op. cit., pp. 465–466 quoting A. I. Arnoldi, and *The Contemporary* of 1837, Vol. VI, pp. 146–147.
31 There is a sympathetic echo of Lermontov's views in the remarks of the Marquis de Custine, whose famous letters about Russia also criticised romantic nationalism and its consequence, war. 'I hope to live long enough to see the shattering of this bloody idol of war and brute force.' See George F. Kennan, *The Marquis de Custine and his Russia in 1839*, op. cit., p. 94.
32 *Russian Literature* by Maurice Baring, op. cit., pp. 120–123.
33 L'Ami and Welikotny, op. cit., pp. 128–129.

Chapter 6 – Last Leave

1 *Chronology of the Life and Works of M. Yu. Lermontov* op. cit., pp. 146–147.
2 V. Byelinsky: *Articles and Reviews*, op. cit., p. 176.
3 *Blackwood's Edinburgh Magazine*, op. cit., pp. 799–800.
4 *Chronology of the Life and Works of M. Yu. Lermontov*, op. cit., p. 152, quoting *Annals of the Fatherland*, Vol. XV section vi, p. 68.
5 Op. cit., p. 151, quoting Countess Rostopchina's *Tales*.
6 Op. cit., p. 148, quoting letter to A. I. Bibikov, of second half of February 1841.
7 Op. cit., pp. 149–150 and p. 155.
8 *Mikhail Lermontov* by John Mersereau Jr. (Southern Illinois University Press, 1962) p. 23.

9 George F. Kennan, quoting Herzen's commentary on Princess Dashkov's Memoirs at the End of '*My Past and Thoughts*' in *The Marquis de Custine and his Russia in 1839*, op. cit., p. 80.

10 S. A. Andreyev Krivitch: *The Omniscience of the Poet* ('Soviet Russia', Moscow, 1973) pp. 202–203, quoting letter to Sofiya Karamsina of May 10, 1841 (not given in full by Manuilov nor by Abramovitch).

Chapter 7 – The Cup of Life

1 *A Book of Russian Verse*, op. cit., p. 39.

2 *Russian Literature Triquarterly* (Ardis Publishers, Ann Arbor, Michigan, U.S.A.) No. 10, Fall 1974.
Article by Helen Michailoff: *The Death of Lermontov*, pp. 279–297. This is a masterly piece of historical reconstruction and Sherlock Holmesian in its analysis, and, to me, correct conclusions. All Lermontov scholars should be indebted to her for one of the few original pieces of fresh and original scholarship in recent years.

3 *Collected Edition of the Works of M. Yu. Lermontov*, op. cit., p. 342. Letter to his grandmother from Stavropol of May 1841.

4 *M. Yu. Lermontov in the Memoirs of his Contemporaries*, op. cit., pp. 302–305 quoting P. I. Magdenko. Transl. for the Author by P. O'Bow-Hove.

5 Op. cit., pp. 310–315 quoting V. I. Chilyaev and N. P. Rayevsky. Transl. for the Author by P. O.' Bow-Hove.

6 L'Ami and Welikotny, op. cit., pp. 41–42. I have been unable to find any corroboration or original source for these verses.

7 L'Ami and Welikotny, op. cit., p. 42.

8 Op. cit., p. 51, quoting Prince A. Vasiltchikov.

9 Op.cit., '*Sashka*', Canto CXVI, p. 327.

10 *Chronology of the Life and Works of M. Yu. Lermontov*, op. cit., p. 164, quoting N. P. Rayevsky in *Niva* of 1885, No. 7, pp. 167–168.

11 *M. Yu. Lermontov in the Memoirs of his Contemporaries*, op. cit., p. 346, quoting Ekaterina Buikhovetz.

12 *Russian Songs and Lyrics* by John Pollen CIE LLd Dublin (London East and West, 1916) pp. 40–41.

13 *A Book of Russian Verse* op. cit., transl. by J. S. Phillimore, p. 43.

14 Op. cit., p. 42, transl. by C. M. Bowra.

15 *M. Yu. Lermontov in the Memoirs of his Contemporaries*, op. cit., pp. 336–337, quoting Emiliya Verzilina (later to marry Shan-Girey).

16 L'Ami and Welikotny, op. cit., p. 46, quoting S. N. Filippov and

F. E. Ansky's Edition of Lermontov's Works, 1892, p. XIII/XIV.

17 Op. cit., pp. 346–347, quoting Ekaterina Buikhovetz.

18 C. E. L.'Ami and Welikotny, p. 47, quoting F. E. Ansky and the memoirs of 'Major' Karpov. 1892.

19 *Chronology of the Life and Works of M. Yu. Lermontov*, op. cit., p. 166, quoting P. K. Martyanov *Deeds and People of the Century* (St Petersburg, 1893).

20 *A Hero of our Time*, transl. by V. & D. Nabokov, op. cit., p. 162.

21 *M. Yu. Lermontov in the Memoirs of his Contemporaries*, op. cit., p. 368, quoting A. I. Vasiltchikov.

22 Original Russian text of Prince A. Vasiltchikov's Memoir, published here for the first time through the kindness of Prince George Vasiltchikov. Prince G. Vasiltchikov further comments:

My great-uncle, Prince Alexander Illarionovitch Vasiltchikoff (a brother of the Vasiltchikoff Capt. Wilbraham talks about) happened to be a close friend of Lermontov's, witnessed the latter's last days and was asked to stand by him at the duel. My uncle published his reminiscences in the eighties in one of the Russian historical journals and these are now regarded as *the* source of information about the tragic duel (with the exception of the biased historians for the reasons we will presently see) as being the work of one of the great 'liberals' of his day and also the only eye-witness account. First of all, one thing appears clearly from these memoirs, despite my uncle's admiration and friendship of the poet; for all his genius, Lermontov was clearly a quite insufferable character and a pain in the neck to all those who associated with him, friend and foe alike. And in this he differed sharply from Pushkin, who was also by no means an easy-going person and who had quite a few enemies, but also many devoted friends.

It so happens that Martynov, though rich was not in the least 'spiteful' but a perfectly harmless and indeed innocuous man. Though he *was* jealous, largely because Lermontov went out of his way to make him jealous by flirting ostentatiously with any girl Martynov happened to lay eyes on and by adding insult to injury and joking to those same girls about Martynov and his jealousy. In general, Lermontov had for some time been seeking quarrels with all and sundry, and he must now have decided that Martynov was just the 'sucker' he needed. And Martynov *was* patient for quite some time. Not only did he not 'foster a quarrel' but Lermontov's friends, including my uncle, kept wondering

how long he would take all this lying down, and worrying over
the inevitable (in those days) consequences of Lermontov's
behaviour. And finally Martynov's patience gave out. After an
evening during which Lermontov had behaved in a particularly
outrageous manner (and quite like Onegin with Lensky, in fact,
who knows, perhaps that was an inspiration?) Martynov called
him out to fight. The whole story was so patently absurd and
Lermontov was so clearly in the wrong, that the four seconds
(including my uncle) had no difficulty with Martynov and quite
a lot of difficulty with Lermontov, in persuading the two young
men that their honour would be saved if they met, and both fired
in the air. Which is why everybody concerned treated the whole
episode with levity until Lermontov, as he reached the firing
line, turned around to his audience and in a loud voice, for all to
hear, announced: '*Aya v etovo duraka streliat' ne budu.*' (I have
no intention of shooting at that fool!) whereupon Martynov,
now thoroughly incensed, took aim, fired and killed him. I knew
an old lady who knew Martynov in his old age. He was a mild old
man, who could never forgive himself that outbreak of temper
that had turned him into the murderer of Russia's second
greatest poet.

23 *M. Yu. Lermontov in the Memoirs of his Contemporaries,* op. cit.,
   p. 368.
24 Op. cit., p. 225, quoting Arnoldi.
25 Op. cit. p. 368, quoting Vasiltchikov.
26 Op cit., p. 340. Emiliya Verzilina quoting M. P. Glebov speaking
   to her.
27 Op. cit., p. 226, quoting Arnoldi.
28 Op. cit., p. 331, quoting N. I. Lorer.
29 *Russian Literature* (Vatsuro, 1974) Vol. 1, pp. 123–124. French
   original, transl. by the Author.
30 Op. cit., p. 120.
31 Extract from letter of W. Keith Neal to the Author on the technical
   characteristics of Kuchenreuters:
   Kuchenreuter, sometimes spelt Kuchenreiter, was the most
   famous Pistol Maker not only in Germany but probably on the
   Continent. The pistol used will have been a smooth bore and
   almost certainly it will have had a calibre of approximately .500
   or half inch bore. It will have fired a round lead ball wrapped in a
   greased linen patch and loaded with a ramrod. The charge which
   of course is poured down the barrel first is black powder and was

H*

roughly one third the weight of the ball. This round ball would be what is known as (about) 36 gauge, which means that 36 round balls weigh a pound. So you can say the round ball would have weighed about half an ounce.

In 1841 the pistol could well have been a flint-lock even though the copper cap ignition came into use in the 1820s, flint pistols remained in use, particularly in Russia right up to past the middle of the last century. This technical description you are getting should clear up this point.

Range. The usual duelling range at this date was 20 to 25 yards, sometimes less according to the whims of the seconds. Kuchenreiter pistols were however often sighted up to 100 yards and would still be deadly at that range. A good shot could hit a man with one of them easily at 50 yards. Duels were not however fired at greater distance than 25 yards.

By comparison with modern weapons, the old duelling pistol was probably deadlier than a modern revolver or automatic and just about as accurate at normal pistol range.

32 *M. Yu. Lermontov in the Memoirs of his Contemporaries*, op. cit., p. 349–350, quoting Polevodin.

33 Op. cit., p. 225. Arnoldi's evidence.

34 Op. cit., p. 344.

35 Op. cit., p. 420, quoting *Russky Vestnik* of 1864, Book 8, p. 224 (Yermolov).

36 Op. cit., p. 332, quoting N. I. Lorer.

37 Op. cit., p. 339, quoting Emiliya Shan-Girey.

38 *Chronology of the Life and Works of M. Yu. Lermontov*, op. cit., p. 173, quoting letter of M. A. Lopukhina to A. M. Hügel of September 18, 1841.

39 *Russky Archiv*, 1863, quoting P. Bartenev, pp. 440–441.

40 *The Sabres of Paradise* by Lesley Blanch (John Murray, 1960), p. 438.

Bibliography

Author's note

I have listed only sources, books and background material that were helpful to me, and therefore this list is in no way 'final', nor fully comprehensive. Lermontov studies, especially under the aegis of the Academy of Sciences (Pushkin House) in Leningrad, have become, in bulk at least, something of a minor industry. Serious students will find in the bibliographies given by Manuilov, Andronikov, Andreyev-Krivitch, Gershtein, Ivanova and Eikhenbaum enough, I trust, to satisfy their most ardent curiosity. Similarly, Lermontov's artistic legacy is well covered by Kovalevskaya and Pakhomov, and musically, by Piccard and Vernadsky (in French and English).

There are, on their respective topics, bibliographies and often useful comment, in Allen on the Caucasian War and in Baddeley's study of it. As for the main aspects of the Decembrists, Nicholas 1st, the Third Department and the Censors, the Russian Army and imperialism, the bibliographies or references provided by Mazour and Zetlin, de Grunwald, Squire and Riasanovsky and Curtiss provide ample cover, where older versions such as Shilder needed amplification.

By 1900 there had appeared, in those perennially interesting volumes of '*Russkaya Starina*' or '*Russky Archiv*' or other reviews of their ilk, any number of memoirs or even half-confessions of Lermontov's former friends, regimental and University companions, by then old gentlemen anxious not to forget and speaking up before they died. Generally I have used such material from that invaluable work edited by Manuilov and Gillel'son '*Lermontov in the Memoirs of his Contemporaries*'. The underlying references can readily be found there. Manuilov's 'Chronology' (*Letopis*) and '*Seminarii*' (1960) gives the other main biographical and bibliographical sources.

As for the English translations of Lermontov's work, there is need for an up-dated version of Heifetz's bibliography compiled in 1942, and also brought forward by Lewandi. But most of the poetry translations worth reading are there. In prose, since the War there have been a number of new translations of '*The Hero of Our time*': *Au choix*: Longworth, and Nabokov, leading the field.

ALLEN, W. E. D. and MURATOV, P., *Caucasian Battlefields 1828–1921*, Cambridge University Press 1953.

ANDREYEV-KRIVITCH, S. A., *Lermontov, Problems of Creativity and Biography*, Academy of Sciences, Moscow. 1954.

– *The Ominiscience of the Poet, Sovietskaya Rossiya 1973*.

ANDRONIKOV, I. L., Lermontov in Georgia in 1837, Zarya Vostoka, Tiflis 1958.

– *Tales of a Literary Man*, 'Detskaya literatura', Moscow 1969.

ARKHIPOV, V. A., *M. Yu. Lermontov, Poeziya Poznaniya i Dei stviya*, 'Moskovsky Rabotchy 1965.

ARZAMAZTSEV, V. P., *Tarkhany, Guide to the State Lermontov Museum, Sovietskaya Rossiya 1976*.

BADDELEY, J. F., *The Russian Conquest of the Caucasus*, Longmans Green 1908.

– *The Rugged Flanks of the Caucasus*, Oxford University Press 1940.

BARING, HON. M., *Russian Literature*, Williams and Norgate 1914.

– *Landmarks in Russian Literature*, Methuen 1960.

BARRATT, GLYN, *The Rebel on the Bridge, A Life of the Decembrist Andrey Rozen*, Paul Elek, 1975.

BAYLEY, JOHN, *Tolstoy and the Novel*, Chatto and Windus 1968.

BELL, J. S., *Journal of a Residence in Circassia 1837–9*, 1840.

DE BENCKENDORFF, COMTE CONSTANTIN, *Souvenir Intime d'une Campagne au Caucase*, Firmin-Didot, Paris 1858.

BERJE, A. P., Article Only: *Nicholas 1st in the Caucasus in 1837, Russkaya Starina No. 8.* 1884.

BERLIN, SIR ISAIAH, Romanes Lecture *Fathers and Children*, Oxford University Press 1972.

BLANCH, LESLEY, *The Sabres of Paradise*, John Murray 1960.

BODENSTEDT, F., *Les Peuples du Caucase et leur Guerre d'Indépendance contre la Russie*. E. Dentu, Paris 1859.

BOWMAN, H., *Vissarion Byelinsky 1811–1848*, Harvard University Press, 1954.

BOWRA, SIR MAURICE, *A Book of Russian Verse*, MacMillan 1943.

BOYD, A. F., *Aspects of the Russian Novel*, Chatto and Windus 1972.

BRYCE, LORD, *Transcaucasia and Ararat*, London MacMillan 1877.

BURTON, A. and MURDOCH, J., *Byron*, A Catalogue, Victoria and Albert Museum 1974.

BYELINSKY, V. G., Articles and Reviews, *School Library, Moskovsky Rabotchy* 1971.

– *Chronicle of Muhammed Takhir al Karakhi about the Daghestan.*

– *Wars in the time of Shamyl*. Institute of Eastern Learning, Academy of Sciences, Moscow 1941.

CORNFORD, FRANCES and SALAMAN, ESTHER, *Poems from the Russian*, Faber and Faber 1925.

COXWELL, C. FILLINGHAM, *Russian Poems*, C. W. Daniel Co., London 1929.

CURTISS, JOHN SHELTON, *The Russian Army under Nicholas 1st 1825–1855*, Duke University Press 1965.

CUSTINE, MARQUIS DE, *Lettres de Russie*, Editions de la Nouvelle France 1946. Translation by Phyllis Kohler, Pelligrini and Cudahy 1951.

DEMIDOFF, PRINCE E. (of San Donato), *Hunting Trips in the Caucasus*, Rowland Ward 1898.

DEUTSCH, BABETTE and YARMOLINSKY, AVRAHM, *Modern Russian Poetry, an Anthology*, Bodley Head 1930.

DUBOIS DE MONTPÉREUX, F., *Voyage autour du Caucase* (6 Vols.) Librairie de Gide Paris 1839.

DUCHÈSNE, E., *Michel Lermontov, Sa Vie et ses Oeuvres*, Plon, Paris 1910.

DUMAS, ALEXANDRE, *En Caucase*, Paris 1859.

– *Adventures in Tsarist Russia*, Translated by A. E. Murch, Peter Owen, 1960.

DURYLIN, S., *Kak Rabotal Lermontov*, Co-operative Publishing 'Mir', Moscow 1934.

EIKHENBAUM, B. M., Articles on Lermontov, Academy of Sciences, Moscow-Leningrad 1961.

FEDOROV, A. V., *Lermontov i Literatura yevo Vremeni*, Artistic Literature, Leningrad 1967.

FENNELL, JOHN, (Editor), *Nineteenth Century Literature, Studies in Ten Russian Writers*, Faber and Faber 1973.

FILIPPOV, C. N., Article only (quoting K. I. Karpov), *Russian Thought* 1890.

FREEBORN, RICHARD, *The Rise of the Russian Novel*, Cambridge University Press 1973.

GAGARIN, PRINCE G. G. and VON STACKELBERG, BARON E., *Le Caucase Pittoresque*, Paris 1847.

– *Scènes, Paysages, Moeurs et Costumes de Caucase*.

GERSHTEIN, EMMA, *Sud'ba Lermontova*, Sovietsky Pisatel, Moscow 1964.

GOLOVIN, IVAN, *Russia under the Autocrat Nicholas the First*, Praeger Scholarly Reprints; First published in English, H. Colburn, London 1846.

GRIGORYAN, K. N., *M. Yu. Lermontov i Romantism*, Nauka, Moscow-Leningrad 1964.

GRIMM, A. TH. VON, *Alexandra Feodorovna, Empress of Russia*, Edmonston & Douglas 1870.

GRUNWALD, C. DE, *Tsar Nicholas 1st.*, McGibbon and Kee, 1954.

GURNEY, B. G., *A Treasury of Russian Literature*, Bodley Head, London 1948.

HEIFETZ, ANNA, *Lermontov in English (Bibliography)*, Bulletin of the New York Public Library, 1942.

HERZEN, ALEXANDER, *My Past and Thoughts*, translated by C. Garnett and revised by H. Higgins, Chatto and Windus, 1968.

HODGETTS, E. BRAYLEY, *The Court of Russia in the 19th Century*, Methuen 1908.

HOLLERBACH, E. F. and MANUILOV, V. A., *M. Yu. Lermontov v Portretakh i Illustratsyakh*, State Pedagogic Publishing, Leningrad 1941.

HOMMAIRE DE HELL, ADÈLE, *Rèveries d'un Voyageur*, Amyot/Dentu, Paris 1846.

HOMMAIRE DE HELL, XAVIER, *Travels in the Steppes of the Caspian Sea, the Crimea, the Caucasus etc.* Chapman and Hall 1847.

IVANOVA, T. A., *Posmertnaya Sud'ba Poeta, Nauka* 1967.

– *Yunost' Lermontova, Sovietsky Pisatel'* 1957.

JARINTSOV, N., *Russian Poets and Poems*, B. H. Blackwell, Oxford 1917.

KENNAN, GEORGE F., *The Marquis de Custine and his Russia in 1839*, Hutchinson, London 1972.

KISCH, SIR CECIL, *The Waggon of Life*, The Cresset Press, London 1947.

KLAPROTH, JULES, *Voyage au Mont Caucase et en Georgie*, Paris 1823.

KORCZAK-BRANITSKY, X., *Les Nationalités Slaves*, E. Dentu, Paris 1879.

KOROVIN, V. I., *The Creative Path of M. Yu. Lermontov*, Prosveshcheniye Moscow 1973.

KOTLYAREVSKY, NESTOR, *M. Yu. Lermontov, the Personality of the Poet, Stasyulevitch*, St Petersburg 1909.

KOVALEVSKAYA, E. A. and MANUILOV, V. A., *M. Yu. Lermontov v Portretakh v Illustratsyakh i Dokumentakh, Utchpedgis*, 1959.

KOVALEVSKAYA, E. A., *Kartini i Risunki Poeta, Sovietsky Khudojnik* 1964.

LACROIX, PAUL, *Histoire de la Vie et du Règne de Nicholas 1er.*, Hachette, Paris 1873.

L'AMI, C. E. and WELIKOTNY, ALEXANDER, *Michael Lermontov, Biography and Translation*, University of Manitoba Press 1967.

LAVRIN, JANKO, *Lermontov*, Bowes and Bowes, London 1959.

– Article only, *Some Notes on Lermontov's Romanticism*, The Slavonic Review Vol. 36, 1957–8.

LEMKE, M., *Nikolayevskiye Jandarmy i Literatura*, 1826–1855. Russian Reprint Series, The Hague 1966. First published St Petersburg 1909.

LERMONTOV, M. YU., *A Hero of our Time*, translated by P. Longworth, New English Library, 1962.

– *A Hero of our Time* translated by V. Nabokov with D. Nabokov, Doubleday Anchor, New York 1958.

– Complete Edition (five vols.) Prof. D. I. Abramovitch, Imperial Academy of Sciences, St Peterburg 1910.

– Complete Edition (IV Vols.) Academy of Sciences 1958–9.

– *The Demon*, translated by A. Condie Stephen, Trubner 1875.

– *The Demon*, translated by R. Burness, Douglas & Foulis 1918.

– *In the Memoirs of his Contemporaries* edited by V. V. Grigorenko and others.

– *Artistic Literature* Moscow 1972.

– *In the Memoirs of his Contemporaries*, edited by V. A. Manuilov and M. I. Gillel'son, 1960 and 1964.

LEWANSKI, R., *The Literatures of the World, Vol. II: The Slavic Literatures*, New York Public Library.

LONGWORTH, J. A., *A Year among the Circassians*, London 1840.

LYALL, R., *Travels in Russia, the Krimea, the Caucasus and Georgia*, (2 Vols.) Reprint, The Arno Press 1970. First published 1825.

LYEBEDINETZ, G. S., Article Only, *M. Yu. Lermontov v bitvakh s Tcherkessami*, 1840. – *Russkaya Starina Vol. 3*, 1891.

MACLEAN, SIR FITZROY, *To Caucasus*, Jonathan Cape 1977.

MAGARSHACK, D., *Turgeniev's Literary Reminiscences*, Faber & Faber 1958.

MAKSIMOV, D., *The Poetry of Lermontov, Sovietsky Pisatel,'* Leningrad 1959.

MANUILOV, V. A., *Letopis' Jisni M. Yu. Lermontova*, 1964.

– Commentary to the *Hero of our Time*, *Prosveshcheniye*, 1966.

– *M. Yu. Lermontov* (Biography) *Prosveshcheniye*, 1976.

and GILLEL'SON, M. I., *Seminarii* (Comprehensive bibliography) *Utchpedgis*, Leningrad 1960.

MARTYANOV, P. K., *Deeds and People of the Century*, St Petersburg 1893.

MAZOUR, ANATOL, *The First Russian Revolution 1825*, Stanford University Press 1964.

MEREJKOVSKY, D., *Eternels Compagnons de Route*, Albin Michel, Paris 1949.

MERSEREAU JNR., J., *Mikhail Lermontov*, Southern Illinois Press, 1962.

MICHAILOFF, HELEN, (Article Only), *The Death of Lermontov*, Russian Literature Tri-quarterly, Ardis Publishers 1974.

MONAS, S., *The Third Section*, Harvard University Press 1961.

NAVORCHATOV, S., *Lirika Lermontova, Artistic Literature*, Moscow 1970.

NEWMARCH, ROSA, *Poetry and Progress in Russia*, John Lane 1907.

NIKITENKO, A., *Diary of a Russian Censor*, Abridged, edited and translated by H. S. Jacobson, University of Massachusetts Press 1975.

OBOLENSKY, PRINCE D., (Editor), *The Penguin Book of Russian Verse*, 1962/1965.

OBRUCHOV, S. V., *Nad Tetradyami Lermontova, Nauka*, Moscow 1965.

OLGIN, M. J., *A guide to Russian Literature 1820–1917*, Harcourt, Brace & Howe 1920.

PAKHOMOV, N. P., *Jivopisnoye Nasledstvo Lermontova*, Vol. 45–46, *Literaturnoye Nasledstvo*, Academy of Sciences 1948.

PEREIRA, MICHAEL, *Across the Caucasus*, Geoffrey Bles 1973.

PICCARD, E., *Mikhail Lermontov*, Edition du Lis, Neuchatel 1963.

POLLEN, JOHN, *Russian Songs and Lyrics*, East and West 1916.

POPOV, A., *Lermontov na Kavkaze*, Stavropol 1954.

PUSHKIN, ALEXANDER, *Complete Edition of Collected Works, Academia*, Moscow 1936.

– *Journey to Erzrum;* translated by B. Ingemansson, Ardis Publishers 1974.

PYPINE, A. N., *Introduction to a critical study of M. Yu. Lermontov*, 1873.

REEVE, F. D., *The Russian Novel*, Frederick Muller, 1966.

RIASANOVSKY, N. V., *Nicholas 1st. and Official Nationality in Russia 1825–55*, University of California Press 1959.

SAYN WITTGENSTEIN BERLEBURG, PRINCE E. DE, *Souvenirs et Correspondances*, Calmann-Levy, Paris 1888.

SEAMAN, W. A. L., and, SEWELL, J. R., *Russian Journal of Lady Londonderry 1836–7*, John Murray 1973.

SEGAL, L., *The Romantic Movement in Russia*, Russian Quarterly Offices, Portsmouth, (undated).

SELEGEY, P., *Domik Lermontova, Guide to the State Museum in Pyatigorsk*, Stavropol Book Publishers 1974.

SHAW, T., Translation of *Ammalat-Bek* by Bestujev-'Marlinsky', in *Blackwoods* Magazine 1843.

SHCHEGOLYEV, P. E., *Duel and Death of Pushkin*, Z. Gis, 1928.

– *The Book about Lermontov*, Priboi 1929.

SHILDER, N. K., *Imperator Nikolay 1, Jisn' i tsarstvovaniye* (2 vols.) 1903.

SIMMONS, E. J., *Leo Tolstoy*, John Lehmann, 1949.

SIPOVSKY, V. V., *Short Course on the history of Russian Literacy*, Bashmakova, Petrograd, 1915.

SOLLOGUP, COUNT V. A., *Vospominaniya, Academiya*, Moscow-Leningrad 1931.

SPENCER, E., *Travels in Circassia, Krim Tartary etc.* (2 vols.) H. Colburn London 1838.

– *Travels in the Western Caucasus*, H. Colburn, London, 1838.

SQUIRE, P. S., *The Third Department*, Cambridge University Press 1968.

STAËL, MADAME G. DE, *10 Years in Exile*, Centaur Press 1968.

STEINER, GEORGE, *Tolstoy or Dostoyevsky*, Penguin Books 1959.

TALIASHVILI, G., *Russko-Gruzinskoye Literaturniye Vsaimootnosheniye*, Tiflis 1967.

TITOV, ALEXANDR, *Leto na vodakh*, Leninisdat 1973.

TOLSTOY, LEO, *Hadji Murat*.

– *The Cossacks*, translated by R. Edmonds, London 1960.

TORNAU, COUNT F., *Memoirs of a Caucasian Officer of 1835*, Katkov, Moscow 1864.

TROYAT, HENRI, *Pouchkine*, Plon. Paris, 1953.

– *L'Etrange Destin de Lermontov*, Plon, Paris 1952.

TURNER, C. E., *Studies in Russian Literature*, Sampson Low 1882.

UKHODOV, T., *M. Yu. Lermontov, his artistic individuality and creative processes*, Voronejh University 1973.

VATSURO, V., Article only; *Russkaya Literature Vol. 1*, 1974.

VERNADSKY, N., Article only; *Lermontov in Russian music, The Slavonic Review*.

VICKERY, WALTER, *Death of a Poet*, Indiana University Press, 1962.

VILDERLING, A. G., *Lermontovsky Muzei Nikolayevskovo Kavaleriiskovo Uchilishche*, St Petersburg 1883.

VISKOVATY, P. A., *Complete Edition of The Life and Work of M. Yu. Lermontov* (6 vols.) Richter, Moscow 1889–1891.

VYRYPAYEV, P. A., *Lermontov, New materials for his biography*, Central Tcherno-Zemnoye Publishing House, Voronejh 1972.

WAGNER, DR MORITZ, *Travels in Persia, Georgia and Koordistan with sketches of the Cossacks and the Caucasus*, (3 vols.) Hurst and Blackett, London 1856.

WEINER, LEO, *Anthology of Russian Literature* (2 parts) Putnam and the Knickerbocker Press 1903.

WILBRAHAM, CAPTAIN R., (7th Royal Fusiliers), *Travels in the Transcaucasian Provinces of Russia 1837*, John Murray 1839.

WOLFF, TATIANA, *Pushkin on Literature*, Methuen 1971.

YAKOVKINA, E., *Posledny Priyut Poeta*, Stavropol 1975.

ZETLIN, M., *The Decembrists*, International University Press, New York 1958.

ZILBERSHTEIN, I. S., *M. Yu. Lermontov v Portretakh*, Goslitmusei, Moscow 1941.

Index

H50 538 481 1